Target London

To the citizens of London,
past and present

Target London

Bombing the Capital, 1915–2005

Peter Reese

Pen & Sword
MILITARY

First published in Great Britain in 2011 by
Pen & Sword Military
an imprint of
Pen & Sword Books Ltd
47 Church Street
Barnsley
South Yorkshire
S70 2AS

Copyright © Peter Reese 2011

ISBN 978-1-84884-122-2

LONDON BOROUGH TOWER HAMLETS		
910 000 00249342		
ASKEWS & HOLT	08-Jul-2011	
942.108	£19.99	
THISWH		

The right of Peter Reese to be identified as Author
of this Work has been asserted by him in accordance
with the Copyright, Designs and Patents Act 1988.

A CIP catalogue record for this book is
available from the British Library.

Typeset in 11/13 Ehrhardt by Concept, Huddersfield, West Yorkshire
Printed and bound in England by CPI UK

Pen & Sword Books Ltd incorporates the Imprints of Pen & Sword Aviation,
Pen & Sword Maritime, Pen & Sword Military, Wharncliffe Local History,
Pen & Sword Select, Pen & Sword Military Classics, Leo Cooper, Remember
When, Seaforth Publishing and Frontline Publishing.

For a complete list of Pen & Sword titles please contact
PEN & SWORD BOOKS LIMITED
47 Church Street, Barnsley, South Yorkshire, S70 2AS, England
E-mail: enquiries@pen-and-sword.co.uk
Website: www.pen-and-sword.co.uk

Contents

Preface and Acknowledgements vii

Prologue 1

PART 1 – Attacks During the First World War 5

  1. The Zeppelin Onslaught 7

  2. The Gothas Take Over 21

  3. The City's Defenders 35

  4. London's Home Front, 1914–18 47

PART 2 – Between the Wars 61

  5. The British Air Service – The Locust Years 63

PART 3 – Attacks During the Second World War 75

  6. Renewed Air Assaults 77

  7. The London Blitz, 1940–1 – Ground and Air Defenders 93

  8. The London Blitz, 1940–1 – Civil Defenders 105

  9. The London Blitz, 1940–1 – Home Morale 123

10. London and the Doodlebugs 135

11. London and the V2s 151

PART 4 – Terrorist Attacks 167

12. The IRA 169

13. Al-Qaeda 183

Epilogue 195

Notes 199

Select Bibliography 215

Index 223

Preface and Acknowledgements

In this book I set out to describe the full range of attacks made on London during the twentieth century, throughout the two world wars and latterly by terrorists.

The men and women who witnessed the first Zeppelin attacks have all but passed away and those who were in London during the Second World War are rapidly diminishing in number. I count myself as one of them, although I was an evacuee during the Blitz before living as a boy in North London during 1943–5 in a house bearing the scars of the earlier bombing. Like others at that time I watched V1s flying overhead and waited fearfully for the rough pulses of their engines to cut out before they tumbled to earth. Although personally unscathed, like others I had a close friend whose home was reduced to a pile of smouldering rubble by a V2. While memories of so long ago may not be fully reliable, my strongest impression of that time was that nothing was allowed to prevent the lives of schoolboys (and other citizens) from following their regular course, which in my case included the regular physical chastisement which, with the young masters away, was delivered by others of advancing years. For me – and hopefully for most readers of this book with no direct experience of them – the number and scale of the attacks upon London during the last century is astounding and the stories about the individuals concerned illimitable.

*　*　*

With regard to my research, I have mined a wealth of correspondence about the raids in the Library of the Imperial War Museum and the Mass Observation Archive at the University of Sussex. Other institutions used have included the Prince Consort's Library, Aldershot, The Army Central Library, London's Guildhall Library, The London Metropolitan Archives, The Library of the Royal Aeronautical Society, The National Army Museum and Farnborough Air Sciences Trust. As in the past, much of the writing has taken place in the Prince Consort's Library where Chief Librarian Tim Ward and his amazing staff are a writer's dream.

The book would never have been completed without the support of commissioning editor Rupert Harding and all at Pen & Sword. As for my own 'support system', Mrs Christine Batten and her computer have again transformed 'old-style' writing into working form.

For personal assistance I would like to thank Mrs Jennifer Prophet for her arduous and vital work in scrutinising the book's first draft, and both her and her son Charles for shouldering the detailed task of compiling the index; my friend Paul Vickers, author, historian and head of the Army Libraries Information Systems, for his production of excellent maps and illustrations and much more besides; Colonel Mike Wellings for discussing at length the book's early tentative form; Colonel Tony Guinan TD for suggesting additional sources, in this case with the ack-ack services; and Mike Cawley who, with distinguished airman Bob Pugh, generously loaned me books from their personal collections.

Finally, above all I would like to thank my wife, Barbara, who over many years has coped with an absent husband at his library desks. This time she has acted as a sounding board for the book's early drafts where her good sense and practicality have, as before, proved invaluable.

Any mistakes are, of course, mine alone.

Peter Reese
Aldershot
September 2010

Prologue

The bombardment of London began during the night of 31 May 1915 with the arrival over the north-east of the city of German army Zeppelin L38, commanded by Hauptmann Erich Linnarz. The airship moved high over the industrial East End before passing across West Ham and Leytonstone. During the course of its flight it released over 2,500lb of bombs, including eighty-nine incendiaries and thirty grenades. These killed seven people and injured thirty-five. The dubious honour of being the first London house to be bombed went to 16 Alkham Road on the outskirts of Hackney where the owner, Albert Henry Lovell, together with his wife, their children and two women visitors, escaped unscathed from the blazing upper rooms.

Unlike the supremacy enjoyed by the British Royal Navy over other naval forces, London's air defences were as yet inadequate, a fact that astonished and enraged its citizens. A warning was received as the airship crossed the coast where the ack-ack response had been limited to machine guns. These opened up during both the Zeppelin's approach and return journeys to London but they failed to damage it. At the time London's ground defences were just twelve genuine anti-aircraft guns and the same number of searchlights. A total of nine aircraft were despatched to meet it but they too failed to locate the massive craft. This was not surprising. One was a very slow FE2a two-seater with a 'pusher' rear engine, whose observer, sitting in his open cockpit in the aircraft's nose, was armed with no more than a rifle and incendiary bullets. This plane failed to reach the 1,500m height required to get anywhere near the Zeppelin and it subsequently crashed on landing, killing the pilot. Another defending aircraft was a Short S81 two-seater seaplane, which was so under-powered that it could not carry an observer and whose armament consisted of a rifle and two grenades resting on its pilot's lap. After failing to make contact, this also crashed on landing, although the pilot survived. Another aircraft involved was an obsolete pre-1914 Deperdussin whose pilot was similarly equipped with a rifle and grenades. This also failed to make contact, although it landed safely.[1]

While the damage inflicted during the initial raid was minor it marked the end of a period lasting almost 900 years when, following its capture by the

Danish King Cnut in 1014 and then by William the Conqueror in 1066, London had been spared from external attack. From its time as a Roman city with an 18ft-high perimeter wall stretching for 2 miles and a single bridge crossing the Thames at a point opposite its forum and basilica, significant changes had already taken place which would continue and accelerate following William's accession. This was fully predictable because, positioned as it was close to the lowest bridging point over the River Thames where routes from the south, west and north of the country converged, and with the river's estuary facing the great waterway of the Rhine leading into the heart of Europe, London was virtually guaranteed commercial success.

This was recognized as early as AD 604 when the Venerable Bede, in his *Ecclesiastical History*, described it as a 'mart of many people arriving thither by land and sea'.[2] Although the original city of roughly a square mile would remain, London was soon to spread rapidly outside its original walls. William the Conqueror's coronation took place at Westminster, in the Cathedral of St Peter, but after Henry VIII's dissolution of the monasteries the church desmenes surrounding the city became Crown lands thereby enabling it to undertake a new expansionary surge. Along with the city's material spread, which by 1915 saw it stretching for over 700 square miles within a 13-mile radius, its population had also grown immensely aided by immigration, with seventeenth-century Flemish, Dutch, Walloon and Huguenot merchants and craftsmen joined during the nineteenth century by other nationals including many Jews who settled in the East End.[3] As a result, by the time of the first air raid the multinational population of London totalled over 7,250,000.

The metropolis, whose palaces, Parliament and other public buildings, factories, docks and private houses were overflown by Zeppelin L38 on 31 May 1915, was also the greatest city in the world. Even with New York reputedly catching it up, Europe's other capitals – Paris, Berlin, Moscow, Madrid, Rome and Vienna – could not compete in terms of population (about a fifth of Britain's population was in London) or in economic importance. While its Square Mile hosted the nation's short-term money market and financed both national and worldwide enterprises, the traditional 'mart' activities took place in its fashionable West End, whose famous shops brought customers from all over the world, to be counterpoised by London's mercantile East End which produced goods of all types and whose industries included ones concerned with printing and paper, machine working, petroleum and chemicals, shoes, clothes, food, drink and tobacco. This area, containing the city's docks, handled twice the number of cargoes passing through Liverpool at that time.

From the windows of the Zeppelin's control car Linnarz calmly recorded his impressions as his missiles rained down: 'One by one, every 30 seconds, the bombs moaned and burst. Flames sprung up like serpents goaded to attack. Taking one of the biggest fires I was able by it to estimate my speed and my drift.'[4] Linnarz's observations would be followed by those of other Zeppelin pilots and by German aircrew in their heavy bombers, until twenty-five years later, during the Second World War, such craft were succeeded by more powerful aeroplanes equipped with sophisticated bomb sights, soon to be joined by pilotless planes and rockets directed onto their great target by gyroscopes.

Towards the end of the twentieth century and during the early years of the next London would become a target for terrorists bringing their own forms of destruction, and they, unlike Linnarz, were far from content to observe the results of their assaults but through them hoped to alert the world's media to their ideological aims.

PART 1

Attacks During the First World War

Chapter 1

The Zeppelin Onslaught

You English! We have come, and we will come again soon, to kill or cure!

Hauptman Erich Linnarz, commander of Zeppelin L38[1]

At the start of the First World War Germany had undoubted superiority in lighter-than-air craft. They owed most here to the remarkable, long-lived Count Ferdinand von Zeppelin, who, with the appearance of the rival dirigible *La France* thirty years before, had become convinced that Germany not only needed such 'air cruisers' but ones specifically for military purposes.

Von Zeppelin retained his belief in such remarkable vehicles, even after a succession of disasters that would have caused a less-dedicated man to give up, and in 1909 founded the world's first airline. By 1911, while embarking on journeys of two hours or so, his passengers seated in wicker chairs were able to enjoy elaborate cold menus and fine wines. By now his airships were 518ft long and 48ft in diameter, with their envelopes holding almost 800,000cu ft of hydrogen gas compared with the 100,000cu ft of contemporary French airships, the 60,000cu ft of the British army's second airship *Nulli Secundus II* (broken up in 1908) and the similar dimensions of the Royal Navy's ill-fated airship *The Mayfly* of 1911.[2] Such advantages in capacity were important because they enabled larger loads, including fuel, to be carried thereby increasing the airships' range and height ceilings far beyond the capabilities of any contemporary aircraft.

By 1914 both the German army and navy had determined to use airships in wartime roles – the army already had thirteen in service which they planned to use by flying over battlefield areas in support of their ground troops, while in 1912 the navy had commenced its own building programme, since with its North Sea Fleet chronically short of destroyers and cruisers it intended to use airships for scouting purposes. A powerful argument in the airships' favour was their six-week construction period compared with the two years required for cruisers.

The navy's first airship was engaged in the strategic fleet manoeuvres of 1913, which took place in good weather conditions, before it was subsequently destroyed after plunging into the sea during a storm. Undeterred, ten larger airships were ordered. These had 955,000cu ft of gas and were powered by four Mercedes Maybach engines, each developing a very respectable 165hp with a speed of up to 70mph. Unfortunately, soon after delivery the first of these burst into flames and crashed, killing all its crew.

Despite, or possibly because of, the evident frailty of such craft the German authorities ordered even larger ones, and after August 1915 ships containing 1,126,000cu ft of gas became standard for both services.[3] By this time the army had already lost three of its earlier airships while supporting its soldiers in France.[4]

Since such hazardous craft were scheduled to be working across the watery wastes of the North Sea, the navy's airship division was made all-volunteer, advertising for men who preferably were unmarried and able to pass a medical examination paying special attention to head, eyes, ears and possible nervous conditions,[5] and an outstanding officer, Corvette Captain Peter Strasser, was appointed to lead it. In addition to the high level of physical fitness required, anyone serving under Strasser had to be highly dedicated, for in addition to Fleet reconnaissance duties he shared the ambitions of Rear Admiral Paul Behneke, the Deputy Chief of the German Naval Staff, for the more hazardous task of crossing over to Britain and mounting bombing raids – with London as the chief target.

For this purpose Behneke attempted to gain the support of his chief, Admiral Tirpitz, and other senior naval colleagues by arguing that German naval inferiority could also be reduced by bombing the London docks and the British Admiralty's headquarters in London. Even so, he revealed his wider ambitions by declaring that such raids 'may be expected whether they involve London or the neighbourhood of London, to cause panic in the population which may possibly render it doubtful that the war can be continued'.[6]

Although the naval airship division saw a rapid increase in its personnel from 352 officers and men at the commencement of the war to 3,740 4 months later (including 25 flight crews of 22 men each and teams numbering at least 300 men that were needed to move the craft in and out of their hangers), it was still chronically short of airships and their capabilities for both tasks were still largely unproven.

Some idea of the dangers to be faced came on 28 August 1914 when a single naval airship on reconnaissance at the Battle of Heligoland Bight not only failed to distinguish itself, but in conditions of poor visibility cost the Germans dear, largely owing to the timidity of its commander. After arriving in the locality at 8.40 am it found German destroyers moving at full speed towards Heligoland with British warships in pursuit. The airship then unexpectedly came under fire from its own destroyers and moved away from the battlefield area. At 8.50 am it radioed to base that it had turned back in the face of fire from an enemy cruiser and was returning due to technical reasons. By leaving the area the airship commander could no longer track or report upon Admiral Beatty's fast-moving battle cruisers, which went on to sink the three light German cruisers *Mainz*, *Koln* and *Ariadne* without loss, and although the alarm felt by an airship commander when fired on in this way needs no emphasis, unless the technical reasons proved very serious it was his duty to remain on station. Such actions were the more blameworthy because this rebuff contributed massively towards the German fleet subsequently opting to stay in harbour for the greater part of the war. In partial extenuation however, it could be argued that the task was far too much for a single airship. Such an event was unlikely to occur again since, during the latter part of 1914, both the navy's and army's air divisions were receiving reinforcements. By the middle of January 1915 the navy had six of the latest types while the army had four, and with the completion of the navy's revolving shed at Nordholz its ships could become airborne whatever the wind direction, thus enabling the division to consider its second task, the strategic bombing of London and other parts of Britain.

The projected bombing of 'defenceless' civilians raised grave moral questions, which would continue with strategic bombing. Discussions about such a policy between Admiral Tirpitz, Chancellor von Berhman-Hollweg and the Kaiser at this time revealed their differing opinions: with Berhmann-Hollweg remaining implacably opposed, Tirpitz gave his support providing such raids concentrated on London, but when on 12 February 1915 the Kaiser finally approved the air war against London, it was still conditional upon the royal palaces being exempted and the capital's residential area spared.

In fact, on 19 January 1915 the naval division had already made its first raid on Britain, although this was in the nature of an experiment. On this occasion 3 Zeppelins, 2 from Fuhlsbuttel (near Hamburg) and 1 from Nordholz, on the Baltic coast, set out to bomb the British east-coast towns. One was compelled to turn back halfway across the North Sea, before its accompanying Zeppelin bombed Yarmouth at 8.25 pm, killing two people and wounding three. The third Zeppelin, having entered British airspace, missed Cromer, which was in darkness, and dropped incendiary bombs along the coast before attacking King's Lynn (which still had its lights on), where two further people were killed and thirteen injured.

By any standard, such casualties were light, although the commanders' reports acknowledged that within the chosen towns their bombing had, in fact, been indiscriminate. Captain Strasser targeted the coastal towns at this time because his airships' deficiencies in range and height capability gave him little confidence to seek targets far inland. Even so, this first raid had a remarkable impact, for as yet there were no defences and it was seen to presage not only a new but a terrifying dimension of warfare.

The attack on King's Lynn was described in dramatic terms by *The Times*: 'The airship circled twice around the town, at times seeming to hang almost motionless. As the bombs fell and explosions occurred great flashes of light leaped up and the reports were terrific.'[7] The German newspaper *Kolnische Zeitung* was understandably both more bombastic and triumphant: 'The first Zeppelin has appeared in England and has extended its fiery greetings to our enemy. It has come to pass, that which the English have long feared and repeatedly have contemplated with terror.... This is the best way to shorten the war, and thereby in the end most humane.'[8]

Compared with raids by hundreds of aircraft later in the century the reaction seems disproportionate, but it brought major reactions in both Britain and Germany: in Britain there were vociferous demands for powerful home defences, while in Germany 'it led the people to renew their demands for the bombing of London'.[9]

If the Germans were really intent on strategic bombing there had to be rapid follow-up raids, particularly on London, the greatest target of all, but in fact Britain enjoyed a respite of almost three months. This was partly because of the adverse weather and the navy's shortage of airships (the two involved in the raid of 19 January were subsequently destroyed in a gale over Denmark), but also because scouting duties were judged to have a higher priority.

Not to be outdone, the German military airship service prepared for raids of its own, using three larger airships operating from recently constructed bases in Belgium. After several light raids by both services on Tyneside and eastern England, in the course of which thirteen people were killed and nine injured and the damage estimated at £23,411,[10] on 31 May came the first raid on London. Flying at a great height, an army airship passed over Hoxton, Shoreditch, Whitechapel, Stepney, West Ham and Leytonstone, dropping 2,636lb of bombs in an indiscriminate fashion, killing seven people, injuring thirty-five and causing £18,396 worth of damage.[11] Not only did London's few anti-aircraft guns fail to locate it but although nine pilots rose in pursuit, only one even caught a glimpse of the ship.

In June, with their own numbers of airships building up, the naval division decided to resume bombing by restricting those involved in North Sea duties to six and using the other three to bomb London. Nonetheless, during the spring and early summer of 1915 the raids were made against largely undefended localities such as Hull and Grimsby, causing twenty-four fatalities and forty injured, as well as targets along the east coast and Kent.

In its determination to raid London the naval service rejected a proposal from the chief of the army's General Staff, General von Falkenhayn, to use both aeroplanes and airships, because it was sure the planes would not become available for some months at the earliest (a fact only too well known to Falkenhayn). Its decision to proceed independently received a powerful boost when, in July 1915, the Kaiser finally removed his restrictions upon raiding the capital's buildings of historic interest.

Like so many operations involving airships, targeting London turned out to be more difficult for the navy than had been anticipated. On 9 August Strasser personally led his five newest airships against the capital, while another three attacked industrial areas north of the Humber. After struggling to find their way through darkness and the fog which habitually hung over the Thames estuary, none succeeded in reaching London and one was lost to coastal gunfire. On 12 August Strasser tried again: after sending one ship as a decoy to Hartlepool he launched the other three against London. Of these, one had to turn back after a propeller shaft became loose over the North Sea, the second experienced engine trouble within sight of Britain and the third turned back after reaching the Thames estuary, following which it encountered an electric storm. In the course of which lightning caused large sparks to come off the ship's wire stays and bluish flames to run along its machine-gun barrels, while on the ship's top platform crew members were encircled with St Elmo's fire, which caused a sort of halo round their sailors' caps.[12] Although all aboard were in constant terror of the ship bursting into flames at any moment, it eventually landed safely at Nordholtz.

On 17 August, two-and-a-half months after the attempts by military airships, London experienced its first raid by four naval ones. They crossed over Walthamstow at 10.34 pm and dropped bombs on Leyton, Leytonstone and Wanstead Flats, killing ten people and injuring forty-eight. On 7 September three craft from the military airship service joined in, two of which reached the capital, but the damage they caused was quite small, amounting to £9,618. More pressing commitments in France made this their last but one attempt to bomb London: it was now up to the naval airships stationed along the North Sea coast at Nordholz and Tondern to rain destruction on the city and terrorize its inhabitants. In fact, the chances of this happening were already lessening, for after Londoners had experienced the first profound shocks of the raids, the capital's ground defences improved, increased numbers of interceptor aircraft stood waiting and a squadron of light cruisers based on the Humber were equipped with anti-aircraft guns to help intercept any airships crossing the North Sea on their way to the capital.

On 8 September when another four airships set off for London only one, under the division's outstanding commander Heinrich Mathy, reached the capital. Mathy was conspicuous among such unquestionably brave and committed men, not only for his flying skills but above all for the confident way in which he handled his perilous vehicle as a formidable weapon of war. On arrival he coolly selected his targets: after dropping a 660lb bomb on Bartholomew Close in the City he inflicted heavy damage on textile warehouses north of St Paul's where, despite the efforts of twenty-two fire engines, the resultant fires destroyed many valuable buildings.

An indication of the capital's improving defences saw his Zeppelin come under continuous gunfire and sought out by approximately twenty searchlights which succeeded in deflecting him from his declared aim of bombing the Bank of England or Tower Bridge, although he did hit Liverpool Street station. Mathy's raid turned out to be the most damaging of any single airship or aeroplane raid of the war and it caused over a sixth of the total air-raid damage within Britain during the conflict. But there was only one Mathy and, successful as his raid was, with the damage at not much over £½ million and casualties at just twenty-two killed and eighty-seven injured, this was no blitzkrieg and far too little to bring the great city, even temporarily, to its knees – although it was guaranteed to bring a storm of protest in Parliament about the capital's inadequate defences.

With his vulnerable craft always subject to adverse weather and now encountering better integrated defences, Strasser experienced the utmost difficulty in maintaining the weight of his attacks. When, 5 days later, 3 of his Zeppelins again attempted to bomb the city only Heinrich Mathy succeeded in even crossing the coast, and in the process sustaining damage from ship-borne guns to 2 of his gas cells and his radio. To make things worse, his port engine failed and it was only through heroic efforts on the part of his crew that he managed to get back to base. Notwithstanding such difficulties and the relative lightness of the damage inflicted on London so far, Strasser appeared delighted with his fleet's achievements.

Further follow-up raids were foiled by the German army authorities rather than the British defences when General von Falkenhayn professed concern that possible retaliation attacks on German cities might result from such unrestricted bombing.

A month passed before the naval airships were allowed to bomb Britain again. On 13 October 1915 five set out for London, with three reaching their target and this time it was the turn of Captain Joachim Breithaupt to distinguish himself. Although illuminated by the beams of searchlights and with gunfire bursting under his ship, he moved across London laying a trail of bombs as he went, first along the Strand to Lincoln's Inn, then from Chancery Lane along Farringdon Road to Limehouse. One bomb fell in front of the Lyceum Theatre, killing seventeen and injuring twenty-one people. In all, Breithaupt's bombs killed 28 people and injured 70, although the other 2 airships were not nearly as successful.

Although the number of casualties was relatively limited, the sight of three such massive craft, stately and mysterious, riding high in the sky, seemingly immune to the probing searchlights and guns, was still able to bring a strong sense of apprehension and wonderment from the onlookers, whether ordinary spectators or experienced newspaper reporters. As Breithaupt's airship crossed the Thames, a representative from *The Times* observed that it was 'played upon by two searchlights and in their radiance she looked a thing of silvery beauty sailing serenely through the night'.[13] In his highly combustible craft it said even more for Breithaupt's cool nerve when he described the scene in similar terms: 'The picture we saw was indescribably beautiful – shrapnel bursting all around (though uncomfortably near us) our own bombs bursting, and the flashes from the anti-aircraft batteries below.... And over us the starlit sky!'[14]

Together with London's theatre land, his bombs fell on the Inns of Court, but when he observed four planes rising in pursuit he broke off his attack and succeeded in climbing rapidly away from them. The other two airships, one under Mathy, achieved far less success, but, nonetheless, the proportion of bombs dropped from these three airships was the highest of the war.[15] On the other hand, the city's airspace had become far more hostile: supported by twenty-six searchlights, more guns placed round its periphery firing explosive shells and even incendiary rockets, while extra aeroplanes stood ready for despatch from their own ring of airfields around London.

The capital was now to enjoy another lull in the raids. The adverse weather during the last two months of 1915 and January 1916 was inimical to the massive craft; unpredictable side winds buffeted them and made it impossible to maintain their intended courses, while strong headwinds wrecked their anticipated journey times. Most importantly, the new commander of the German High Seas Fleet, Admiral Reinhard Scheer, was far more adventurous than his predecessor and he markedly increased the airship division's commitments with the fleet.

The next Zeppelin raid, on 31 January 1916, was directed against Middle England, which was less well defended than London. Although conditions promised to favour the attackers, they experienced major difficulties in navigation and target spotting that were increased by extensive light reductions in many of the towns. These precautions restricted the casualties to some 70 killed and 128 injured, with just £53,000 worth of damage being caused.

Although the airship raids had been taking place for more than a year, during which time they had enjoyed undoubted moments of success – especially Mathy's raid of 5 September the previous year – Strasser realized that their influence on the war as a whole had been relatively limited. This was something he was determined to change.

*   *   *

Strasser planned to lift German home morale, at the time deeply affected by the heavy and continuing casualties during their battles with French forces around Verdun, by mounting a series of attacks across Britain – from London to Edinburgh – which he intended to continue for a week or more. By now he had no illusions about the strength of the London defences, the responsibility for which had been assumed by the British War Office, but over the country as a whole he knew they would be far less effective.

In the event his attacks mounted during the week 31 March–3 April proved very disappointing. Only one airship, commanded by Captain Breithaupt, succeeded in even reaching the outskirts of London and in so doing suffered such damage that he crashed off the coast when attempting to make his way home. Successes elsewhere, including the destruction of bonded warehouses in undefended Edinburgh, hardly compensated for this. In any case, the total casualties of 84 people killed and 227 injured were far too light to affect British resolve to keep fighting.[16]

During May, when his raids were likely to be resumed, Strasser had once more to put strategic bombing plans aside in favour of supporting the High Seas Fleet during the Battle of Jutland, where poor weather badly degraded the airships' performance. Nonetheless, Strasser's hopes for bombing Britain were again raised by the delivery of the first so-called super Zeppelins, each more than two football pitches long with a gas capacity of 2 million cubic feet and six engines capable of carrying a much-improved bomb load.

Unbeknown to him, the British were developing a weapon that spelled likely destruction for any Zeppelin, however large, to replace the 20lb explosive bombs and incendiaries with which it had been hoped to attack Zeppelins from above, but which proved to be useless. This was combustible ammunition upon which work had been deferred due to the mistaken belief that the airships had eliminated their most extreme fire risks by directing inert gases around their hulls. Once this was disproved, a million rounds of explosive and phosphorus-carrying ammunition had been ordered for the home-defence aircraft.

Strasser wrote to his chief, Admiral Scheer, spectacularly advocating the prospects for his 'super Zeppelins': 'The performance of the big airships has reinforced my conviction that England can be overcome by means of airships in as much as the country will be deprived of the means of existence through increasingly extensive destruction of cities, factory complexes, dockyards, harbour works with war and merchant ships lying there, railroads ...'.[17] With these he planned another sustained offensive from the end of August and throughout September 1916, this time chiefly against London. On 24 August he personally led 13 airships towards the capital, but just 1 ship under the resolute and skilful Mathy reached London, where, despite heavy gunfire, he bombed Deptford causing damage worth £130,000, killing 9 people and injuring 40. A second raid was cancelled due to bad weather, but on 2 September twelve navy Zeppelins, together with four army ships, set out for London in the largest raid so far. In the case of the army's ships it was a melancholy tale: the first failed to reach Britain, the second rapidly dropped its bombs at Tilbury before making its best way home, while the third dropped its bombs on the coastal ports rather than risk London's defences. Only the fourth, commanded by Wilhelm Schramm, succeeded in reaching north-east London, where it dropped some bombs before encountering an aeroplane piloted by Lieutenant Leefe Robinson. Once the aircraft came within range it proved to be no contest, and after being hit by the plane's deadly bullets its great opponent was consumed from end to end by fire before plunging down near Cuffley.

As the first pilot to shoot down a Zeppelin, Leefe Robinson was awarded an immediate Victoria Cross and he subsequently described the effectiveness of his ammunition. 'I was very close – 500 feet or less below – and concentrated one drum on one part (underneath its rear) ... I hardly finished the drum before I saw the part fired at glow. In a few seconds the whole rear part was blazing.'[18]

With the odds becoming so adverse, the army airship service never again attacked Britain and it was disbanded within a year. What was more, the horrific sight of the huge airship blazing from end to end caused the naval Zeppelins who were approaching London from the eastern counties to drop their bombs prematurely.

While Strasser might conceivably have been able to shrug off the loss of an army airship, however portentous, the outcome of his next raid must have been unquestionably daunting. On 23 September 11 ships set out, with the 8 older ones bound for the Midlands and his 3 new super 'thirties' under Mathy targeting London. Only one of the older ships reached the Midland cities but the super Zeppelins fared even worse. L33, commanded by Captain Bocker, bombed two warehouses along the Thames causing two of the most dangerous fires of the war[19] but in the process suffered such severe damage that it crashed near Mersey Island. The wily Mathy dropped his bombs on south-east London before escaping through a blanket of mist, but the third ship, after being illuminated by searchlights, was caught by a BE2C plane piloted by Second Lieutenant Frederick Sowrey. Another British airman watched his bullets strike home and said it looked as if the Zeppelin 'was being hosed with a stream of fire'.[20] The stricken craft plunged down over Billericay and, ablaze from end to end, it shed a brilliant light over the neighbouring countryside.

The loss of two out of three super Zeppelins and their experienced commanders and crews was a grievous blow, while the damage to London from September's raids was far lower than expected. Strasser acknowledged the potency of London's defences when he ordered his commanders to exercise caution in clear weather and, when it proved to be a star-filled night, the proposed raid for 25 September was diverted from the city.

At the beginning of October, Strasser despatched eleven Zeppelins in stormy weather to attack London, but whereas this was bound to affect the defenders' visibility it also made things especially difficult for the ships when the squally winds were laced with hail and snow, and only the indefatigable Heinrich Mathy succeeded in reaching the city. During the last week of September in a letter written to his wife, he had already revealed his growing awareness of the shortening odds against his survival: 'During these days when you lay our little daughter down to sleep, a good angel will see you and will read what is in your heart, and he will hasten to guard my ship against the dangers which throng the air everywhere about her.'[21] On the October raid, after skilfully avoiding the ground defences, he met his nemesis in a way he must have most feared, from a defending aircraft armed with the latest ammunition flying at the same altitude as himself. Its pilot, Second Lieutenant Tempest, described the effects of his deadly bullets against which Mathy could find no escape: 'As I was firing, I noticed her begin to go red inside like an enormous Chinese lantern and then a flame shot out of the front part of her ...'.[22]

The airship came down in fields near the suburb of Potters Bar, where the spectators found a dying officer away from the debris lying on his back, half embedded in the soil. Around his neck was the identity disc imprinted with the words 'Kaptit Mathy L31'. Following their multiplying difficulties, the effect of Mathy's loss upon his fellow airship commanders and crews needs no emphasis. Heinrich Bahn, a German Petty Officer, believed that with Mathy's death the life and soul went out of the airship service,[23] although the indefatigable Strasser persisted with his attacks.

The aircraft's fast-growing supremacy was also about to be felt outside London. The next airship raid, on 27 November (almost two months after Mathy met his death), was aimed at the northern counties. It was here over Hartlepool that another of 'the originals', Max Dietrich, was attacked by an aeroplane piloted by Second Lieutenant Ian Pyott, and after bursting into flames his airship fell into the sea, while a second was pounced on by three aeroplanes and also came down in the sea, about 10 miles from Lowestoft.

Strasser was compelled to extend his order against attacking London during clear weather to anywhere in the country. By now, despite his ability to mount much heavier raids, the balance had tipped strongly against him. During 1915, for instance, when 47 airships set off for Britain, 27 succeeded in entering the country's airspace, but during 1916, when 187 ships set out and 111, including super Zeppelins, crossed into Britain, the total damage inflicted was down by a third.[24] Their losses were also much higher and these included the newest and best airships; what was more, they were patently failing to hit their main target severely enough.

Characteristically, Strasser still refused to admit defeat, although when, at the end of 1916, he again appealed for Admiral Scheer's continued support, he no longer claimed his airships could defeat Britain. Although he stressed the raids' serious collateral effects, the dread of airships by a wide strata of society, the disturbance of transportation and, above all, the occupation of very considerable materiel and military personnel,[25] most tellingly he no longer promised his chief that he could destroy London.

By now the Zeppelins' limitations as bombers were generally acknowledged. As a result, with Germany's stocks of rubber and aluminium in very short supply, these materials were diverted to other weapons such as U-boats that could still conceivably win the war, and for heavy aircraft also capable of overflying the North Sea and carrying out strategic bombing.[26] Henceforth, Zeppelin replacements would be down to the equivalent of half a ship per month.

Even now, Strasser decided to adopt a new approach. Paring down his airships by such devices as removing an engine, thinning out their metal framework, reducing the thickness of their gas bags and diminishing wind resistance by treating their outer envelope with dope, he believed they could be made to fly at significantly higher altitudes. When flying at 16,500ft to 20,000ft they could again outstrip the defending British aircraft, whose maximum ceilings were 13,000ft, and also fly above the anti-aircraft fire. What Strasser and the German navy's medical department had not fully anticipated was their crews' physical problems during a sixteen- to twenty-hour flying sortie within the sparse, freezing atmosphere some 4 miles high, which, among other physical problems and despite the subsequent issue of liquid air, brought about altitude sickness. The sub-stratosphere was plagued by increased wind velocities and violent storms, and it also caused serious mechanical problems, including a severe loss of engine power, which reduced flight ceilings to levels where they remained vulnerable to aircraft.

The first raids by the 'height climbers' confirmed such difficulties. On 23 May 1917 Strasser sent five 'to attack London', but none reached the capital and two were very fortunate to get home after experiencing horrendous weather conditions. During the next month another six set out but only two reached Britain and none got as far as London, while after experiencing engine trouble the ship commanded by Strasser's deputy, Viktor Schutz, was caught at 13,000ft by an aeroplane piloted by Lieutenant L P Watkins and, following three short bursts, 'the Zeppelin caught fire and fell burning'.[27]

With his airships badly in need of some success, on 19 October 1917 Strasser left 'fortress London' alone and despatched eleven ships for Middle England. On the journey they encountered appalling weather which blew them off course and led to the loss of an unprecedented five ships, four of which came down in France. Remarkably, one airship that lost its way actually bombed the capital.

While the 'height climbers' continued to offer a shadowy menace to British cities they would never be entirely irrelevant, but the main responsibilities for bombing had passed to German heavy bombers and any hope of airships regaining the chances offered in 1916 appeared to have gone. Amazingly, during the last few months of the war the ever tenacious Strasser planned an attack on London equal in scale to those of the German heavy bombers. With notable rashness, on 5 August 1918 he personally led a raid – in daylight – on 'south or Middle England' under clear skies, when low barometric pressure prevented his craft from reaching the high altitudes required. Off Great Yarmouth five airships were flying in formation with Strasser leading, when they were caught by a DH4 aircraft, flown by Major Egbert Cadbury and Captain Robert Leckie, powered by a Rolls Royce Eagle engine producing a remarkable 375hp. Its bullets rapidly tore a hole in the tail of Strasser's ship before fire spread along the craft and it plummeted into the shallows off the Lincolnshire coast. There were no survivors, and Strasser's body was subsequently recovered and buried at sea.

If with Mathy the German airship service lost their troubadour, with Strasser they lost their father figure, the one man with unshakeable faith in the airships' abilities. In the event, however resolute and skilled his crews – and whatever the undoubted achievements of the defenders – this proved over optimistic due, primarily, to the inherent limitations of these air Titanics that were not only fiendishly difficult to fly but, with their immense gas bags, all too ready to ignite.

An account of an accident gives a vivid picture of the hazards facing such crews, and their ships' vulnerability in a raid:

> During the night a (raiding) Zeppelin had become stern heavy through loss of gas in one of her rear gas cells. Her crew dropped rear ballast and moved fuel and bombs to the fore end of the craft. At dawn she descended through thick fog to try and get her bearings with the ground. Through a sudden change in air temperature the gas expanded and she became nose heavy. The engines were set at full speed to try and increase the speed of air flowing over her control surfaces and give her dynamic lift. At the height of 200 to 300 feet she broke out of the fog and the crew saw the ice-covered estuary of a River below them. The engines were immediately stopped and forward ballast was dropped. The bombs that had been moved forward could not be dropped because at this height they would have probably destroyed the airship. Its course continued downwards until the control car smashed hard on to the ice. One crew member fell out and was able to make his way to shore in spite of an injured foot. The airship then shot back up into the air to 3,300 feet, but since the damaged control car threatened to tear itself off and the escape ladder to the body of the airship had been smashed the lives of the men still inside the control car were hanging by a thin thread indeed.[28]

The airships' increased size made them even more vulnerable to adverse weather conditions, particularly in the high atmosphere and yet larger barn-door targets for opposing aircraft.[29] In any event, the Zeppelins were never used to best effect as bombers because of the other tasks to which they were assigned (which they were also not best able to perform). Due to inter service rivalry they rarely united in bombing raids, with the result that when London was almost defenceless it escaped virtually unscathed, and by the time enough ships were made available Londoners had found ways of coping with the raids and the capital's defences, including its aircraft, had become too strong for them.

Even so these singularly vulnerable craft had a massive impact. Londoners' initial wonder and bewilderment at the sight of such giants hovering overhead rapidly changed to outrage and anger at what they saw as cowardly and indeed immoral attacks, an anger all the more violent because in the early stages at least there seemed no effective way of countering them.

Although they could never meet the unrealistic expectations of Admiral Behneke, a relatively small number of such uniquely unsuitable craft actually achieved far more than could reasonably have been expected and, equally important, their experiences paved the way for heavy aeroplanes far better equipped for the task.

Chapter 2

The Gothas Take Over

Night shatters in mid-heaven – the bark of the guns,
The roar of planes, the crash of bombs

'Air Raid' by Wilfred Gibson[1]

In addition to its airships, by 1914 Germany possessed 180 aeroplanes of varying kinds, almost as many as Britain and France combined which, like those of its opponents, were mainly intended for reconnaissance purposes and not equipped for genuine air combat. However, following the expected success of its planned thrust through neutral Belgium to the Channel coast, some of these could conceivably be despatched to bomb London, the political and commercial heart of Britain's worldwide empire lying just 70 miles west of Calais. From the beginning of the war this initiative had enjoyed the support of Oberste Heereslitung (or OHL, the army's high command) and Major Wilhelm Siegert, an air battalion officer, had in fact been appointed to command a dedicated bomber squadron given the innocuous cover title of 'the Carrier Pigeon Detachment of Ostend'.

After the great offensive was checked short of the Channel coast – due in part to the skilled defence shown by a small British Expeditionary Force, and despite one or two 'hit and run' raids on London by individual adventurous pilots, any squadron bombing of the capital was beyond the range of most aircraft of the day. The 'Carrier Pigeon' formation was deployed instead on bombing the Channel ports along with other targets behind the allied lines, leaving the bombing of London to the longer range airships.

As a result of serious and growing problems experienced by the airships during 1916, interest revived in using aircraft for strategic bombing. Here the example of the brilliant Russian aeronautical engineer, Igor Sikorski, who before the war designed both two- and four-engined aircraft, had already inspired German designers and by the winter of 1914 they were testing a twin-engined aircraft of their own. This would subsequently develop into their famed Grosskampfflugzeug, or battle aeroplane, but because of the extended trials required and the urgent need for fighter planes on the Western Front, comparatively few GI and GII machines were operational by 1916.

Even so, the growing importance of air warfare and allied successes in the air during that year resulted in an upgrading of the German Combatant Air Forces (Luftstreitkrafte) to the equivalent of an army wing commanded by a General Officer. Whatever his concerns in France, General Ernst von Hoeppner decided that since airship raids on London had become so difficult, attacks by aeroplanes should be mounted as soon as practicable[2] by machines such as the advanced versions of the Grosskampfflugzeug, and orders were placed for thirty such planes (Gotha GIVs) from the Gothaer Waggonfabrik factory for delivery by 1 February 1917. This was a grotesquely small number for such a massive task as it had been calculated that 18 bombers, each carrying 660lb of explosives, would be needed to achieve the destructive capacity of 3 Zeppelins (although 3 Zeppelins had, in fact, never yet reached London together). In fairness, Hoeppner had additional plans for a second squadron of much larger multi-engined planes – the Riesenflugzeugen or Giants – scheduled for use against Britain in the near future.[3]

Following OHL's approval for a bombing campaign of Britain – codenamed Turk's Cross – orders were issued for the construction of three permanent aerodromes on the outskirts of Ghent, beyond the marauding planes of the Royal Naval Air Service (RNAS) but also a full 170 miles from London. Like those men recruited for the airships, the squadron looked for especially good candidates who were confident of flying across wide expanses of water. Hoeppner outlined their objectives which, while still highly ambitious, stopped short of the Zeppelins' aim of preventing Britain from continuing the war. The Gothas were 'to disrupt the British war industry (in London and elsewhere), disorganise the communications between coastal ports and London, attack the supply dumps of the coastal ports and hinder the transport of war materials across the channel'.[4]

By attacking London and creating destruction and panic there, it was also hoped to cause further planes and guns to be re-directed from the Western Front which, after the initial impact of the Zeppelin raids, had been returned there. Between February and May 1917, for instance, 77 pilots trained in night flying were withdrawn from the British Home Defences and sent to France, leaving 107 against a full establishment of 198.[5] Conversely, London would unquestionably be the hardest nut for the bombers to crack. In the case of the two single light aircraft that had raided the city during 1915 and 1916, their bombs had injured just ten people and inflicted the smallest of pinpricks on such a huge target.[6] Hoeppner hoped that massed raids by his heavy Gotha bombers would have quite different results.

With so much depending on this strategy, the commander of such an elite squadron (answering directly to OHL) was obviously of the highest importance and for this task Hoeppner selected Captain Ernst Brandenburg. A 34-year-old infantry officer who had been severely wounded in 1914 and was no longer fit for service in the trenches, he had become an air observer, where he proved himself to be a natural leader. The tall and balding Brandenburg had a massive brow and a strong presence; an ardent chess player and student of philosophy, he was more intellectual than the archetypal German officer and soon showed that he had good judgement and was capable of making rapid decisions.

The problems experienced by the Zeppelins left Brandenburg and his men in little doubt about the magnitude of their task, but by the standards of the day their bombers were undoubtedly impressive: the Gotha GIV biplane was larger than any other in service, with its long, angular wings measuring 78ft, a figure unequalled by any German aircraft of the Second World War, and a slim fuselage over 40ft long. When on the ground the plane's nose and forward cabin towered impressively above any spectator. In its lower wing two Mercedes six-cylinder engines, each generating 260hp, gave it a respectable cruising speed of 80mph and the ability to reach an impressive height ceiling of 18,000ft. It was designed to carry six 50kg bombs. Although its three-man crew had the disadvantage of being in open cabins, they had three machine guns to protect them, one of which fired through a tunnel designed to counter any aircraft from attacking under the plane's tail. Angular and by no means handsome, the Gotha proved surprisingly manoeuvrable in the air, although perilously unstable when it came in to land unladen.

Brandenburg was thorough in his preparations. Each plane was tested for at least twenty-five hours before he considered it ready for operations and when he found their performance below his exacting standards he returned many of the engines to the Mercedes factory, for by 1917 defective materials were customarily being used in the manufacturing process. In spite of such precautions, engine failures would remain a conspicuous feature of the Gotha raids. Following his test flights, Brandenburg decided that auxiliary fuel tanks were required to extend the planes' flight times by approximately two hours. He also trained his crews to fly in close formation the better to meet opposing fighters, but with no radios yet in operation he was compelled to use a system of coloured flags to signal any required changes of direction.

Cold was a major factor for the Gotha airmen; to help them remain efficient at 15–18,000ft they were given heavy gloves, high boots and a half-length coat to go over their uniforms, and issued with small cylinders of compressed oxygen which they accessed through a mouthpiece resembling an oriental smoking pipe. As with the Zeppelins, Brandenburg's aircraft faced serious problems from the elements: in windy conditions, for instance, their massive wings met with high air resistance. While this was entirely predictable the weather patterns were far less so, for the continental ones tended to follow those over Britain and the squadron's meteorological expert could never depend on the timing of expected storms over the North Sea that threatened their return flights. From the outset predicting the weather was a major factor. For the England Squadron it was of crucial importance to predict the weather as accurately as possible. The squadron's first operation, for instance, following a storm warning, ended at Nieuwmunster airfield on the Belgian coast, where (prior to the fitting of supplementary fuel tanks) the planes were accustomed to top up their tanks. During their second raid of 25 May 1917 the weather again proved important[7] for, after crossing the English coast between the Crouch and Blackwater rivers, Brandenburg and his twenty-one raiders came upon cloud banks some 7,000ft thick that completely masked the London area. Upon this he decided to turn coastward and bomb the military camps at Shorncliffe and Cheriton together with the port of Folkestone, from where so many soldiers crossed over to Europe, even though it meant sacrificing the elements of surprise in his bombing capability.

After splitting up to bomb the military camps with their many hundreds of Canadian troops, the squadron reunited for a formation attack on Folkestone. For no explicable reason the town had not received a warning, despite Dover's reporting the bombers' approach an hour and a half earlier. Although the sound of the bombs must have been heard in Folkestone, the town's citizens were not alarmed since they were accustomed to hearing regular explosions during the military exercises nearby.

So it was that on a beautiful spring evening in 1917 Folkestone's streets thronged with unsuspecting families and wounded servicemen. In the absence of any warnings, even after they caught sight of the planes (rather than airships), most of the onlookers were curious rather than apprehensive and the watching Edith Cole, for instance, described them flying at some 15,000ft as 'beautiful with the sun on their wings'. Their bombs soon started dropping on Tontine Street, into which numerous lanes and alleys converged.[8] Here, people were gathered outside its major shops such as Gosnold's Drapery Store and Stoke's Greengrocery, and one bomb fell among a queue outside Stoke's which brought the shop's roof down and caused a large number of casualties. In all, the raid caused 95 deaths and 195 injured.[9]

Although thirty-seven pilots from both the Royal Flying Corps and the Royal Naval Air Service attempted to intercept the raiders, without radios they were unable to co-ordinate their sorties, and the few who were capable of reaching the height of the German bombers took so long climbing that they arrived after the bombers had moved away. No Gothas were downed over the target and, after dropping further bombs on Dover, they moved off without molestation, although much closer to their bases they were attacked by Nos 4 and 9 squadrons of the RNAS based at Dunkirk. One Gotha was destroyed and another crashed near Bruges, with the Germans claiming three of the attackers.

As with the earlier Zeppelin raids, this more disciplined and effective foray by heavy bombers brought angry reactions, primarily about the inadequacy of the defensive measures. As a result a so-called 'Indignation Meeting' was held in Folkestone, while in London a conference was convened at the War Office under General Sir David Henderson, the Director General of Military Aeronautics, to consider the most appropriate response. While regretting the Folkestone raid, it understandably focused on strengthening the defences of more sensitive targets against this new menace and an extra forty planes were made available for the defence of London, compared with an additional nineteen for the coastal areas. The conference also decided that any further reallocation of aircraft would be to the detriment of the Western Front, and that with the increased numbers of defending fighters there would be no longer any likelihood of the enemy avoiding 'an engagement with our fighting machines'.[10]

With Brandenburg's hand now revealed he had every reason to launch his bombers against London. Yet again, on 5 June, bad weather prevented him from reaching the capital, and instead his twenty-two aircraft attacked coastal installations at Shoeburyness and Sheerness on the Isle of Sheppey. Of the forty-seven people killed or wounded on this occasion, only twelve were civilians. Despite the War Office's confident expectations over intercepting the attackers, of the sixty-six planes attempting it, only five got near enough 'to deliver brief but ineffective attacks'.[11] The anti-aircraft guns at Sheerness and Shoeburyness had better luck, shooting one plane down into the sea off Barton's Point, but although a number of RNAS pilots based at Dunkirk again attempted to intercept the returning bombers, German fighters from Flanders engaged them and no further Gothas were lost.

* * *

The first bomber attack on London finally came on 12 June 1917, six weeks after the raid on Folkestone. This followed a prediction by the squadron's weather expert, Lieutenant Cloessner, of clear skies over Britain during the next few days, a forecast that he later modified to likely thunderstorms on the afternoon of Wednesday 13 June. After diverting four planes to confuse the defenders, Brandenburg led fourteen bombers in a diamond formation towards the capital. At 11.35 they were looking down in amazement at the size of a city stretching outwards in all directions. In contrast, from ground level the correspondent of the *New York Times* based in London was looking up at 'the enemy aeroplanes with their throbbing engines journeying through the clouds like little silver birds'.[12]

Along the city's outer defences the guns opened up in a noisy crescendo, although their shells proved ineffective against planes flying 3 miles high which, following a white flare from Brandenburg's leading aircraft, scattered to drop their bombs individually. These struck four main localities within the city between East Ham and the Albert Docks, around Liverpool Street station and upon Southwark and Dalston. The main attack lasted just 2 minutes but the casualties amounted to 162 killed and 432 injured, the largest total of any bombing attack during the war. The worst incident occurred at the Upper North Street Schools, in Poplar, where a 50kg bomb smashed through the 3-storey building to explode on the ground floor amid 64 very young children and their teachers, killing 16 children and injuring 30 more. The mood, like that of German citizens during the RAF and USAF bombing of Germany during the Second World War, was vengeful. Following a service conducted by the Bishop of London, the children were buried in a common grave and the floral tributes included one that read, 'To our children murdered by German Aircraft'.   MONUMENT IN   PARK "POPLAR"

Whatever the emotions aroused, Brandenburg and his crews had struck far more effectively than the Zeppelin pilots of the previous year. They not only reached London but flew over it in broad daylight to select their targets, before resuming a close formation for the homeward run. Their attack was so swift and unexpected that none of the ninety-two planes sent against them registered a single kill. However, this time they were also very lucky. Tired and cold as they surely were, all the Gotha pilots managed to land safely before a violent storm carrying giant hailstones pelted the grounded planes – half an hour later and Brandenburg's whole squadron could have been destroyed.

However well led, a raid by fourteen bombers crewed by fewer than fifty airmen carrying explosive bombs of just 50kg or 12.5kg could not reasonably be expected to damage the great capital unduly, nor have any significant effect unless it could be repeated day after day.

The reactions on both sides were predictable: pride in Germany and fury in Britain. German pride was seen in an official communiqué announcing that 'Today our airmen dropped bombs on the Fortress of London' and in the Kaiser's award to Brandenburg of the coveted blue and gold cross of the Pour le Mérite for his achievements.

With the British, while the casualties bore no comparison with the daily losses of the Western Front or the ¼ million men soon to be lost during the coming autumn offensive there, the effrontery of such an attack on innocent men, women and children living in the nation's capital inevitably raised the most furious questions yet about the continuing poverty of the home defences. At its meeting that same afternoon the War Cabinet voted for a massive expansion in the Royal Flying Corps, increasing its 108 service squadrons to 200, and recommending a corresponding expansion in the Royal Naval Air Service. It also considered taking revenge on a German town, such as Mannheim, although this proposal was rejected in favour of immediately bringing two squadrons from France to reinforce the home defences and moving another to Calais to help intercept raiders on their return. In fact, after an uneventful fortnight these squadrons were returned to the Expeditionary Force.

In retrospect, this first raid on London marked a high point in the England Squadron's fortunes. No one, for instance, could have anticipated that as Brandenburg was returning from his visit to the Kaiser his Albatross would crash on take off, badly injuring him and killing his pilot. His successor, Captain Rudolf Kleine, also chosen by Hoeppner, had already been twice wounded in the air but he never attracted the same affection, and from then on the bombers would face ever improving defences. In any case, the chance of rapidly following up the first raid was soon lost. Following a succession of unfavourable weather reports, the next attack did not take place until 4 July, almost a month later, and with the weather still uncertain this proved to be no more than a hit and run raid on Harwich naval base. Out of the twenty-five Gothas that set out, seven were forced to return with engine trouble. Although the remainder succeeded in damaging the docks at Harwich and Felixstowe the casualties were light with just seventeen employees killed and thirty injured. Although eighty-three defending planes were scrambled, the bombers had turned for home before they could be intercepted and, despite the RNAS force in Belgium receiving fast and manoeuvrable Sopwith 'Pups', all the Gothas returned safely.

Three days later, on 7 July, came London's second daylight raid, by twenty-one planes flying in the now traditional diamond formation. These attempted to retain surprise by approaching the city from the north and north-west, but they failed to escape harassment from the London barrage. Passing across the City and the East End they dropped bombs as they went, killing 54 people and injuring 190, considerably fewer than on the first raid. Seventy-eight pilots of the Royal Flying Corps and seventeen from the Royal Naval Air Service rose in the city's defence, but again failed to make contact. Apart from thirty contemporary fighters that had recently been supplied, there were still twenty-one other models, many of which were of limited value.[13] This was shortly to change and, in any case, the raid was not without loss for the attackers: one Gotha was pounced on while flying low over North Foreland and was shot down into the sea, while three others crashed as they attempted to land.

Although less costly than the first, this raid created an even greater outcry. At a Cabinet meeting held the same day, the fact that the bombers had succeeded in flying in full daylight across Britain before reaching London provoked a reaction that General Sir William Robertson said was 'akin to the world coming to an end'. The *Daily Mail* added to the clamour, declaring that Britain had not been so humiliated and disgraced since the Dutch fleet ravaged the Medway in 1667.

Field Marshal Haig was again ordered to send two good fighter squadrons to Britain, and the proposal to retaliate by bombing Mannheim was revived. Haig accordingly despatched the two squadrons without delay but he maintained his strong opposition to any bombing of Mannheim, both as a matter of principle and because it would compel him to reconsider his own planned operations in support of his troops. In the event, just one fighter squadron was kept back from France and any bombing of Mannheim was postponed, although twenty-eight other fighters intended for France were also retained in Britain.

Apart from such immediate reactions, the government decided to set up a committee under the Prime Minister (in which the work was effectively carried out by his special adviser, Lieutenant General Jan Christian Smuts) to examine any arrangements necessary for home defence against air raids, and to consider improving the direction of air policy. Smuts' proposals are examined later, together with other arguments in favour of a separate air arm, but those he put forward for home defence were primarily concerned with the London area. He left little doubt about its importance when he wrote that 'London occupies a peculiar position in the Empire of which it is the nerve centre, and we consider that its defence demands exceptional measures'.[14] After echoing the generally sombre mood of the day and predicting that London would become part of the battlefront, his main proposals included both improved ground defences and extra fighter squadrons. He also recommended that a 'senior officer of first rate ability and practical air experience should be placed in executive command of the air defence of London'.[15]

Smuts, who was appointed on 11 July, presented his report just eight days later and by 5 August Brigadier General Edward B Ashmore had been selected to work out the plans for the London air defences.

Hoeppner's aim to divert further much-needed resources from France was about to be achieved, but henceforth things would become ever more difficult for Kleine and his men. The weather again caused the majority of their problems. More than a fortnight passed before conditions seemed reasonably favourable for further air raids, and even then the Gotha squadron was reluctant to go far inland, limiting itself to a raid on Harwich and the naval air station at Felixstowe, where although an amazing 121 aircraft rose in response, none succeeded in sighting them. At this time Leutnant Walter Georgii, the squadrons' new meteorological officer, was not regarded favourably by Kleine, for while the weather seemed good enough on the continent, Georgii advised against further raids because of the strong west winds he knew were blowing across Britain. His caution was proved right when one raid authorized for 29 July failed to reach Britain and another, on 12 August, launched at very short notice with just twelve bombers, was forced to limit its attacks to coastal targets. After 2 planes turned back with engine trouble just off the British coast, the main body were approached by 133 aeroplanes. After attacking Southend they quickly turned homeward but this time they lost five bombers, four of which crashed on landing.

The next attack on London was scheduled for 18 August, 6 weeks later, for which Kleine assembled his largest force so far, of 28 aircraft, including 2 'Giant' bombers. The latter were, in fact, the only planes that in any way approached the range and carrying capacity of the much frailer Zeppelins. These had previously operated on the Russian Front and were commanded by Captain Richard von Bentivegni, a regular German officer of Italian extraction who received his orders directly from Hoeppner. Such massive biplanes had an even larger wingspan than the Gothas, measuring 138ft 6in, longer than that of British Halifax bombers of the Second World War and only 3ft shorter than the American B29 Super Fortresses of that era. In many ways they were ahead of their time. Their four Mercedes Maybach engines, each of 245hp facing both front and rearward, gave them a range of 300 miles and the ability to carry a bomb load of 2 tons, normally in the form of eighteen 220lb bombs that could be released electronically. Their crew of between 7 and 9 had the option of firing up to 6 machine guns (although 3 became standard). Each plane had a wireless (and an operator who could check their position by radio signal) and all the crew members were equipped with electrically heated flying suits, oxygen for altitude flying and (unusually for the time) parachutes. Considered the ugliest aircraft of the First World War, they proved more than a match for British fighters. Their disadvantage was that they needed protracted and labour-intensive servicing and, because they were not transferred to Germany until the autumn of 1917, they came too late – and crucially were too few – to play a major part in the strategic bombing of the British capital.

The raid of 18 August proved disastrous for Kleine, although not as a result of the air defences. Despite his meteorologist's warnings of severe winds and poor weather over Britain, he overruled him and set off. After flying for three hours into strong headwinds which caused much-increased fuel consumption, Kleine finally realized the operation had to be abandoned, but by now his aircraft had insufficient fuel to reach their home airfields and as a result eleven of them were lost – over a third of his total force.

Just four days later the obdurate Kleine had his surviving bombers out again. He was down to just fifteen airworthy planes, four of which had to turn back with engine trouble. This time it was not London that was the objective, but even with the closer target of the coastal towns a combination of accurate gunfire and marauding aircraft forced his planes to turn back before they could cause much damage. This time there were 137 defending aircraft, 17 from the RNAS and 120 from the RFC. Consequently, 3 Gothas were shot down, 2 by gunfire and 1 by a plane piloted by Flight Sub-Lieutenant Drake of the RNAS.

This raid brought the Gothas' daylight operations to an end. With the coastal defences also proving their effectiveness, those for London had undoubtedly become too strong. If he continued with the same tactics, Kleine knew he was bound to suffer an unacceptable level of wastage and, to make good such losses, he would need to accept inferior machines and less-experienced crews.[16] Seeking an alternative, on 3 September 1917 he mounted a trial attack by night upon Chatham, using five of his most experienced crews whose only navigational aid at the time was a compass. To his surprise four of the five Gothas reached Britain successfully and, thus encouraged, he ordered an attack the next night against London. When the five bombers involved reached the capital they found its defences unprepared, the gunners unable to find them and no answering British fighters, although one of his bombers was lost to gunfire off Sheerness. In such circumstances, attacking London had again become a viable option.

Although obliged to take part in raiding the continental Channel ports through which thousands of troop reinforcements were passing, OHL also allowed Kleine to continue with his strategic raids. While it was accepted that inflicting major damage upon London had become more difficult, they would at the very least prevent the capital's defences from standing down and serve to keep Londoners' nerves on edge. OHL also gave permission for the Giants to be included in the force. Kleine made full use of this opportunity and from the week commencing 24 September 1917 it was said that the threat posed from successive raids by a small number of German bombers succeeded in holding 'sway over millions of Londoners'. Anticipation of further raids by the England Squadron against which, as yet, there seemed little or no satisfactory reply, the Squadron not only kept Londoners in suspense but caused alarming rumours to run rife. Charles H Grasty, a London correspondent for the *New York Times*, was, for instance, told in all seriousness by an American air officer that 'a fleet of 500 Gothas would come to London within a few months'.[17] In reality, just 3 planes bombed London on 24 September, killing 14 people and injuring 36; 13 more were injured by anti-aircraft fire. In any case, London remained unnaturally dark and cheerless, with its streets deserted since petrol restrictions had reduced motor traffic almost to zero. To add to the general apprehension on the day of the raid a fleet of ten Zeppelins were seen off the Yorkshire coast, which went on to raid Hull. The Gothas were out again the following night, although their bombing was even less severe. On 28 September, after being grounded for forty-eight hours by rain and bad weather, they were again despatched to London. This promised to be a major raid with all Kleine's 25 Gothas, together with 2 Giants, involved, but because of thick cloud they failed to reach the city and only 16 Gothas survived. No less than six planes crashed while landing and three others were shot down by gunners along the coast. The two Giants returned safely, although also without bombing the capital. On the following night only two Gothas and one Giant managed to reach London, but by the standards of the time the city was said to have suffered heavily. Houses in Notting Hill, Kingsland and Kennington were hit and twelve people were killed, with sixty-two injured.[18]

These 4 raids in less than a week[19] caused some 300,000 Londoners to seek shelter in the Underground transport system. Not only did such crowding prevent ordinary passengers from boarding their trains, but the whole network soon reeked of unwashed bodies. On 30 September came another raid but, although houses were hit in the East End near the docks, the overall damage was slight. By Sunday a good proportion of Kleine's surviving airmen were exhausted and one of his wings had to be stood down. For the projected raid on 1 October he resorted to new tactics, sending out eighteen Gotha aircraft in relays between 6.50 and 10.00 pm in an attempt to bring the warning systems close to breaking point. In material terms, this last raid of the series was not particularly costly, with only 8 bombers reaching London where they killed 10 people and injured 28.[20]

Never again would the England Squadron mount such a sustained campaign as the so-called 'Raids of the Harvest Moon'. As before, London continued to prove very difficult to reach: of the 92 Gothas despatched during the week only 55 succeeded in crossing the English coast and less than 20 reached the capital. Of the five sorties made by the Giants, only one succeeded in reaching London. Even so, although it also proved expensive in terms of the aircraft lost, and caused relatively small numbers of casualties, the effects of the first mini-blitz brought profound psychological concerns for the city's population.[21]

Almost a month after the 'Raids of the Harvest Moon' Kleine again rang the changes, by sending twenty-two Gothas to raid London, Ramsgate and Dover with bombloads of 10lb incendiary devices. In practice, when dropped over relatively wide areas of the city these proved far less successful than expected, and he lost six planes. On 5 December, nineteen Gothas and two Giants again raided London with incendiaries and this time they attempted to drop them more densely, but although they succeeded in igniting four large fires, these were, however, rapidly extinguished by the London Fire Brigade. By now it was clear that their incendiary bombs, about which so much was expected, needed further development[22] and in early December Kleine also felt obliged to send a special report to Hoeppner acknowledging that with London's ever strengthening defences the cover of night could no longer protect his raiders.

Soon afterwards he was himself shot down and killed while attacking British troop encampments near Ypres. Kleine was succeeded by Oberleutnant Walter, one of his best flight leaders, under whom sporadic raids continued before, in February 1918, Brandenburg arrived to reassume command. Although he now had an artificial leg and other scars from his crash, his enthusiasm remained as strong as ever. When he saw the state of the squadron he rated it non-combatant for six weeks while setting about retraining and refitting it. It needed to be in good heart for he had in mind a larger raid than ever before, but in the meantime he sent out the Giants, under Captain Bentivegni, on a series of 'tip and run' attacks to keep Londoners on edge and the capital's defences at full stretch.

These proved effective. On 29 January four Giants reached London and, after dropping their bombs, all returned safely. Just over a fortnight later, five repeated the process and this time one dropped a bomb of a metric ton, the heaviest of the war to date, causing great devastation to Odhams Printing Works near Covent Garden, whose basement at that time was in use as a public air-raid shelter. The casualties at this one site were 233, including 67 deaths. The next day a single Giant reached and bombed London before evading the 69 planes sent against it and returning safely to base. On 7 March all 6 mounted another attack, although only 3 reached the capital and this time 2 crashed over Belgium on their return.

By mid-March Brandenburg again had his Gothas primed for raiding Britain, although they had first to support the German offensive of April 1918 against Haig's British forces. Then, following more frustrating delays due to bad weather, Brandenburg launched his revitalized squadron against London. This numbered 38 aircraft, including 2 with single engines, together with the remaining 3 Giants. On reaching the capital they found things very difficult, losing 6 aeroplanes over London and 4 elsewhere. The defences forced them to split up and as a result their bombing was spread over a wide area, but

1,000 premises were destroyed and 45 people killed with 181 injured, most of them Londoners.

This proved to be the England Squadron's last throw. Although the London defenders fully expected another wave of bombings like those of the 'Harvest Moon', with Germany rapidly losing the war, Brandenburg's aircraft were required to support the German armies recoiling from the allies' counter-offensives, and to attack the British Handley Page aircraft presently bombing the German homeland.

*   *   *

As with the Zeppelins, Brandenburg's more robust Gotha and Giant aircraft failed either seriously to disrupt London and its war industry or disorganize its communications with the coast.

Apart from the strengthening British defences, they encountered other serious problems, notably resulting from adverse weather: 1917 was the worst summer and autumn in living memory, and this undoubtedly played a major part in the Squadron's inability to mount regular attacks on London. There were also engine failures that limited the weight of such attacks and led to one in every eight planes having to turn back before crossing the English coast. Nothing could be done about the weather, but despite the massive strides in aircraft technology as a whole the higher priority given elsewhere led to an actual decline in the squadron's engine efficiency. In its first raid it succeeded in reaching altitudes of 16,000–16,700ft, while by the third this had dropped to between 12,500 and 13,500ft.[23]

Although the England Squadron did not suffer from the inter service rivalry that had so affected the Zeppelins, it was similarly not used as effectively as it might have been, with the German High Command deploying it on a series of varied tasks, including battlefield support and bombing the Channel ports, rather than allowing it to concentrate on the strategic bombing of London. When it was used on bombing, too little thought was given to the timing and concentration of such attacks. Although the autumn raids of 1917 succeeded in forcing Douglas Haig to send fighter squadrons home from France, there was no attempt to make the night bombing raids of February or March 1918 coincide with the German offensive on the British Third and Fifth armies in France.

However much the England Squadron might have been better employed or not, the principal reason for its failure was that its destructive capacity proved inadequate. Although during 1917–18 its raids on London caused £1½ million worth of damage, as well as killing 487 people and injuring 1,434[24] (and they were twice as destructive as those mounted by the Zeppelins during 1915–16[25]), when seen against Greater London's population of 7 million or so stretching across a radius of some 13 miles, they were troublesome rather than grievous. In the hysterical atmosphere of the time it might have been different if the England Squadron had actually been given the 100 bombers that OHL believed were needed to make an effective strike,[26] or if its incendiary bombs had genuinely proved effective. But the German production of heavy bombers was never high enough and a doubling in the number of bombers still seemed too little against such a massive target. There could be no denying that the squadron tried its best, for its human casualties amounted to almost twice its original strength and it lost 60 Gotha aircraft, 24 of which were shot down over Britain or disappeared into the sea, with a further 36 lost in crashes.[27]

In retrospect, while representing a far greater menace than the gigantic but frail Zeppelins, the small number of strategic aircraft which, up to May 1918, never exceeded twenty-seven on any raid, faced an insuperable task. In such circumstances the conclusion of the official historian for the British air war that 'on military grounds the air attacks were overwhelmingly justified by the results'[28] appears somewhat surprising. In fact, he was referring specifically to the continued and growing diversions of men and materiel sent from the battlefronts to bolster home defence, especially for London.

It was, of course, far easier for a historian writing after a victorious war to weigh up comparative costs in this way. For those actually involved in safeguarding the nation's war efforts, when the throb of the Gothas' engines over London (however few in number) could cause such fear and anger and represent such a menace to the country's nerve centre, different standards would have applied. The raiders had to be stopped and, before radar and inter-ceptor planes were equipped with radios, attempts to develop some form of early warning system and to erect a novel defensive screen across the skies round London were bound to be demanding of both men and materials. Whatever the costs, by the later stages of the war they were undeniably proving successful and if the raiders had been able to mount larger raids the defenders' success rates would surely have been more marked still.

Chapter 3

The City's Defenders

*The raids even at their worst entirely failed to produce the despondency
expected by the German High Command.*

Major General E B Ashmore,
Commander London's air defences[1]

As for London's defences at the beginning of the war, despite the warnings
of visionary writers like H G Wells, there is no evidence that the British
establishment expected it to be seriously attacked from the air. Was it not
only six years since the first flight of a British aircraft and had not the 1907
Hague Convention (unsigned by Germany) forbidden the bombardment of
undefended places 'by any means whatever'? Admittedly, Article 2 of its Naval
Convention acknowledged that military installations in undefended places might
be bombarded, but aeroplanes were still comparatively frail and of short range
and Germany's supreme warlord, Kaiser Wilhelm, had forbidden his airships –
theoretically capable of reaching London – from bombing the English royal
palaces and other historical monuments. In Britain the prevalent feeling towards
such attacks, expressed by General Sir David Henderson, Commander of the
recently formed Royal Flying Corps, was that 'no enemy would risk the odium
such action would involve'.[2] General Henderson had no doubt his service's
primary task was to support the British Expeditionary Force despatched to
France to assist their French allies. With no attack expected, London needed
no defences.

But in Germany opinion was different. By 20 August 1914 Admiral Behneke,
Deputy Chief of the Naval Staff, was already advocating aerial attacks on
London, if primarily for tactical reasons, because of the major role played by its
massive docks and because the British navy's nerve centre was in Whitehall. If
such attacks had been mounted they would probably have faced little or no
opposition, for by 13 August 1914 four of the Royal Flying Corps' squadrons
were with the Expeditionary Force in France, thus removing all their current
pilots and almost all the country's serviceable aircraft, sixty-three in all.[3] Their
transport included requisitioned vehicles, one of which was painted scarlet and

had gold letters on its side proclaiming 'The World's Appetizer'. Although the 116 aeroplanes remaining in Britain were theoretically available for Home Defence, all but 20 were either obsolete, damaged or worn out. The prime responsibility for the other fifty or so aircraft in Britain belonging to the Royal Naval Air Service was to protect the naval installations and ships.

In spite of General Henderson's conviction that London and other capitals were safe from attack, the bombing of Antwerp by German airships on 26 August 1914 soon caused the British war minister, Lord Kitchener, to recognize his country's new vulnerability and to extend the responsibilities of Winston Churchill as First Sea Lord for all naval installations to include protection of the country as a whole. Churchill's reaction was typically spirited and pugnacious. Well aware of the resources and time required to construct a national defence system, he immediately advocated a policy of 'forward air defence' against possible strikes from the German Zeppelins by attacking them 'as near as possible to their point of departure'.[4] In their attempts to implement this policy, during the first twelve months of the war RNAS pilots operating from their base at Dunkirk succeeded in destroying six Zeppelins, but once the airships' bases were moved back from the Belgian coast the Zeppelins could no longer be prevented from setting out for Britain.

Churchill therefore decided the best option was to station a force of aeroplanes along Britain's east coast to intercept such raiders before they entered the country's air space. With typical confidence, if not relish, Churchill told the House of Commons that 'any hostile aircraft, airships or aeroplanes which reached our coast during the coming year would be promptly attacked in superior force by a swarm of very formidable hornets',[5] and to this end he caused to be assembled on airfields between London and Dover sixty aeroplanes of different types, armed with rifles firing incendiary bullets which (he assured his listeners) had proved their capacity to destroy a Zeppelin.[6] Churchill also made clear his intention to defend London by placing his few guns and searchlights where they could protect its vulnerable points, such as power stations, magazines and oil tanks, rather than trying to cover the whole of the city neighbourhoods. Such measures were to be combined with a policy of passive defence such as darkening localities to confuse the attackers.[7] Churchill's policy of forward air defence however would be put aside following his resignation as First Sea Lord late in 1915, and the main emphasis placed on defending London itself.

At first the defensive measures were very limited. There were only thirty-three guns that could even be considered of use and these were of very variable standard. One was a relatively large 12-pounder[8] that the Royal Horse Artillery in London had ingeniously emplaced in a vertical position, but which needed major disassembly before it could be traversed or even adjusted. In addition, some 1-pounder 'pom-poms' of Boer War vintage had been positioned on the roofs of important government buildings, such as the Foreign Office, the Admiralty, the Office of the Crown Agents and Woolwich Arsenal.[9] Such ordnance, even when supplemented by a few howitzers, caused General Pile, the Commander of Anti-aircraft Command during the Second World War, to acknowledge that in those early days 'the ribald dismissal of the anti-aircraft gun as one of the three most useless things in the world' seemed amply justified.[10]

Churchill had been fully aware of these deficiencies when in 1914 he had appointed a senior naval officer, Rear Admiral Tudor, to produce a scheme for the capital's defence. This commenced by identifying London's vital nerve centre containing senior executive and administrative personnel as extending from Buckingham Palace to Charing Cross. Tudor's defences were necessarily limited, although they included placing three pairs of searchlights in the area, supported by guns and controlled from a pivotal gun position at Admiralty Arch. In addition, special lookout posts were to be established on the city's periphery, connected to Tudor's control centre by telephone and, most important of all, he put forward proposals for a ring of aeroplane stations along a 10-mile radius from Charing Cross.

By September 1914 Churchill's recommendations for London's passive defence had resulted in the Home Office issuing regulations for the extinction or dimming of lights, to prevent marauding enemy airmen from recognizing salient points on the ground. Attempts were also made to break up the uniformity of lights along 'easily recognised thoroughfares such as the Mile End Road and the Victoria Embankment and on bridges'.[11] Conversely, the London parks with their large telltale patches of dark were to be provided with lights. From 1 October 1914 – eight months before the first airship raid – all-powerful outside lights in London were required to be extinguished from sunset to sunrise, the street lamps shaded and lights on omnibuses reduced to no more than was necessary to collect the fares. Whether effective or not, this meant that from the earliest months of the war the airship menace had become all too apparent to Londoners. (Similar steps were taken to reduce lighting in the coastal towns and in Birmingham.)

London escaped very lightly from the first Zeppelin raids during the spring and summer of 1915, until on 8 September a single Zeppelin (commanded by the brilliant aviator Heinrich Mathy) moved across London with apparent impunity, coolly selecting his targets as he went, and this raised such serious doubts about its defences that a storm of petitions and protests demanded their improvement. Four days later a naval gunnery expert, Admiral Sir Percy Scott, was appointed as defence controller. He straightway discarded the pom–poms and requested an extra 104 larger anti-aircraft guns – both 13- and 18-pounders – to be supported by at least 50 searchlights. These were to be supplemented by 75mm auto-cannon from France, capable of firing high-explosive anti-aircraft shells mounted on motor vehicles powered by 100hp engines, together with 3-pounders carried on open lorries. Accompanied by mobile searchlights, they were capable of speeding to the threatened areas and life in such detachments was undoubtedly exciting: Commander Rawlinson, Admiral Scott's second in command, described 'a breakneck drive at speeds of up to 56 mph along Oxford Street to the Artillery Ground in Moorgate Street, before opening up on a Zeppelin'.[12]

In practice, they proved far from effective. By the time they started firing, the Zeppelins had usually moved on.[13] At this time Commander Rawlinson was involved with improving the fuses of anti-aircraft shells to avoid earlier problems of premature detonation in the gun barrels and, most importantly, to ensure they fragmented in the air, thus protecting Londoners from the dangers of complete or large portions of shells falling back to earth and inflicting injuries or death, together with serious damage to buildings.[14]

Scott also established a semi-circle of 13-pounder gun positions across the eastern approaches to the city (the most common direction of attack) in an effort to engage raiders before they reached the central area,[15] and on receiving further guns it was planned to have a second mobile brigade stationed in East Anglia to take on the airships as they crossed the coast. To provide earlier warnings of the intruders, Scott began to place observer posts on a radius of 13, then 60 and finally 80 miles from London across Essex and Kent. On the Zeppelins' approach these were required to release different coloured rockets to warn the gun and searchlight crews, together with the waiting Home Defence pilots who, it was hoped, would now have enough time to climb to the required 8,000ft before the Zeppelins arrived. Under Scott, more stringent blackout measures replaced the earlier dimming regulations. Shop and street lighting was further reduced and the lake in St James's Park was drained to cancel its reflection. Gas lamps had to be permanently extinguished and heavy curtains became standard at windows, while pedestrians were sometimes obliged to grope their way along walls adjoining the streets, or follow kerbs that had been whitened.

Whatever the improvements to the ground defences, Scott showed his commitment to aerial warfare by advocating night-flying training for pilots stationed on the east coast because he expected 'when trained (they) would be the Zeppelins' worst enemy',[16] and specially trained pilots were stationed at London's Hendon and Chingford aerodromes. Following the Zeppelin raid of

13 October 1915 during which the airship commanders reported a great increase in London's gunfire, the defending RFC pilots called for better illumination of their targets from the searchlights, and as a result Scott established an inner ring of lights.

Much to Commander Rawlinson's regret, on 16 February 1916 responsibility for London's defence passed from his highly regarded chief, Scott, to the army's Field Marshal Lord French who, after being superseded in France by Douglas Haig, was appointed Commander in Chief of the Home Forces. During his five-month period of command Scott had undoubtedly succeeded in making massive improvements to London's defences. On taking up his duties there were just twelve assorted anti-aircraft guns, inefficiently mounted and of unsuitable calibre. At his departure fifty guns (properly mounted) were in place and a further ninety-eight emplacements nearing completion. Such guns now had sufficient and better ammunition, which posed a much lesser risk of injury to the city's inhabitants, and a proper defence organization had been established with gun and searchlight crews fully aware of the need to operate with defending aircraft. Even so, Scott left with his plans incomplete, for he had estimated that the full scheme would need an incredible 475 guns (including 72 mobile) and 500 searchlights.[17]

On taking over, French continued with Scott's plans which included pairs of interceptor aircraft, manned by pilots specially trained in night flying, to be on standby at ten airfields – Hounslow, Wimbledon Common, Croydon, Farningham, Joyce Green, Hainault Farm, Suttons Farm, Chingford, Hendon and Northolt – encircling London, some of which would become even better known during the next war.[18] The long-term air-defence plans for the Home Forces were for 10 aircraft squadrons, 2 of which were allocated to London and 4 more – 2 at Harwich/East Anglia and 1 each at Chatham/Dover and Portsmouth/Newhaven – covering likely approach routes to the city. By no means were they all up to strength and there was a pressing need for improved machines to replace ones whose pilots reported as 'incapable of flying even in favourable conditions'.[19] Delivery of more modern planes was, of course, affected by the demands of the Western Front and the see-sawing aerial combat there.

Even so some progress was made with, for instance, the delivery of a new single-seater aircraft (BE12) developed from the eminently stable but desperately slow BE2. (The provision of Sopwith Camels or Pups in any quantity would not take place until August 1917.) Another important development was that of explosive bullets, the first 500 of which were apparently made by the wife of their inventor, John Pomeroy, in a top-floor room in the Home Defence Wing Headquarters at Adastral House in London.

While the London defences could not of course stop the Zeppelin raids being mounted, by the autumn of 1916 they had largely mastered them by means of searchlights illuminating the great craft as targets for both the ack–ack guns and the planes, some of which could rise high enough to attack with explosive ammunition. Their achievements may not compare with those of the British air aces in France during the following year, such as Albert Ball, James McCudden and Mick Mannock, but the first pilots to destroy Zeppelins over Britain also came to receive popular appreciation. Pilots like Frederick Sowrey, Egbert Cadbury, Robert Leckie and William Leefe Robinson also gained public recognition.

Successes gained against the Zeppelins led to cuts to the Air Defence squadrons in favour of the Western Front, but with aircraft attacks in the offing Marshal French complained furiously about the way his forces were being reduced to a dangerously low point and one that 'does not enable the general scheme of defence . . . to be carried out'.[20] His warnings seemed justified by the 162 deaths and 432 injuries sustained during London's first aircraft raid on 13 June, a total that had never been approached by the airships.

As already stated, the resultant outcry from across the capital brought a further major review and an extension to London's defence arrangements. The system was integrated into what became known as the London Air Defence Area (LADA) – which also included the defence resources of south-east England – and it was given a new commander, an experienced artillery officer and pilot, Major General Edward 'Splash' Ashmore. Ashmore was despatched peremptorily from Ypres to London and he shared the general surprise in France at the time that, despite such relatively few casualties, London should be allowed to affect the build up for Douglas Haig's massive battle of Passchendaele. He made his feelings clear through his breezy observation that 'the fact that I was exchanging the comparative safety of the Front for the probability of being hanged in the streets of London did not worry me'.[21]

Even so, Ashmore was not only very capable but had already studied anti-aircraft defence and had definite ideas about what should be done. His first aim was to improve co-ordination between listening posts, anti-aircraft batteries and air squadrons. When he took over, the Gothas were still mounting daylight raids and, although certain they would soon commence night raiding, he set about constructing a new barrier line of guns about 20 miles to the east of London. This aimed to break up their formations which could then be attacked by his air-defence fighting squadrons working inside the 20-mile line of guns, where they had priority of action. Ashmore also set up a control system at Horse Guards (which was not formally declared operational until 12 September 1918) that became a model for the next war's defences. He established an operating room featuring a giant map table (lit from beneath) that was divided into map squares whereby the position of enemy raiders could be pinpointed as they moved towards their targets and where from a dais overlooking the table senior operations officers had an overall view.

The system relied on a well-practised sequence of events. Upon the duty officer receiving and confirming the news of an impending raid – generally before the enemy had crossed the coastline – he summoned his staff and tele-phone operators – who were already on duty – to their action stations. Ashmore expected this to be accomplished in half a minute at most. Such readiness did not just apply to the controllers, for all defence personnel, whether pilots, those manning gun positions, searchlights or aerodromes, together with the police and fire brigades, would be given pre-arranged orders. Once the raid was confirmed, the pilots were to fly on to their respective beats.

The raid's progress would then be tracked by ten so-called plotters in the control room who, wearing telephone headsets, received their messages directly from the twenty-six sub-control centres, including the observer cordon and other reporting stations. Acting on the information received, which in the final stages of the war was aided by radio telephony, they were able to move appropriate symbols – a disc for a single enemy aircraft and a rectangle for a formation, with arrows indicting their courses – across the squares. (Defending fighters were represented by aircraft-shaped counters.) Ashmore had a switch-board allowing him to cut into the plotter's line should he want extra information or to give instructions to a sub-commander. The relevant Air Force commander standing at his side had direct-line communications with his fighter wings.

Ashmore made other significant changes: he ended the previous practice of ordering barrage fire before the invaders had been picked out by searchlights. While useful against airships, he considered it too slow for attacking aircraft. He also cancelled the earlier order for all searchlights in a given area to wave their beams about the sky to frighten off attackers. Henceforth searchlights were only to be used when an aircraft was heard or already illuminated by another searchlight.

Upon the commencement of night attacks, Ashmore instigated his own system of barrage fire which, after picking up the sounds of their engines, put up a curtain of bursting shells in front of incoming aircraft. With his defending aircraft now also regularly operating at night, Ashmore removed any guns from within the London barrier line and replaced them with searchlights to help show his pilots the direction from which the enemy was coming. Such guns were used to help complete his intended full circle of ordnance round London.

To supplement his gun defences Ashmore set about constructing what he called a balloon-apron barrage, consisting of sets of three balloons joined horizontally by stout wires from which weighted wire streamers hung at fixed intervals. By 1918 ten aprons of three balloons, each with streamers and capable of reaching 10,000ft, were installed. Designed to force the enemy planes to fly in the narrow range between the height of the aprons and their flight ceilings, it was hoped that, in the London area at least, defending aeroplanes would have a far greater chance of locating the intruders.

Despite such aprons, and the growing predictability of the attackers' lines of approach, more effective ways of following their movements were developed, although prior to radar the ability to locate German aircraft at a sufficient distance for the defensive aircraft to move into ambush positions was never fully achieved. The defenders were provided with sound locators specifically designed to track the incoming craft, which were to prove very valuable when combined with searchlights, and particularly after the Germans switched to night bombing. Although the belief in some quarters that 'had it not been for the sound-locators the German night aeroplane campaign would never have been faced so successfully' surely goes too far,[22] they undoubtedly became an integral part of London's Home Defence.

Originating from the 'Claude Orthophone' used by the French army, they consisted of two trumpets or kettle drums pointing skywards that could be rotated along a horizontal axis to track and amplify the sound of an approaching enemy, together with his distance and position.[23] Although relatively effective, a persistent difficulty for the operators came from extraneous sounds, such as the squalling of gulls near the coast. 'A later, more sophisticated, pattern employed four 24 inch trumpets connected to stethoscopes, enabling the operators to assess direction of a target in elevation and azimuth up to an effective range of 10,000 yards'[24] – but only in favourable weather conditions. Large sound mirrors of a parabolic contour, built of concrete to a diameter of 20ft or more, were also positioned along the south-east coast and equipped with microphones to give warning of the approach of German bombers from Belgium. These sometimes succeeded in detecting aircraft 15 or 20 miles from the coast.[25]

Ashmore's new defence arrangements faced their first major test during the autumn of 1917. In early September, prior to the more serious raids expected over the next moonlight period, he was still working on them to the accompaniment of continuing strong criticisms in the press. One commentator maintained that 'the official view appears to be that these raids cannot be prevented, and that there is nothing to be done', while another observed that 'the commander of the air defences who cannot defend the capital is evidently in the wrong place'.[26] In reality, apart from his major improvements to the ground defences, Ashmore had finally received twenty of the latest and most efficient interceptor planes for each of his three Home Defence squadrons.

The anticipated 'Raids of the Harvest Moon' commenced on 24 September, when in favourable flying conditions attacks were mounted on 6 of the 8 nights between 24 September and 1 October. From the beginning, the improvements in defence were evident in the limited damage the Germans inflicted on London. On the first night, only 3 of some 20 aeroplanes penetrated to the London area, and 1 of these was shot down by an anti-aircraft gun off Sheerness. During the second, 1 of the 3 aeroplanes aiming for London was forced to veer off because of the defence's barrage fire. On 28 September, although 20 planes were involved and some reached London's outer barrier, none penetrated to the city. On the following night, of the 19 planes directed at London only 4 succeeded in bombing the city. During the final 2 raids, of 30 September and 1 October, the damage inflicted was light. Ashmore calculated that over the series of raids, 'it took rather over two bombing aeroplanes to kill one person'.[27] This was striking evidence of his defences' success. Yet for those in Britain, and there were still many of them, who believed that true success could only come, by inflicting heavy and unsustainable losses on the attackers, this was still not being achieved – during the 'Raids of the Harvest Moon' only two of the robust and well-armed bombers were brought down. Even so, by October much of the heat in the earlier criticisms was giving way to a growing appreciation of the Home Defence's work. Apart from sporadic Zeppelin attacks, which continued until near the end of the war but which no longer offered serious threats to London, by late 1917 the aeroplane raids were also fewer in number, although much of this was due to deteriorating weather conditions.

On 31 October eight of the twenty-four bombers that set out reached the capital but the casualties were light, as they were again during the next raid of 5 December. However, on 18/19 December the defending aircraft, in this case Sopwith Camels armed with upward firing Lewis guns, shot down a Gotha, while during the first raid of 1918 on 28/29 January, a pair of Camels shot down another Gotha in flames.

When the Gotha squadron was temporarily grounded while Brandenburg brought it back to efficiency the raids during the first quarter of 1918 were carried out by the Giants, none of which were downed over London, although its defences were necessarily kept on full alert. With never more than five over the city at any time the damage caused was limited and even the ultra-critical MP William Joynson-Hicks – scourge of the air defenders – acknowledged that 'Day by day, or night by night, when these raids come, although it is perhaps impossible to secure complete immunity we are satisfied that the defences are infinitely better than they were a year ago'.[28]

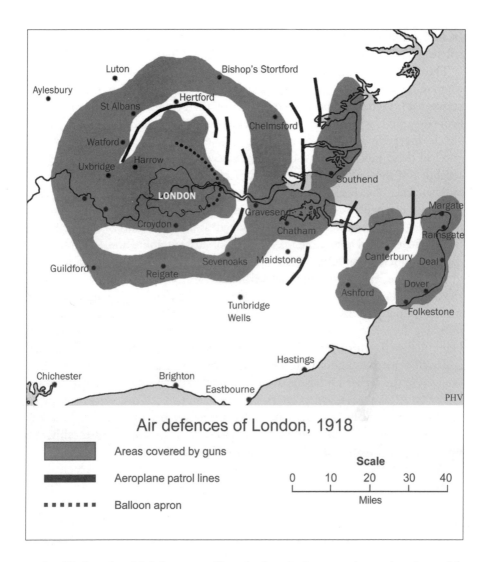

Air defences of London, 1918

Areas covered by guns

Aeroplane patrol lines

Balloon apron

Scale

0   10   20   30   40

Miles

PHV

On Wednesday 19 May came Brandenburg's last attack on the city, with forty-three planes, thirty-three of which reached London, giving the defences a good opportunity to show their effectiveness. By now the defending aircraft were vastly more effective with a large proportion of Sopwith Camels and Bristol fighters rather than the relatively ineffective BE2s and BE12as. Again it was also a clear moonlit night and the planes shot down three Gothas, the guns two others and a sixth crashed over Essex with engine failure. In addition, 4 others failed to make their bases, bringing about an unsustainable rate of attrition for just 49 people killed and 177 injured. With such disappointing results and the tide of war turning against Germany, the bombers were reassigned to other tasks and the last Zeppelin raid took place on 8 August 1918.

Although by now things had moved in the defenders' favour (with continuing improvements to their system, such as the fitting of the night fighters with radio telephones), there was no doubt that the relatively small number of German Zeppelins and bombers had succeeded in provoking a remarkable response. This was, in part, due to the demands from Parliament and the people of London who had never before experienced what they considered were barbarous attacks, which had to be stopped. Conversely General Ashmore, a forceful idealist, knew that 'no scale of defence, however great, can secure complete immunity from bombing', although he hoped that 'by suitable arrangements the attacker may be made to suffer such casualties that his efforts will die out'.[29] In the event, unforgiving public opinion and Ashmore's professional pride led to the British building up a massive, if not disproportionate, defence system unequalled elsewhere. By the time of the last aeroplane raid on Britain (by planes that had succeeded on reaching London on just 114 occasions) the ground defence forces totalled 469 anti-aircraft guns, 622 searchlights, 258 height finders and 10 sound locators manned by 6,136 officers and men.[30] A further 82 officers and more than 2,000 men were with the balloon barrage, although many of them had medical grades that precluded them from being sent to France. In addition, the fighting strength of the Home Defence aircraft had reached 355 aeroplanes, 660 officers and 4,000 airmen, across 16 squadrons,[31] although in June 1918 less than half of these were yet considered efficient. Nonetheless, by now they had a core element of good aircraft – 145 Camels and 55 Bristol fighters – that could conceivably have provided 10 full-strength fighter squadrons and some night bomber units for the Western Front.

Apart from such tactical considerations there was the remarkable expenditure involved, each Sopwith Camel cost around £1,500 and a Bristol fighter twice that figure, and the material costs of constructing and maintaining the Home brigade's 35 main aerodromes and 139 other landing grounds was immense. With the fixed defences it was not just the price of the anti-aircraft guns but that of their ammunition. At times of barrage fire, up to 20,000 rounds or more were used in a single raid with the cost of each shell being £2. With the life of a 3in gun standing at about 1,500 rounds this brought the consumption of guns up to (an average of) 13 or 14 a raid.[32]

There were additional costs associated with the passive measures. When warnings of raids were received it was the practice for 75 per cent of munitions workers in some areas to cease work, with output continuing to be restricted for twenty-four hours after the raid ended. At Woolwich Arsenal, for instance, after the Germans instigated night attacks, during the night shift of

24/25 September 1914 output dropped to an amazing degree: that for .303in ammunition diminished to a sixth of its normal level and the production of 7.62mm ammunition and rifle grenade cartridges dropped proportionately.[33]

On psychological, military and economic grounds the German authorities could therefore justly feel their air attacks on London, first with highly vulnerable airships and then with the world's first strategic bombers, were overwhelmingly justified, despite the ultimately limited results and their own high costs. The total bill for their airships, for instance, exceeded £12 million and the costs of each Gotha and Giant aircraft were the equivalent of £9,000 and £19,000, quite apart from the fifty-man ground crew for the Giants that included a large number of specially trained mechanics, electricians and radio technicians.[34]

Such cost comparisons have obvious limitations; although the London defences were unquestionably expensive it is unrealistic to consider material costs above everything else, particularly in the case of London with the unique role it played in the war and its own treasure house of productive and distributive assets. With their Zeppelins and heavy bombers the Germans were (until the late stages of the war) not only in advance of other nations but seemingly capable of startling developments as well, such as the dropping of revolutionary incendiary devices. These also appeared capable of frightening Londoners as nothing else could and, with so many of the city's sons absent away serving their country, no risks could be taken over a possible collapse in civilian morale.

Whether or not the defence of London absorbed a disproportionate amount of national resources during the First World War, the lessons it provided for the next war against longer and more sustained attacks would prove highly valuable.

Chapter 4

London's Home Front, 1914–18

Leaving Guildhall at about ten o'clock, the guests found the streets of the City dark, empty and silent. Very few of the street lamps were burning and those were so masked that their light fell only at one's feet.

London district[1]

During the First World War the aerial attacks on London were bound to excite strong emotions among those who experienced them, when the Zeppelins or Gothas were not only able to bypass the strength of Britain's land and naval forces but (in the days before efficient wireless) the bulk of the Royal Flying Corps defenders[2] as well. To circumvent the other services in this way before striking at the heart of London, particularly when the Royal Navy had always acted as London's shield, seemed iniquitous, a sentiment echoed by *The Times* when, in June 1915, it declared that 'while armed airships might be a proper means of attacking armies and navies, it was an entirely new and barbarous practice to use them as weapons against defenceless civilians'.[3] For such reasons, apart from mounting military countermeasures, the British government was understandably concerned about how London's civilians – whether office staff in the City, munitions workers, dockers in the East End or housewives – would react.

Such concerns were understandable when the means of communicating with them were so limited compared with those of the Second World War. Valve transmitters began to be used during the war but it was not until 1920 that a broadcasting station was sending out two half-hour daily programmes of news items and live and recorded music to private homes, and not until 1922 that the British Broadcasting Company began operations. The British Broadcasting Corporation,[4] which gave political and other leaders an opportunity to address a sizeable proportion of the population, was established five years later. As for people contacting each other, at the beginning of the First World War slow and unreliable telephone calls had to be relayed through a succession of telephone exchanges, while private telephones were strictly for the homes of the more affluent.

Although 'picture palaces' had already sprung up in most sizeable towns, their flickering movies relied on subtitles and the music of accompanying pianists to help convey their meaning (sound did not come in until 1927). Some films were made during the war by production companies that paid for the privilege of filming in France before selling such films back to the government for propaganda use, but only a proportion gained wide popularity. These included *The Battle of the Somme* (1916), which for much of its seventy-seven minutes showed frames of dead or wounded soldiers. More contemporary facts about the fighting came from bi-weekly newsreels introduced in 1917, although these were still heavily dependent on re-enactments of engagements produced in Britain rather than on photographs taken in France and elsewhere.

With no system of national broadcasting, a rudimentary telephone system and no newsreels until 1917, the government relied on an efficient and widely used postal service to carry information and instructions about what they required of individual households. It delivered the dreaded telegraphs informing them of the wounding or death of their relatives, as well as providing the opportunity of writing to their loved ones at the front. At this time the newspapers also had a vital role to play in communication. In pride of place came the national dailies, ranging from the authoritative *Times* – the only paper that had consistently argued for war between the great powers – and more populist ones like the *Daily Mail*, the *Daily Express* (which almost doubled its circulation before the end of the war) and the recently established *Daily Mirror*, which by 1916 averaged daily sales of 1,307,000. These were supplemented by weekly papers published in all the districts of London, together with others such as the *Illustrated London News*,[5] *Great War Illustrated* and *John Bull* which, as well as their accounts, carried large numbers of photographs or etchings. *John Bull*, for one, sold 2,000,000 copies per issue by 1918.

In its anxiety to maintain civilian morale in the face of air attack and the appalling casualty figures coming from the Western Front, the government imposed strict censorship on the papers for the first time. Under the Defence of the Realm Act (DORA) passed on 8 August 1914, it prohibited reports or statements in any newspaper, periodical or other printed publication that was liable to undermine loyalty to the King, recruitment or confidence in the country. So strict were such measures that *The Times* journalist Michael MacDonagh was driven to comment that:

> No news, civil as well as military, was allowed to be published which might be useful to the enemy. Everything relating to the War in London had, nevertheless, to be covered (as we say), although in the circumstances it might be productive of little or no copy which

the censor would pass. In fact the more an event was of consequence from a newspaper point of view the less about it was, as a general rule, permitted to be printed.[6]

In such circumstances, when negative reactions could not be printed about the raids, there are obvious difficulties in discovering Londoners' true reactions. The problem is made no easier because there are no longer any eyewitnesses to events that occurred almost a century ago and because, unlike the next war, no mass-observation surveys were subsequently conducted. While as a generation Londoners were fiercely proud and patriotic to the point of jingoism, with even closer family and community ties than in the succeeding war, the meagre and partisan reports of the air raids issued by the government's Press Bureau in Whitehall undoubtedly influenced what the newspapers were able to print. This was undoubtedly the case with Michael MacDonagh's articles in *The Times*.

Whatever the compelling psychological impact of the first raid by the giant German airships in June 1915, its death toll of just four was not likely to produce mass panic. Even so, whether it justified the studiously dismissive language used by the Press Bureau, which referred to such raiders as 'visiting London', is more questionable. After informing its readers that ninety bombs, mostly incendiaries, had been dropped, *The Times* plainly felt obliged to assure them that 'all were promptly and effectively dealt with and adequate police arrangements, including the calling out of special constables, enabled the situation to be kept thoroughly in hand throughout'.[7]

This allusion to 'specials' reflected the Asquith's government's residual fears about a possible breakdown in public order, such as happened during the previous century at the time of the repeal of the Corn Laws and Chartist agitation. Therefore, in 1914 the Special Constables' Act was passed a few days after the declaration of war, appointing such officials 'for the preservation of the public peace and for the protection of property'.[8] Within a few weeks 30,000 men (rising to a maximum of 33,000) from all walks of life were embodied for the duration of the war (unlike the 150,000 specials enlisted for the short duration of the Chartist riots): they included barristers, lawyers, Members of Parliament, clerks, shop assistants and labourers, the vast majority of which had daily business responsibilities. Their symbols of authority came in the form of an armlet and two badges – one to be worn on the buttonhole of their coats, the other in front of their caps – a warrant card, a truncheon and a book of instructions and regulations. (By 1915 they had also been issued with a uniform coat.) Specials were accustomed to performing their duties on four-hourly shifts, mostly at night, where their greatest challenge undoubtedly came at the time of the air raids when, as their historian acknowledged, 'no individual could consider himself absolutely safe if he was within the area of a raid'.[9]

This prevailing sense of vulnerability, felt by both specials and ordinary Londoners alike, to what were never more than relatively light and rarely sustained raids, was in no way revealed by official releases from the government's Press Bureau. However restricted the death toll might be, it was the first time that defenceless citizens far away from the battlefronts could be killed in their beds by sky raiders who came at them unawares.

The first two raids were followed by the much more serious one of 18 September 1915, when there were 162 casualties and, following a request from the Home Secretary, *The Times*' report was made by a so-called impartial observer (whose identity was not revealed but whose language was undoubtedly chauvinistic). With a headline like 'Random Murder' there could be little doubt about its tenor and purpose. It had to be condemnatory:

> Almost all the unfortunate people who have been killed have not only been non-combatants but non-combatants of a kind which it has been hitherto the honourable practice of civilised warfare to exempt from attack, that is to say women and children, small shop keepers and working men, the sacrifice of whose lives can effect no military purpose whatever, either morally or materially.

A week later *The Times* published another report, this time by a 'neutral' rather than an 'impartial' observer, in this case Mr William G Shepherd, a correspondent of the United Press. This was, in fact, a full-blooded and highly affectionate account which he had sent to the American newspapers:

> Seven million people of the biggest city in the world stand gazing into the sky from the darkened streets.... Great booming sounds shake the city. They are Zeppelin bombs – falling – killing – burning.... Suddenly you realize that the biggest city in the world has become the night battlefield in which 7,000,000 harmless men, women and children live. Here is a war at the very heart of civilisation, threatening all the millions of things that human hearts and human minds have created in past centuries.

Shepherd then noticed a soldier embracing his girl, whom he suggested typified London and Britain – unchanged one iota by this Zeppelin raid that only ended in the loss of twenty harmless lives. His final sentence then informed his readers that 'on the next day recruiting tripled'.[10]

The other newspapers were similarly obliged to follow the Press Bureau's directives. The *Daily Mirror*, for instance, recalled Mr Balfour's contemptuous words upon the Zeppelin attacks which he made to a correspondent during August 1915, namely that 'they have been brutal but so far they have not been effective. They have served no hostile purpose, moral or material.'[11]

Such censorship naturally extended to the bitter fighting on land, but agonisingly long casualty lists made the newspapers' invariably optimistic stance irritating for individual readers and attracted a degree of scepticism. In fact *The Times* soon succeeded in finding ways of getting round the Press Bureau releases, such as publishing the official German reports on the raids. It also chose to publish individual letters from its readers: like one on 22 April 1915 coming from F E Hamer, President of the National Union of Journalists, that was unequivocal in his criticism of such press restrictions: 'The question of the official control of the British Press affects so vitally the rights of the public no less than the rights of the Press, that the Government cannot, without risking a serious loss of credit, afford much longer to ignore public and professional feeling on this matter.'[12]

Such partial comment was unlikely to bring about concessions, but from November 1915 onwards *The Times*' leaders included some that referred specifically to the bombing, although their observations had to be made within a patriotic framework. In its leader of 26 September 1916 the paper concluded that 'excitement and curiosity, as this last instance has again demonstrated, are the predominant feelings these raids arouse at the moment, while they leave behind them a deepened anger and a more resolute will to subdue these methods of barbarism'.[13]

During 1917 *The Times*'s published letters on the raids increased in number and on 10 July of that year, following the raid of the previous Saturday, nine appeared on the same day. These included one by AJC of London EC, demanding that the German bombers should be made to suffer the same risks as allied bombers attacking Berlin, which was five times further from their bases. The same correspondent also stated that there was no analogy between the fact that soldiers are bombed daily and that an enemy is to be allowed to come unscathed and drop bombs leisurely on densely packed masses of undefended women and children. In early September 1917 *The Times* printed a powerful letter by aeronautical authority Lord Montague of Bealieu advocating the need for reprisals by bombing the German aerodromes at the front and bombing their towns behind the lines.[14] Despite the DORA restrictions *The Times* and the other newspapers found additional ways of getting round them, often through a succession of 'campaigns' overtly aimed at intensifying the British war effort. Although these aimed at boosting the sales of War Bonds and encouraging recruitment, their accompanying headlines even extended to suggesting possible changes to the senior military commands in France and elsewhere and to 'chivvying insufficiently bellicose ministers', even to attacking prime ministers. During September 1917 *The Times* not only published letters relating to bombing Germany but, together with the *Daily Mail*, took up the need for reprisal bombing, criticizing the slowness of government decisions here.[15] *The Times* also weighed in to advocate a great fleet of bombers carrying out retaliatory strikes.[16]

The continuing independence of the press was of undoubted importance when, whether for the best intentions or not, wartime Britain was by stages coming to resemble a police state: all letters sent home from the battle fronts were subject to censorship and the Press Bureau, assisted by the Secret Service Department, scrutinized over 38,000 literary articles, 25,000 photographs and 300,000 private telegrams in 1916 alone.[17] Lloyd George acknowledged that whereas the public 'knows only half the story, the press knew something more like three quarters'.[18] This was the same Lloyd George who, as Munitions Minister, had limited the opening of public houses to five hours a day, reduced the alcoholic content of beers and prohibited the practice of buying rounds of drinks for one's friends. To such a politician committed to winning the war by whatever means possible, it was vital that the press be kept on side and also brought under a measure of control. In particular, this meant the Harmsworth brothers, who had built up Britain's biggest newspaper group, the elder becoming Lord Northcliffe and the younger Lord Rothermere. Rothermere accepted the post of Air Minister – thus tying himself into the establishment – which had earlier been held by the lesser press baron Lord Chandos, proprietor of the *Westminster Gazette* and the *Star*.

Despite the presence of state censorship, the public's appetite for material relating to the war increased the power of the media and Lloyd George gave peerages to no less than twelve press barons in return for their co-operation before, in 1918, creating Northcliffe director of public propaganda in enemy countries and making Max Aitken (Lord Beaverbrook) his Minister of Information.

Such attempts to control the press caused Londoners and others to remark to each other, 'Oh the newspapers. Don't we know they are muzzled?'[19] They had no reason to change such beliefs when official reports on the airship raids by Lord French, commander of the Home Forces (published in the news-papers), followed by others on the Gotha raids during the autumn of 1917 strongly emphasized London's improved air defences. They were accompanied by references to allied air raids into Germany, allegedly producing 'good results', and such reports continued into 1918, when Londoners read that they were apparently taking all such raids in their stride: 'The public had plenty of time to take shelter which they did quickly and in an orderly way as people now thoroughly accustomed to such work. Indeed they now appear to do so nowadays in the most unconcerned way possible.'[20]

Following the Gotha's final raid of Whitsun 1918 the heavy German losses were given great prominence, while civilian morale in the damaged areas was said to have received a massive boost from a visit by the King and Queen accompanied by the Assistant Commissioner of the Metropolitan Police. As far as the papers were concerned, all was apparently moving steadily towards an inevitable victory.

A much rounder story is revealed in the unpublished correspondence held in the Imperial War Museum between those who, during the First World War, either witnessed raids or received accounts of them from their loved ones. Unsurprisingly, these gave an altogether less predictable picture, where strong chauvinism and unashamed hatred, together with competing strains of patriotism and individual self-interest, were accompanied by genuine and persistent fears. At the outset the images of huge and seemingly cataclysmic airships hovering over London brought fright bordering on terror to people of all classes. Redoubtable cricketer W G Grace, for instance, then in his sixties, whose heroic and stubborn qualities had brought him 100,000 runs and 7,000 wickets, was particularly affected and the raids were widely believed to have contributed towards the stroke that led to his death in October 1915.

Similar reactions were experienced by Londoner W A Phillips, who in his letter of September 1915 describing a Zeppelin raid over his home in Muswell Hill said, 'The noise of the guns and shells bursting and the bombs exploding was terrific and most awesome. It was a great sight but I hope to be spared seeing it again. Women simply went off their heads and were difficult to control.'[21] In the same vein a letter by a Miss Finucane, describing a Zeppelin raid the month before, ended with the words 'I really can't write any more about it, it was too awful'.[22]

It might have been expected that soldiers who were removed from the horrors of the Western Front would have taken such relatively light raids in their stride, but this was far from the case. During one memorable afternoon at St Thomas' hospital, where Mrs M Rattray was nursing wounded soldiers, five operations had been carried out. The relatively crude anaesthetics of the day and the nature of their wounds caused some to return in extreme distress – 'what a night we had with the growing yells of someone being constantly sick'. Then 'to crown it all. . . . We had a Zeppelin raid . . . nearly all the patients . . . panicked and all the day nurses dressed and came down to the wards to soothe them'.[23]

It was not just poor wounded Tommies. Mrs Purbrook, a housewife from Hornchurch, wrote in her diary about the London poor who were terrified of living so close to munitions factories and the docks. Not believing what they read in the newspapers, they were prey to the latest and most colourful rumours about future raids, 'And rushing from their homes they flocked into any underground place, such as Tube stations, church crypts and underground cellars.'[24] So great was this exodus that a total of 86 Underground railway stations had to be made available as air-raid shelters, with a capacity of 250,000 persons. The East Enders, with their children, flocked there night after night to sleep head to toe on platforms where the air quickly became foul. Among the most popular stations were Finsbury Park, where 12,000 people regularly gathered, and King's Cross, which attracted upwards of 9,000.[25]

It was not just the old, sick and the poor – some people, whatever their background, were constitutionally susceptible to such assaults from the sky. 'With some people their judgement seems to go and you can't reason with them. If you say the explosions are a long way off and the searchlights are pointing miles away all they say is "there might be other Zeps right overhead etc"'. As this particular correspondent concluded, 'Shakespeare was right when he said, "Cowards die many deaths". . . .'.[26]

Such widespread and persistent fears fuelled the remarkable belief that whatever their numbers, if the raiders actually succeeded in penetrating London's airspace the defences had been defeated. The strains imposed by repeated raids also seemed to be cumulative. A regular correspondence between a nurse on a London cancer ward and her husband who was serving overseas reveals that she had little sleep and was losing weight. He responded by imploring her to leave London and lovingly chided her, 'If you go on like that (losing 10lbs) you will be getting ill and breaking down and then when I get home you will be a wreck instead of being fit to stand the strain of my coming home and our next honeymoon!'.[27]

While many were exceedingly nervous, other Londoners, often from the more affluent parts, were aware of the small chances of their suffering injury or death and went – as the authorities repeatedly claimed – to the other extreme, exposing themselves brazenly to the dangers of the bombs or to the more widespread fragments of shrapnel from the anti-aircraft guns. Neither group, of course, would have recognized themselves from an urbane leader of *The Times*, which in 1917 maintained 'that neither in London nor the provinces was there any trace of panic. England has become inured to air raids and regards them with reasonable calmness as in the past'.[28]

Londoners not only felt most strongly about the raids but their angry reactions had remarkable consequences. With such limited communications, rumours abounded. One early result was a fixation about possible spies, the hunting down of whom became a popular activity, if not a compulsion. One story going around was that of a Brixton woman who cleverly saw through the disguise of four German spies and had them arrested. In another actual incident an elderly correspondent of *The Times*, when sitting alone at the press table during a meeting to enquire into the actual existence of the Hidden Hand, a secret German society, had his notebook seized by a woman who believed his individual system of shorthand was in fact German script.[29]

More seriously, during 1915 German provision shops were wrecked and looted across London. In Deptford High Street several, notably pork butchers and bakers, suffered. In some cases the strongest motives were for individual gain: eyewitnesses spoke of looters leaving ruined premises carrying sacks of flour, and in one instance a man was seen with a whole pig's carcase across his shoulders. It is likely, however, that attacks on individuals were even more extensive than the authorities acknowledged at the time, for twenty years after the war a Londoner who became a sergeant in the Thames Division of the Metropolitan Police chanced to look through an old Dead Book Register, where particulars of all bodies recovered from the Waterloo Pier section of the Thames were recorded. Under those for 1915 he was struck by the number of people with obvious German names such as Carl, Otto, etc., and the high percentage of people with German surnames whose bodies had been recovered from the river during that year. He wondered whether some might 'have been suicides induced by the wrecking and looting and the general anti-German feeling that prevailed everywhere' (he also wondered if any of them were deliberately pushed or thrown into the river).[30]

Whether his suspicions were correct or not, the strength of such reaction can be gauged by the animosity shown to a Scottish publican in the East End, whose name of Strachan was foreign enough for him to have his windows smashed.[31] Such feeling, backed by certain sections of the press, also reached individuals at the highest levels, with the First Lord of the Admiralty, Prince Louis of Battenburg, being forced to resign. He was in fact of Austrian extraction but felt compelled to change his name to Mountbatten. Even the King, whose family name was Saxe-Coberg-Gotha, adopted the more British sounding name of Windsor.

The Zeppelin raids, which were also rightly held responsible for such diverse things as clocks no longer being allowed to chime during the night-time hours and the virtual cessation of buses or trams after dusk, contributed strongly to such hatred, which was by no means restricted to the less well educated. Clergyman M F Foxell, for instance, included the Belgian atrocities, the execution of Miss Cavell, the bombardment of Scarborough and the sinking of the *Lusitania* with the Zeppelin raids, to mount a broadside against 'the Germans' deliberate and organised frightfulness which has sullied their armies and made them the bye word in the war'.[32] He was no more extreme than technical editor J H Stapley who, in a letter to a soldier friend, ended with the statement 'better be tried and condemned by my own country for preaching the extermination of foul fiends than ever be in the power of these foul devils'.[33]

Mrs Purbrook could be equally condemnatory. 'If even a small fraction (of the stories we have are true) war must have turned this once decent and enterprising nation into something more savage and frightful than wild beasts ... his armies are unspeakable ...'.[34] And medical orderly J B Evans, whose mission was to help the sick and wounded from both sides, was incandescent when writing to his mother about the German bombing of an infant school in the East End: 'If ever a crime called to heaven for vengeance that one does. I hope they will speedily be repaid with interest.'[35]

Together with the hatred and contempt felt in many quarters for the raiding Germans, their success in reaching and bombing London also brought surprising anger against the British government for being unable to prevent it. This owed much to servicemen's feelings of rage and impotence to learn that, while away fighting, their loved ones at home were also in danger, a fact made all the worse because the actual details were suppressed. In this regard, *The Times* echoed their grievances that not enough was being done. Its editorial of 1 October 1917, for instance, concluded that 'it would be absurd however to infer that the problem of aeroplane raids either by day or by night has been successfully tackled'.[36] One of the letters it published that supported air reprisals against such attackers came from the author Arthur Conan Doyle.[37] In her private diary Miss Winifred Toner also criticized the government for not providing better protection against air raids, and attended meetings in favour of air reprisals.[38]

Unsurprisingly such criticisms were not intended for those actually manning London's guns and other defences but for their senior policy makers. Lance Corporal S G Pittaway, for instance, writing to his family in London declared,

> [The Germans] seem to be able to get over and back again quite easily and I think it is a shame that we cannot do or build something that can prevent them from coming to England. We chaps out here are fighting so that the Germans shall never get to dear old England and yet the War Office cannot do something to prevent those blighters from killing our women and children.'[39]

In his letter to a soldier friend, another fighting soldier, Lieutenant A G Stevenson, adopted a different anti-government criticism: 'If the censor had censored all the rot about Germany running out of ammunition and food that was in the papers during the winter instead of censoring war news it would have been more to the point.'[40]

However much Londoners in their darkened, cheerless city might vent their feelings against both German nationals and their country's senior politicians for not better organizing its defences, it was undoubtedly the sight of a gigantic Zeppelin, compared by journalist Michael MacDonagh to John Keats's 'a new planet swimming into his ken', that provoked their strongest reactions,[41] particularly when they watched one falling to earth in flames. The letters were not entirely of mindless delight, and A T Wilkinson proved himself far more aware of the German crewmen than most. After observing the whole sky being lit up as the flaming mass dropped slowly to earth and people standing and cheering in the street, he observed that they were 'oblivious to the fact that human bodies were plummeting to earth to be smashed to pieces'.[42]

A description of the Zeppelin, destroyed by Flight Sub-Lieutenant Warneford, left its reader in no doubt about the public's delight. 'The next thing we saw was a light above the Zepp and a small bomb dropping which seemed to burst into flames as it hit the Zepp. The Zepp began to turn upon its end and as it dropped it was a mass of flames as high as the monument and about twice as wide. It lit up all the streets and the people were all cheering and shouting.'[43]

After a seemingly endless series of misses anti-aircraft gunner A Lockwood could not believe it as he watched a Zeppelin sink to earth: 'We could but think a Zepp had been destroyed before our very eyes and I said to Maddie probably our gun did it.'[44] In the event, his optimism proved unfounded for the airship had, in fact, been destroyed by an aircraft.

More than anything else it was the sensational nature of such huge ships of the sky being consumed by flames that caught the imagination of the spectators. An accomplished description by a Mrs Daynell-Browning, for instance, included the words 'These deaths must be the most dramatic in the world's history. They fell – a core of blazing wreckage, thousands of feet – watched by 8 millions of their enemies'.[45]

Surely the most remarkable account of this nature came from Lieutenant W Leefe Robinson, the first man to shoot down a Zeppelin, in the form of a letter to his mother and father. He began by saying that he was so tired of the subject that he felt he never wanted to mention it again, but:

> when the colossal thing actually burst into flames of course it was a glorious sight – wonderful. My feelings? Can I describe my feelings?

> I hardly knew how I felt ... I gradually realized what I had done and grew wild with excitement. When I had cooled down a bit, I did what I doubt many people would think I would do and that was thanked God with all my heart. You know darling old mother and father I'm not what is popularly known as a religious person so it was strange that I should pause and think for a moment after the first 'blast' of excitement, as it were, was over and thank from the bottom of my heart that supreme power that rules and guides our destinies ...

The sound of cheering came up to him in the clouds, 'it swelled and sank, first one quarter of London, then another. Thousands one might say <u>millions</u> of throats giving vent to thousands of feelings ... and the cause of it all – little me sitting in my little aeroplane above 13,000 feet of darkness! – it's wonderful!'[46]

For most Londoners there was the unalloyed delight in Leefe Robinson's and the other kills, with just a few mindful of the German crews. The aerial leviathans had been felled and the day after Leefe Robinson's success it was said that almost three-quarters of the city's population went to marvel at the pathetic remains of the airship, a complex skeleton of aluminium girders blanched by the intense fire.

With Londoners' feelings of fear and anger about the raids, and their delight at a raider's destruction, the correspondence revealed other sentiments, including the strong Christian beliefs possessed by most writers and their faith in the providence of God. C T Newman, a devout Christian who had been decorated for bravery, wrote from France to his beloved wife Winnie acknowledging that he was 'inwardly a coward', but that he had proved God and found him true, although 'presently both of them were in the hard path of duty'.[47]

Not all possessed Newman's confidence. After learning about the death of his elder brother Oswald in battle, medical orderly and practising Catholic J D Evans faced the terrible task of having to write to console his mother. After promising her he would try to follow in Oswald's footsteps his rawly emotional letter ended with the desperate cry, 'I can only pray that God will console you and all of us'.[48]

Quite separate from any religious feelings, virtually all Londoners, except for 'a small group of Socialists in the House of Commons and those members of the poorer and more discontented class who ask why should they fight',[49] were patriotic and fiercely proud of their city. For them the Zeppelin raids made them aware of their new responsibilities concerning what was generally becoming known as the Home Front. Writing to his son in Canada, retired headmaster R Saunders, in a burst of pride (not without a trace of self-pity) told him, 'You can't live in town at the present time without feeling an atmosphere of restless excitement (that tells on the nerves)'.[50]

Towards the end of the war journalist George Sims echoed such pride when he wrote specifically about the importance of London's Home Front in two articles featured in the *Daily Chronicle*:

> The final issue may be fought not on the land or on the sea or in the air but in the homes of the people of London[51] ... where the struggle is carried on bravely by combatants who have not the clash of arms and the thunder of the guns to stir the blood and brace the nerves.[52]

By January 1918, the initial sharpness of the different emotions was giving way to a greater acceptance. When a Gotha raid inflicted massive damage on Odhams Press building in Long Acre, journalist Michael MacDonagh, covering the incident for *The Times*, was surprised that 'in the large crowd that looked on I heard no resentment voiced against the raiders. This I thought was a curious thing. ... Today it is taken for granted ...'[53] By now Londoners had come through the initial alarms at aerial attack to show much of the resolution and fortitude already ascribed to them by the press.

A willingness to undertake novel duties in a city transformed by war was seen, for instance, when women took the place of men that had joined up to fight the Germans. Londoners quite enjoyed the sight of the conductorettes on trams and buses in their smart jackets, short skirts to the knees and leather leggings!

By the end of the war such letters included references to a whole series of government measures, including the rationing of food and fuel supplies, the requests not to buy new clothes so that the spare money could be invested in War Bonds, and the exhortations to grow vegetables on every spare foot of ground. For similar dictatorial instructions Londoners had to look back to General Monck's Committee of the Privy Council during the Great Plague of 1665–6, but by 1918, together with an acceptance of the greater egalitarianism within their society, Londoners had undoubtedly more confidence in the improved measures against air attack. Although nothing could make a city as large as London invulnerable, they realized that their chances of being harmed during such raids were now many thousands to one in their favour. In any case aeroplanes, although more effective and capable of delivering far greater destruction on the city if used in sufficient numbers, were much less terrifying than the gigantic airships.

While the raiders kept coming, nothing, of course, could remove from Londoners the overriding awareness of their city being under siege, a sensation underscored by the stringent blackout regulations and its near empty streets. But beyond such individual concerns, the need to protect the nation's capital against future marauding bombers had given a powerful impetus towards the founding of an air arm, separate from the other two armed services.

PART 2

Between the Wars

Chapter 5

The British Air Service –
The Locust Years

*[By 1920] the whole organisation of the [London] defences with the
exception of a small school of anti aircraft artillery for the Regular Army
had completely disappeared.*

General Sir Frederick Pile[1]

The second Gotha raid on London on 7 July 1917 had a momentous effect on
the development of British air power. Although the earlier Zeppelin raids had
brought demands for London's better protection, it was this chillingly efficient
attack by German heavy aircraft in daylight that led to demands for retaliatory
raids on Germany. By making such demands, men like Member of Parliament
Noel Pemberton Billing not only recognized the ability of airpower to gain
overall success against an aggressor but the need to create a separate air arm,
both to help defend London and the rest of the country and to be able to mount
offensive operations against would-be attackers. As senior RAF officer Air
Vice-Marshal Joubert de la Ferté freely acknowledged, 'it was the successful air
raid of July 7 1917 that crystallized the rather scattered discussions which had
been proceeding for some time over the higher direction of our air forces'.[2]
Without its impact a merger of the Royal Flying Corps and Royal Naval Air
Service would have been unthinkable during wartime, and in the subsequent
climate of massive military cutbacks it was most unlikely to have taken place
during the early post-war years.

While an Air Board had been set up in May 1916 under air enthusiast and
ex-Viceroy of India, Lord Curzon, it was a purely advisory body with nothing
like the stature of its equivalent in the other two services and a subsequently
reconstituted and strengthened Board still lacked the power to rule upon the
proper use of aircraft, despite its President, Lord Cowdray, and his assistant,
Sir William Weir, being early believers in strategic bombing.

It was the furious reaction in London to the July raid – in some ways akin
to that following the shock caused by the 9/11 terrorist assaults on New York

during 2001 – that led Prime Minister Lloyd George to appoint the South African Jan Christian Smuts to examine both the arrangements for defence against air raids and (more important still) the organization for 'the higher direction of aerial operations'.[3] Smuts was considered by the Earl of Swinton as 'the greatest Empire and Commonwealth statesman, splendid – quick, penetrating and decisive'[4] and the Prime Minister's solid backing (only Lloyd George and Smuts were named on the Committee) ensured his reports would be taken seriously. After consulting senior figures from the armed services and home forces, including Sir David Henderson and Hugh Trenchard, Smuts' conclusions and recommendations proved far-reaching.

His first report relating to Home Defence (particularly that of London) was released on 19 July, eight days after he had received the assignment. It was, however, his second of 17 August 1917 that understandably provoked the greatest reactions. This assumed that the recent air raids on London were bound to become more intensive, and that 'The time is rapidly approaching when the subordination of the Air Board and the Air Service (to the Army and Navy) can no longer be justified'. In fact, Smuts was sure that the Air Service could conduct war operations far from, and independently of, both the army and navy. What was more, 'as can presently be foreseen there is absolutely no limit to the scale of its future independent war use' and 'in such a situation the day may not be far off when aerial operations with their devastation of enemy lands and destruction of industrial and populous centres on a vast scale may become the principal operations of war to which the older forms of military and naval operations may become secondary and subordinate'.[5]

Following such conclusions, Smuts recommended the establishment of a single air service under its own Air Ministry and own air staff which should incorporate within it the two older air services. What was more, he proposed that the necessary legislation should be agreed by Parliament during the coming autumn and winter. Smuts stressed such urgency because of the great surplus of planes expected to become available for independent air operations by the following spring and summer. Although he acknowledged the need for aircraft to operate with the other two services, the essence of his report (on the assumption that Germany was planning further strategic raids against London and Britain as a whole) was for air power – working independently – to carry the war deep into Germany. Smuts recognized that Germany would respond with counter-efforts and because of this 'we should not only secure air predominance, but secure it on a very large scale; and having secured it in this way we should make every effort and sacrifice to maintain it for the future (for it) may in the long run become as important a factor in the defence of the Empire as sea supremacy'.[6]

Such was the amazing response to a raid on London that killed just 54 people and injured 190, allied with Smuts' expectations of large numbers of surplus aircraft promised by Sir William Weir, the outstanding protagonist of long-range bombing fleets.[7]

With this headlong challenge to the two older services it was hardly surprising that the creation of a separate air force should neither be as smooth nor as rapid as Smuts hoped. There were other powerful reasons – after July the daylight raids tended to peter out and Prime Minister Lloyd George was compelled to retire for a time from active leadership as a result of overwork and depression. It was therefore not until the commencement of night raids upon London during September 1917 that under Smuts' chairmanship a series of committees helped push the project through and draft the necessary legislation.[8] Understandably, the other two services did not give up their air establishments without a fight. In the case of the army Haig and Trenchard were the most prominent opponents, although the navy's appointed representative, Admiral Mark Kerr (an air enthusiast), was less so. In fact, Kerr became convinced that the night raids on London were, in fact, training exercises for pilots who would later be flying several hundred bombers every night, capable of carrying several tons of explosives and destroying Woolwich, Chatham and other parts of London as well as the workshops of south-east England. Such exaggerated expectations would become a characteristic of the thinking about mass bombing that would continue up to and during the Second World War.

The source of Kerr's facts was unknown, but with the commencement of aeroplane raids on London by night, *The Times* and the *Daily Mail*, together with air power advocates such as Pemberton Billing and Joynson-Hicks, joined in the agitation for aerial reprisals. During October *The Times* called for a giant fleet of bombers to be used in raids against Germany for 'only when we attain that ideal London may know peace at night'.[9] The air raids had again acted as the catalyst and on 16 October the Cabinet approved a draft bill for an independent air service. This passed through Parliament and received the Royal assent by 29 November, with the Royal Air Force coming into being on 1 April 1918.

Smuts' arguments for the new service had relied heavily upon the over-blown estimates of bombers provided by Sir William Weir and there were, of course, no German air fleets standing by. (Their limited bombing offensive would actually falter badly.) Nor, on the other hand, were there large surpluses of British aircraft ready for use on the Western Front, while the hoped for supplement of aircraft from the USA following its entry into the war on 6 April 1917 – expected to be an amazing 200,000 planes – never materialized.

By 1919 much increased numbers might possibly have been attainable, but during 1918 aircraft shortages helped make the early days of the new service difficult, along with its serious problems at senior command level. Just eleven days after the RAF officially came into being Hugh Trenchard, its first Chief of the Air Staff, resigned following what had become irreconcilable differences between him and his then Air Minister, press baron Lord Rothermere.

The early story of the RAF and its possible roles, including the defence of London, would become inseparable from Trenchard, who was shortly to return as its Chief of the Air Staff and continue in that post for a full decade, where his ideas would prove all powerful. During the previous year, following the London raid of 17 June 1917, both Haig and Trenchard, as Haig's air commander in France, had been called back to the War Cabinet when Trenchard's chief concern was to give adequate support to the ground forces on the Western Front, rather than countering what he felt were not overly destructive raids on London. He argued that the best way to stop the bombing of London was for the army to capture the Belgian coast where the Gothas had their bases and, failing this, to bomb the Gotha airfields, operations that would require more pilots and planes in France rather than allocating some of them to Britain.[10]

In truth, the need for more aircraft in France at this time was partly due to the methods by which Trenchard conducted air operations there, in the course of which he suffered proportionately higher casualties than the French air units, which placed more emphasis on observation. When told by the War Cabinet in June 1917 that two squadrons should be sent back, even temporarily, from France, Trenchard's immediate reaction was to point out that it was bound to allow the Germans an advantage over the front lines. At the same time he also felt compelled to warn the Cabinet against unrealistic demands for reprisal bombing attacks upon German towns because 'At present we are not prepared to carry out reprisals effectively being unprovided with suitable machines'.[11]

Notwithstanding this, during the autumn of 1917 the War Cabinet directed that arrangements be made for conducting offensive operations against German towns with factories producing munitions of all kinds – although the inaccuracy of bombing made the targeting of such factories decidedly optimistic. Trenchard was ordered to establish No. 41 Wing at Ochey in France by uniting two RFC and one RNAS bomber squadron prior to the force's anticipated expansion for a strategic bombing offensive against Germany during early 1918.

So it was that Trenchard, who went to strategic bombing reluctantly convinced that bombers were not yet capable nor numerous enough to win the war (while it could be lost if air superiority was surrendered on the Western Front), joined an Air Minister who, with his brother Northcliffe, was committed to bombing at the expense of other operations in France. The net result was Trenchard's resignation. But the high regard felt for him, both within the air service and in the royal household, resulted in him being offered a new command with the so-called Independent Air Force, formed in June 1918 from the three squadrons of bombers that Trenchard had earlier sent to Ochey in France to raid Germany. Commanded by Lieutenant Colonel Cyril Newall, these proved more successful than Trenchard could ever have imagined, even causing a delegation of Rhineland mayors to demand that the German authorities bring the raids to a halt in a similar way to some authorities in London in the face of moderate German raids. Trenchard was not an advocate of such methods of bombing[12] nor happy in a command where he had to report to the new Minister for Air, Sir William Weir, bypassing not only his former military chief, Douglas Haig, but also Ferdinand Foch, the allied commander in France, and Colonel Sir Frederick Sykes, who had replaced Trenchard as the Chief of the Air Staff in London.

In practice, the Independent Air Force contained an overwhelming preponderance of British planes and full operations could not be undertaken until 'the imperative requirements of the land fighting have been satisfied or during intervals of the fighting'.[13] During both September and October 1918, Marshal Foch demanded help from the IAF in bombing railways close to the front,[14] but when strategic raids could be undertaken the weather, which was 'poor in September and really bad in October', intervened.[15] One most important outcome was that, as with the German attacks on London later in the war, Trenchard met greater opposition from German fighters than he had expected and he was compelled to ask for help from allied fighters and direct one-half of his force to bomb the German airfields.

While the raids were not particularly heavy, nor very accurately delivered, as an early believer in strategic bombing Lord Weir believed that it was 'not the destructive effect but the effect of what we cause the Germans to do' that mattered.[16] Right or not, Trenchard's own losses were considerable, which was unsurprising when the operations were conducted before gaining air supremacy. In fact, from the 120 planes made available to him for bombing, he lost 74 between August and Armistice Day, although some were due to bad weather and pilot errors, rather than to direct enemy action.[17] Despite such losses Trenchard was now confident that, if the war continued, his reinforcements, including the gargantuan Handley Page V/1500 bombers with their 126ft wingspan and a bomb capacity of 7,500lb (also capable of carrying large loads of incendiary devices and poison-gas projectiles) would transform the scale of such bombing. The war ended before he could work with the American air commanders on his intended raids against the Ruhr, the Rhineland and eventually Berlin[18] and the effects of allied strategic bombing remained unproven.

Whatever the high hopes for strategic bombing, in January 1919 Lloyd George made the surprising decision to wind up the Air Ministry as a separate department, which might well have happened had it not been for the opposition of Winston Churchill, who at the time was both Secretary of State for War and Air. (The ambitious Churchill would, in fact, have liked to have been Minister of Defence covering all three services.) Churchill asked Trenchard to propose an establishment for the RAF that Parliament could accept and on 11 December 1919 the White Paper outlining its organization was accepted by the House of Commons. This was for 50 squadrons, only half of which would be at full strength, amounting to a total establishment of 28,000 other ranks and 2,800 officers – just a tenth of the air force at the war's end – costing a mere £15,000,000, or the equivalent of just one-and-a-half battleships.[19] (Within two years RAF personnel would be reduced to 25,000 men and its earlier fleet of 22,000 planes was down to a minuscule 200,[20] although the White Paper considered it possible – in times of national emergency – that the force could become the predominating factor in all types of warfare.) Trenchard decided that to enable the RAF to play a vital role in any future hostilities the requirement was to build a highly trained service with its own distinct 'air Spirit', and he determined to spend much of his small budget upon buildings rather than on war equipment. Plans were made for an imposing Air Force Staff College at Andover, a Cadet College at Cranwell and an Apprentice School at Halton, together with other training bases. It was crucial that officer training at Cranwell should be of a high standard – for Lord Derby had remarked to Stanley Baldwin in 1923, 'Really the calibre of the young officers who are taken in now is very low'.[21] For a technical service, continued research was also considered vitally important and the existing establishments at Biggin Hill, Martlesham Heath and Grain had to be retained and developed.[22]

As early as 1921 Trenchard had already had the chance to demonstrate his service's flexibility (and its claims for equal treatment with the other two) by assuming the prime responsibility for policing duties along the North West Frontier between India and Afghanistan, in Somaliland and especially in Iraq. During the latter operation the RAF was granted overall command for operations conducted with the army. While the bombing of native villages inevitably raised a number of serious moral questions – and might well have given him undue expectations where the bombing of European civilians was concerned – during its first year in Iraq the RAF helped reduce the policing expenses from £20 million to £6.6 million, and this saving continued into the second year.

Notwithstanding this, the RAF's right to exist continued to be challenged by the other two services. When, in 1921, a series of inquiries were raised by the Committee of Imperial Defence (CID) into the part played by the different services in the nation's strategic plans, Trenchard's arguments in favour of the RAF hinged upon its ability to mount strategic bombing for both deterrent and defensive purposes.

In a nutshell, he was maintaining that only the RAF could protect London and Britain as a whole. Following predictable howls of protest from the other two services at such a claim, former Prime Minister Arthur Balfour was called upon to arbitrate. Somewhat surprisingly, he came down in Trenchard's favour, concluding that 'in the case of defence against air raids, the army, and navy, must play a secondary role' and that 'any attempt to reduce the new force to an inferior position will seriously hamper its vigorous development'.[23]

Trenchard fought off another serious challenge to his service in 1923 and at the same time France's occupation of the Rhineland, which for a time raised the possibility of conflict between the two war-time allies, gave the RAF a most welcome opportunity to expand what came to be called its 'Home Defence Squadrons' to fifty-four, increases scheduled to take place over the next five years.[24] Significantly, with his belief in bombing he decided these should have a ratio of two bomber squadrons for each fighter one – which, with the extra cost of bombers to fighters, made the true ratio something like 6:1 in favour of bombers.

With the growing obsolescence of many RAF first-line aircraft Trenchard's doctrine of defence relying on the deterrent power of his bombers reinforced by heavy counter-bombing was certainly flawed when he put it forward in 1924, and with the development of effective early warning systems and potent monoplane fighters it would become unsustainable.

In fact, as early as 1925, following the Treaty of Locarno which offered a new sense of rapprochement for Europe, the credibility of such a doctrine had already become unrealistic. With its budget reduced by another 3 per cent the RAF was still required to expand its number of squadrons by 10 per cent a year. As France had nearly three times more fighters and bombers than Britain, Trenchard's short-term remedy was to keep a show of strength by retaining the number of his squadrons in being, but reducing their strength from eighteen aircraft to twelve. Further constraints by the Chancellor of the Exchequer, Winston Churchill, continued to fall particularly hard on the smallest and youngest service that received just 3s in the pound – 15 per cent of the total defence budget – over the years 1924–9. This was particularly serious for a force so dominated by equipment. Although some long-delayed developments, such as the issuing of parachutes and the establishment of a Department of

Aviation Medicine, took place, the RAF's aircraft grew ever more dated, with its standard interceptor continuing to be of 1916 vintage, and a third of its bombers still from the same era.

Trenchard's force, now a shadow of its earlier self in 1918, was withering away for lack of funds. In such a situation, whatever Trenchard's strategic non sequiturs and inexplicable bias against certain aircraft, his decision to construct a framework for a skilled service capable of rapid expansion with a unique pride and characteristic flamboyance appeared all the more important. Even so, when in 1929 Trenchard handed over to his successor, Geoffrey Salmond, there had been no loosening of the government's purse strings, and the state of the air force had become so bad that the editor of the *Observer*, J L Garvin, concluded that 'in terms of defence we are relatively weaker than we ever were in our whole history since the Norman Conquest. This was all the more culpable because owing to the dense degree of our industrialisation we are the nation in the whole world vulnerable to air power'.[25]

In such a situation the great sprawling city of London and its attendant industries in south-east England were, of course, especially vulnerable. Whether or not Trenchard began to have some belated doubts about his strategy, during his last three years as Chief of the Air Staff he started annual exercises between attacking and defending forces. The one held in 1927 brought disaster for the defenders, who were forced to abandon London and remove the national government to Manchester. Although an exercise, it could not have given the London authorities massive confidence in their aerial protectors, or Trenchard's current strategic doctrine.

Then in 1929 a full-length book appeared, written by General Ashmore, Smuts' candidate for masterminding the defence of London during the First World War, which ran directly counter to the Trenchard doctrine. Ashmore had long kept silent despite his basic disagreement, but the results of the 1927 air manoeuvres persuaded him that he must speak out. Central to his book was the conviction that London was indispensable 'to its nationals to a degree unequalled in any country in the world. Paris, Rome, Berlin, Moscow are all less easy to attack, less vulnerable to air targets, and less vital to the existence of their respective countries'.[26] He was not convinced about the validity of the recent air manoeuvres, in which the staff involved had little experience of defence beyond that on the Western Front during the First World War, and he directly questioned why thirty-six of the RAF's projected fifty-two squadrons should be bombers. His book contained a number of searching queries for the air commanders.

'How [he asked] would these [bombers] be used in the event of war? Would the British want to get their strategic blow in first? If so, could they justify it morally? Or did they have to wait until London was bombed before launching a counter-bombing offensive/defence?' This led on to the most important question of all. 'Could they trust that the mere existence of our bombing squadrons will prevent our being attacked?'[27]

Ashmore's conclusion was quite clear. 'We are relying too much on the defensive power of offensive bombing which has led to under reliance on fighter aeroplane defence. Such planes must be increased proportionately for unless we can defend our capital from air attack we shall find ourselves existing by favour of continental nations.' He went a step further. 'In fact, it appears certain that defence in this country will put a stop to raiding in a much shorter time than any counter-bombing could hope to do ...'.

Ashmore ended his book on a strong moral note. Regardless of outside influences, 'we have the right to protect ourselves by defences in our own country. Whether the world is armed or disarmed, we are liable to air attack.... If we maintain an efficient air defence, we may never be attacked; if we have no air defence ...?'.[28]

Such a powerful message from London's former chief defender was not only at variance with Trenchard's retaliatory doctrine, but with his often declared belief that the moral effect of bombing stood to its material effects in a proportion of twenty to one. It was patently at odds with the darkly sombre findings of the Air Raid Precautions Committee established in 1924 during the crisis with France, that in the event of London being bombed there would be likely failures in public morale. And it was even more out of sympathy with doom merchants such as Captain MacNeece Foster who, writing in the *RUSI Journal* of May 1928, had forecast that London could not hold out for more than weeks against air attacks which would have it 'flooded with gas, set alight with incendiary shells and bombed by high explosives'.[29]

*   *   *

Ashmore's ideas about developing a genuine air defence system centred on London were based on those he formulated during the First World War, including the use of its fighter planes.

As yet, Ashmore's ideas would not find favour with the British government, where the 1929 Wall Street financial crash was followed by a short-lived era of disarmament which brought even more cuts in defence expenditure to accompany the continuing unreal expectations for bombers illustrated in 1932 when Prime Minister Stanley Baldwin gave his famous warning about Britain's vulnerability. His conclusions were utterly bleak:

I think it is well for the man in the street to realize that there is no power on earth that can protect him from being bombed. Whatever people may tell him, the bomber will always get through. The only defence is offence, which means that you have to kill more women and children more quickly than the enemy if you want to save yourselves.[30]

At this time, under the auspices of the League of Nations, a number of disarmament proposals were being considered, including ones for cutting down the unladen weight of military aircraft to 3,000lb, which would have done away with anything but light bombers and (as intended) deal a fatal blow to their powers of deterrence.

Although over half of Britain's bombers were indeed light, these would not have been permitted, but in any case such attempts to cap air power were brought to a swift end in 1933 by Japan's offensive moves against China. This led the British Chiefs of Staff to call finally for the cancellation of the ten-year rule (by which the possibility of war within the next decade was ruled out). It was not a moment too soon, for in the following year Adolph Hitler was elected as German Chancellor and Germany joined with Japan to leave the League of Nations.

* * *

In 1933, with the worsening international situation, the British government appointed a Defence Requirements Committee to advise it on how to repair the worst deficiencies in its national defences, including those of London. In early 1934 London's vulnerability also became the subject of the first of Winston Churchill's dire prophecies resulting from Britain's unpreparedness: 'With our enormous metropolis here, the greatest target in the world, a kind of tremendous, fat, valuable cow, tied up to attract the beast of prey we are in a position in which we have never been before.'[31]

During the same year recommendations were made for a dramatic increase in the Metropolitan Air Force from 30 to 84 squadrons over the next 5 years. It was suggested that the fighter forces be increased to twenty-eight squadrons, although they would still be heavily outnumbered by the bombers. By 1935, in view of the accumulating conflicts across Europe, including Italy's hostilities against Abyssinia and the outbreak of civil war in Spain, the five-year programme appeared far too long. More serious still for the Royal Air Force, after visiting Germany two British ministers, Sir John Simon and Mr Anthony Eden, reported that the German air force had reached parity with it and now intended to overtake the total of 2,000 planes reportedly possessed by the French air force that were designed for close support only.

Remarkably, just prior to Germany being identified as Britain's most likely enemy and when more attention was at last being paid to would-be interceptor planes, a scientific committee under Sir Henry Tizard, the Scientific Adviser to the Air Ministry, decided to support a revolutionary early warning system that would replace the earlier locators and acoustical mirrors for detecting incoming aircraft. This relied on a system of radio waves, which in the first place had raised unrealistic hopes for a form of death ray to explode bombers and kill their crews. In the spring of 1935 the new system was demonstrated by R A Watson Watt of the National Physical Laboratory, and as a result a radio research station was set up under his direction at Orfordness on the Norfolk coast. Within weeks aircraft were being successfully tracked at a range of 40 miles, by what came to be called RDF (radio direction finding) and later RADAR (radio direction and ranging). By October 1935, six towers 350ft high (for transmitting) and others (for receiving) were being built out of an intended twenty that would cover the coast from Southampton to the Tyne. This remarkable system was allegedly independent of the three main obstacles of mist, fog and nightfall that had so affected its predecessors[32] and its range was soon extended to 100 miles from where a bearing could be taken on approaching enemy aircraft to ascertain their number and height.[33] Work also began on another series to detect aircraft flying beneath 300ft, and all RAF aircraft were fitted with a transmitting device to enable their 'signature' to be distinguished from those of the enemy. The essential advantage with such a system was that incoming planes could now be located early enough to avoid interceptor fighters having to spend valuable time and fuel on standing patrols.

However good such an early warning system might be – and it would, in fact, prove invaluable during the early part of the war – modern interceptor planes were also needed. Their new responsibilities were recognized with the forming of a dedicated command, along with Bomber, Coastal and Training commands. Fighter Command began to operate on 14 July 1936 under Air Marshal Sir Hugh Dowding, whose headquarters was at Bentley Priory near Stanmore. Contrary to most other senior officers in the RAF, Dowding had long believed that fighters would prove superior in battle to bombers but only if they were the faster, metal monoplanes rather than the wooden biplanes still in existence. He therefore decided that the RAF's thirty fighter squadrons due to become operational by 1939 must be equipped with these – something which would only become possible with an increase in fighter aircraft production beyond all expectations.

Remarkably, the Air Ministry still placed its main emphasis on bombers, requesting an increase to ninety squadrons compared with relatively modest increases in fighters. What was more, the bombers were expected to become larger. The medium-sized Whitleys, Hampdens and the more powerful Wellingtons that had reached the production stage by 1936 were expected to be replaced by genuine long-range aircraft such as the four-engined Stirlings and Halifaxes and the twin-engined Manchester (which, when equipped with four engines, would become the legendary Lancaster), although these were not expected to come into service until 1942. Fortunately for London and the country as a whole, these proposals were opposed by the then Minister for Co-ordination of Defence, Sir Thomas Inskip, who maintained that German bombers could be better destroyed over Britain by a fighter force than by bombing their aerodromes and factories.[34] Moreover, he recommended that it would be better in the short term to develop medium and light bombers. As a result the new Secretary of State for Air, Sir Kingsley Wood, ruled that fighters should have first claim on production – at which Dowding straight away asked for his fighter squadrons to be increased to forty-five and for anti-aircraft guns, searchlights and balloons also to be provided for London's ground defences. Likely attacks from a revitalized German Luftwaffe had finally forced the Air Staff to give way over their long-held doctrine of strategic bombing.

Despite this last-minute conversion, there were the gravest doubts over whether sufficient fighters could be produced in time: to stand any chance unprecedented measures would have to be taken towards mass-production. The adverse balance between the RAF and the Luftwaffe (combined with the unpreparedness of the other two services) was already in Prime Minister Neville Chamberlain's mind when he yielded to Hitler at Munich, thereby gaining a breathing space of almost a year. The need was unarguable, for at the time of his going to Germany only five of the RAF's fighter squadrons had modern aircraft and London's ground defences, together with the country's radar chain, were still far from complete.

How the RAF, which had been so depleted during the locust years, acquired the men and machines needed to bring it up to establishment in 1940 and how they and their radar defences would meet the massive and repeated attacks from the fighters and bombers of a rampant German air force on London and the south-east was about to be revealed.

PART 3

Attacks During the Second World War

Chapter 6

Renewed Air Assaults

'He died who loved to live', they'll say
Unselfishly so we might have today!
Like hell. He fought because he had to fight
He died that's all. It was his unlucky night.

'Luck', Wing Commander Dennis McHarrie[1]

During the autumn of 1940, despite the RAF bombing raids on German invasion barges, it was Fighter Command who faced the massed assaults of the German air force upon the home country. At the time the Luftwaffe, with its '2,550 serviceable aircraft including 900 bombers, 250 dive bombers, 800 single-engined fighters and 200 twin-engined fighters',[2] was the world's premier formation and once it had succeeded in shooting down the opposing British fighter planes and ravaged their airfields and aircraft factories the way would be open both for air assaults on London and the south-east and for the Luftwaffe to give direct support for an invasion of Britain by German land forces. To this end the main weight of the early attacks fell on the south-eastern airfields and radar installations guarding London. Spectators from the counties to the south and east of the city soon became accustomed to the flash of wings and uneven waves of sound from snarling engines as the Royal Air Force's interceptors, Hurricanes and Spitfires which Max Hastings considered 'the most beautiful aircraft the world has ever seen',[3] attacked the German bombers and duelled with their more battle-hardened opponents accompanying them.

Whatever claims they might have for beauty, in speed, manoeuvrability and potency such fighters were light years ahead of the British biplanes which only weeks before were being used to help defend the skies in France and the Low Countries against German invaders. Given that Trenchard had never believed in massed fighter-to-fighter engagements as a proper use of air power, it was remarkable that such advanced British planes contested the skies with the Luftwaffe. After years of financial contraction during the 1920s and early 1930s that inevitably favoured conventional designs, it was unlikely that the RAF would have progressed beyond Hawker Fury or Gloster Gladiator biplanes had it not been for the conjunction of an international air race with a far-seeing and dedicated British designer.

The race in question was instituted in 1912 by Jacques Schneider, son of a French armament maker, to encourage the development of long-range, ocean-going planes: following the First World War, it captured the imagination of leading aeronautical nations including Britain, USA, France and Italy (Germany was, of course, not allowed an air force) during a period of massive retrenchment and neglect. Britain's appetite for a challenge seen in its relish for Polar expeditions and for the air races organized by the *Daily Mail* was well proven. However, its successes in the Schneider Trophy owed much to the young designer Reginald Mitchell, who, working at the relatively small company of Supermarine Aviation, won the 1922 race with an elegant biplane suspended on floats called *Sea Lion II*, powered by a British Napier engine.

In Baltimore, USA two years later, his entry, now a lively monoplane, reached a speed of 226mph, thereby breaking the world speed record across water. Then in 1927, by which time the Americans had turned their main attention to transport planes, Mitchell raised his speed to over 300mph, although by now his plane's Napier engine was approaching the limits of its development. Prior to the 1929 race an ageing Henry Royce was persuaded to build an engine for Mitchell's now all-metal, heavily streamlined airframe. After repeated setbacks and myriad modifications, a new cocktail of aviation fuel was adopted which propelled Mitchell's S6 aircraft to victory and a few days later, upon being fitted with a new propeller, it reached a speed of 358mph.

Despite such an achievement, Mitchell's chances of participating in the 1931 race were slim when faced with opposition from both the British Treasury and the Air Ministry. The Chancellor of the Exchequer, Philip Snowdon, was also opposed to what he saw as a 'pernicious rivalry', and somehow Trenchard and his successor, Sir William Salmond, both convinced themselves that the cost of subsidizing Mitchell was out of all proportion to any benefits from the research and development involved. For some peculiar reason Trenchard also considered it bad for RAF morale. It was finally left to a female philanthropist, Lucy Houston (former mistress of a rich brewer and widow of a very wealthy baronet), to pledge the £100,000 required. In the event, the 1931 race never took place, although the course was over flown and Mitchell's S6 aircraft with its Rolls-Royce engine set a new world speed record of 379mph. This still did not satisfy the designer and on 29 September Mitchell finally succeeded in exceeding 400mph, an achievement not formally bettered until after the Second World War.

Although suffering from cancer, for the next three years until his death in June 1937 Mitchell worked tirelessly on a new aeroplane that embraced the virtues of his trophy winners, an all-metal fighter aircraft with elliptical cantilever wings and monocoque fuselage for which Rolls-Royce developed their legendary Merlin engine. The resultant Spitfire, whose development owed remarkably little to support from the RAF's hierarchy – except for the maverick Hugh Dowding[4] – was described by Harald Penrose, eminent test pilot and aviation commentator, as 'the most exotic and awe-inspiring fighter ever produced'.[5] Mitchell's achievements finally convinced Sydney Camm, chief designer for the Hawker Company, about the advantages of the monoplane design, although his Hawker Hurricane retained the conventional tubular frame construction and fabric covering. Coming midway in development between the advanced Spitfire and Camm's Fury biplane, the Hurricane would prove more robust and easier to build than the Spitfire and, while its performance was somewhat inferior, when equipped with the Merlin engine it acted as a worthy and, in numerical terms, major partner to the Spitfire in the coming battle against the Luftwaffe. Both aircraft were equipped with long-range armament of eight American Browning machine guns fitted in their wings, capable of firing 1,000 rounds a minute. While the prototype Hurricane flew in November 1935 and the first Spitfire in March of the next year, the problems of producing both types in sufficient quantity for the autumn of 1940 was to prove a saga of its own, the success of which owed much to the eccentric press baron Max Aitken (later Lord Beaverbrook), whom Winston Churchill had selected for the task.

On the German side the headlong development of their air force to its premier position since it was re-established in 1935 was equally noteworthy and they too had a remarkable interceptor aircraft in the Messerschmidt Bf 109. This was the brainchild of Willy Messerschmidt, an erratic if undoubted genius, but it also had its detractors, notably Erhart Milch who masterminded the secret development of the German air force. The Messerschmidt 109 was only saved when Ernst Udet, the ex-fighter ace appointed by Goering as Director of the Luftwaffe's Technical Department, despite misgivings of his own, preferred it over a Heinkel contender. Although more delicate than the Hurricane, it had the most aerodynamically efficient airframe for its size, with a top speed virtually identical to that of a Spitfire but a much better performance at altitude. Its projected armament was a combination of two machine guns on the engine crankcase and two further cannon in the wings.[6]

For their projected attacks, in addition to their star Bf 109s the Luftwaffe had longer range escorts, Messerschmidt 110s which, although faster in level flight than the Hurricanes, had relatively poor acceleration and a wider turning circle that made them vulnerable to both Hurricanes and Spitfires. As for their bombers, the most notable at this time was the Stuka dive-bomber which had terrorized both troops and civilians during the German advances across Europe, although when opposed to the RAF fighters it was found to be relatively slow, with no protective armour and a shorter range than the Messerschmidts.

As a result of the previous ban on a German air force their three main classes of bomber were only medium sized, although capable of not only striking at RAF airfields and other installations in southern England but also London and the English provincial cities. These were of three types. The oldest, the Dornier Do 17, nicknamed the 'Flying Pencil' because of its ultra-slim fuselage, had nominally been designed as a high-speed mail carrier and was obsolete by 1939 due to its slowness, vulnerability and inadequate bomb load. The Heinkel He 111, although capable of carrying twice the Dornier's bomb load, also lacked armour and efficient defensive armament, which from mid-September 1940 caused it to be relegated to night bombing. The third and latest aircraft, the Junkers Ju 88, had progressed from the drawing board to its first flight in December 1936. Directly comparable with the later RAF Mosquito, it was not only fast but by far the most versatile of the German bombers. At the beginning of the war, however, the semi-obsolescent Dorniers and vulnerable Heinkels still made up the bulk of the German bomber fleets.

Whatever their aircrafts' respective technical merits, the Luftwaffe enjoyed a clear numerical advantage over Hugh Dowding's Fighter Command. How clear remains open to some debate with the picture further complicated by the air fighting that took place over Europe prior to the British withdrawal from Dunkirk.

Dowding calculated that he required a minimum of fifty-two squadrons of Hurricanes and Spitfires (with twelve operational aircraft each) for the defence of Britain, but the successes of German forces in Norway, the Low Countries and France brought frenzied calls for some of Britain's Home Defence aircraft to augment the allied air detachments there. During the winter of 1939 two squadrons were accordingly despatched to Norway with the consequence that in May 1940, following the destruction of the Dutch and Belgian air forces and the decimation of the French air force, the RAF's Advanced Striking Force in France of 400 largely obsolescent bombers and fighters was left to face most formidable odds and quickly lost half its planes. As a result, on 12 May a further four squadrons of Hurricanes were sent out, rapidly followed by another thirty-six aircraft. The French Premier Paul Reynard then appealed to Churchill for ten more squadrons.

At this point, fearing potential disaster, Dowding presented the British Cabinet with a graph showing the numbers of Hurricanes that had been taken from the home defences so far, a policy which, if continued, would lead to Britain's inevitable defeat. As a result a compromise was agreed; although six further Hurricane squadrons were assigned to missions in France, it was on condition that they returned each day to their home bases in Britain. Notwithstanding this, by the time of the French surrender on 22 June 1940 the RAF losses of 66 aircraft in Norway had been increased by a further 959 in France, some half of which were fighters. Dowding's home defences were now reduced to 331 Spitfires and Hurricanes, supported by 150 second-line machines of questionable value, facing some 800 single-engined and 200 double-engined interceptors, apart from considerable numbers of German bombers.

Of equal, or greater, importance to Dowding was the loss of nearly 450 of his experienced pilots when the RAF received a maximum of 200 pilots a month from its training schools, where the quality of the training was imperfect[7] given the prospect of immediate action. Dowding also competed for both pilots and aircraft against Bomber Command, within an Air Ministry still holding on to its traditional belief that the cardinal purpose of aerial operations should be the mounting of strategic attacks, particularly on German oil supplies.[8] Fortunately this standpoint was amended, if temporarily, when Prime Minister Churchill told Lord Beaverbrook that 'in the fierce light of the present emergency the fighter is the need and the output of fighters must be the primary consideration until we have broken the enemy's attack ...'.[9]

It was Churchill's appointment of the acerbic, unorthodox and ruthless Beaverbrook that led to a startling rise in the production of fighter planes, his Civilian Repair Organization alone contributing about a third of the 'new aircraft' during the Battle of Britain. By 1 July 1940 Dowding's aircraft fleet had risen to a total of 639, although not all were Hurricanes and Spitfires, and its defensive responsibilities included the rest of Britain. Fighter Command was divided into four groups, each under an Air Vice Marshal, 10 Group in the south-west, 11 Group in London and the south-east, 12 Group in Lincolnshire and South Yorkshire and 13 Group in North Yorkshire and the Scottish Borders. Of these, 11 Group was by far the most important, with 348 planes compared with 12 Group's 113 and 13 Group's 178,[10] and by 1 August the numbers in 11 Group had again increased.[11]

Whatever the weaponry and the numbers involved, like all conflicts the personalities and performances of the respective commanders proved of immense importance. In Dowding, who had assumed his post with Fighter Command in July 1936, the British had a better commander than they realized and one who certainly deserved better treatment from his senior colleagues following the main battle.

Dowding took up his newly created command with one clear advantage. He had formally been the RAF's Member for Research and Development where he had not only strongly supported the use of metals in the construction of modern aircraft, but fully recognized the technical significance of radar. In the RAF hierarchy a posting to Bomber Command would have carried greater weight and Dowding's appointment came after he had been passed over as Chief of the Air Staff. Yet in this austere, enigmatic, highly principled, unpopular and self-opinionated man, utterly committed to his pilots although rarely meeting them face to face, Fighter Command gained a champion who was prepared to oppose anyone, including Churchill, to keep the squadrons he felt necessary for his Home Defence system, with its early warning (RDF) radar and co-ordinated operations rooms linked to his own at Stanmore.

Dowding was convinced that, in the circumstances, his command's needs should prevail over any other branch of the armed services, 'except those of the Royal Navy' (because) 'Britain's security resting on command of the air and sea approaches must have absolute priority over defensive action'.[12]

To command 11 Group, with its vital task of defending London and the south-east, Dowding chose the cool and measured New Zealander Keith Park. Coming from a humble background, during the First World War he had served as a private soldier at Gallipoli. Having subsequently become a distinguished First World War pilot, it was Park's custom, unique among senior officers, to fly his personal Hurricane and, having fought with it in the skies over Dunkirk, he was easily the most experienced man in the RAF in the disposition and control of fighters in action.[13] Dowding preferred Park to the more excitable and more senior Trafford Leigh Mallory, who, in comparison, lacked fighter experience, although he kept Leigh Mallory in his post as commander of 12 Group covering East Anglia and the Midlands, which he had held since 1937.

Park's was a crucial appointment, for Dowding was confident he fully under-stood his own priorities, namely to keep the fighter screen covering London in being at all costs. This entailed his pilots concentrating on breaking up the bomber forces rather than choosing to attack their fighter escorts. Fewer numbers meant squadrons had to be used sparingly and local reverses accepted. Such tactics were understandably not fully understood by Dowding's more cavalier pilots or by his belligerent Prime Minister, who would send Dowding's old enemy, Trenchard (who considered Dowding too soft on his pilots during the First World War), to look at and report back on the hard-pressed squadrons during the battle. In fact, Trenchard reported to Churchill that 'the pilots and junior commanders 'are less tired and rattled than some of the senior officers', and he even went as far as to acknowledge – belatedly – that he had under-estimated Dowding's leadership qualities.[14] This did not prevent Dowding's compulsory retirement in November 1940 while his fighters were still involved with the continuing German attacks upon London. His brutal removal was inevitably followed by that of Park on 18 December 1940 (although by then the climax of the battle was past and their tactics had been justified) in an act that is now generally regarded as both vindictive and highly unjust.[15]

The reclusive Dowding's opponent, Reichsmarschall Hermann Goering, German Air Minister and the Luftwaffe's Commander in Chief, was a markedly different character. As a fighter ace during the First World War he had shown undoubted bravery, and by 1940 after the Luftwaffe's successes in Poland and the West he became the most powerful military figure in Germany. Unlike Dowding, who arrived at his headquarters at Bentley Priory unannounced and unattended, Goering revelled in the trappings of power, including gaudy uniforms, a diamond-studded Marshal's baton and his personal railway train. But whatever his undoubted intelligence, by temperament he was an opportunist and more importantly for the coming battle lacked the crucial appetite for technical matters so vital for the commander of an air arm. This made him over-confident about his superior numbers of aircraft (including the vulnerable Stuka dive-bombers) and the dedication and skills of his airmen to achieve results beyond their capabilities when up against a formidable and determined enemy. Because of this he was forced into a series of tactical U-turns that favoured Dowding.

Like Dowding, Goering had a political leader who thought he knew better than his commanders but, unlike Churchill, he took over strategic control of his forces, often with disastrous consequences. By any standard Hitler was undoubtedly the wrong man to receive Goering's unrealistic promises about subduing the RAF.

For the commanders on both sides the battle's preliminaries did not turn out as anticipated. The British Air Staff expected initial bombing exchanges rather than the concentrated German attacks on Channel shipping. In the case of the Luftwaffe commanders, Goering's rash offer to Hitler to attack Britain straight away scarcely gave them time to move their air fleets to the Channel coast before they had to open the campaign. Such haste led to serious weaknesses of intelligence about the British defences, a lack of agreement over target selection and an over estimation of the RAF's fighter strength, particularly the Spitfires' performance capabilities. Albert Kesselring, who commanded the Luftwaffe's Air Fleet 2 opposing Park's 11 Group, and Hugo von Sperrle, leader of Air Fleet 3 with its headquarters in Paris, knew little about Dowding's command structure, including his operations rooms and, above all, they had scant appreciation of the importance of British radar facilities.[16]

The opposing commanders faced contrasting tactical problems. The attackers could choose their points of attack and undoubtedly had the resources to assemble large numbers of aircraft for the purpose, although they were hampered by the short operational range of their best fighters.

The defenders priorities were different. They had to scramble early enough to gain the required height to meet their assailants on equal terms, although the advent of radar, whose information was processed in Dowding's operations rooms, enabled the raiders' approaches to be tracked with some accuracy and in time to intercept them. What was more, if such interceptions occurred close to their home aerodromes, the defenders could expect to make multiple sorties, thereby cancelling out their deficiencies in numbers.

As for the respective personnel, by July 1940 most of Goering's aircrews – all full-time professionals – had acquired some battle experience. Whether in Spain, Poland, France or the Low Countries, the results had always turned in their favour, and during such operations, the relationships between officers and NCOs had understandably grown closer than in the other German armed services – or for that matter in the RAF. With Dowding's squadrons the RAF's best pilots were likely to have opted for bombers and he had already suffered the misfortune of losing more of his experienced pilots than the Luftwaffe while flying inferior aircraft in France. In the case of 85 Hurricane Squadron, for instance, 'out of its normal establishment of 18 pilots, it lost, in the space of 11 days, 8 killed or missing in action and 6 wounded'.[17] Its commanding officer was among the dead and Squadron Leader Peter Townsend was sent to rebuild it.

Such losses were the more serious in Fighter Command because it relied heavily on reservists, which led to a remarkable 25 per cent of its pilots coming from the auxiliary air force and volunteer reserve, both officers and NCOs, some of whom, in the early stages at least, were somewhat under trained and others past their peak in terms of age. Dowding believed that 26 was the upper age for fighter pilots, although many would distinguish themselves at 30 years or more as a result of shortages. Other pilots came from the university air squadrons, the Fleet Air Arm and the Commonwealth, including 127 New Zealanders and 112 Canadians, who returned to fight for the home country. From occupied Europe there were Czech, Belgian, French and Polish pilots, all relishing the chance to fight the hated Germans. Of these, 88 came from Czechoslovakia and 145 from Poland, with the Polish pilots achieving the greatest proportion of kills overall. Such a disparate group needed to bond together as quickly as possible.

Contrary to popular belief the majority of the British pilots did not come from public schools – only about 200 of the 3,000 involved, with Eton providing by far the most. Even so, Fighter Command's officers' messes undoubtedly had a public-school ethos and in 1940 its sergeant pilots were strictly segregated from their commissioned counterparts and provided with their own messes and accommodation. Still further segregation occurred among the NCO pilots, with reservists tending to be cold-shouldered by those who had trained at Halton's apprentice school. Unsurprisingly, Peter Townsend noticed that the imminence of danger soon broke down many of these barriers, particularly between the new and the old RAF recruits.[18]

The confrontation between the two air forces, which Churchill was to call the Battle of Britain, that commenced in early July and went on until late September, took two main forms. The first saw the Luftwaffe attacking coastal shipping, before moving on to the radar installations and RAF airfields covering London, while attempting to shoot the defending fighters out of the sky. The second saw it mount massive bombing raids on the British capital itself, which, apart from the devastating damage expected, would finally force the RAF defenders to seek combat with their seemingly superior Bf 109s. During the Luftwaffe's initial attacks on the British coastal ports and shipping in the Channel, most of the advantages lay with the attackers, for such sweeps were carried out within the range of their best fighters and British radar proved of relatively limited use against aircraft that did not venture inland. Without the benefits of early warnings the defenders were obliged to react to every threat, even those from individual planes.

Together with such problems, Park's determination to keep a proportion of his units in reserve and insist that his pilots concentrate on attacking the German bombers also brought bewilderment and even anger within certain squadrons. His pilots always seemed to be outnumbered and, when there were superior numbers of 109s, they undoubtedly suffered heavily. It represented a harsh learning curve for the less experienced and, although coming before the main battle, both sides suffered heavy losses. The best estimates of these from early July to 11 August 1940 were 180 planes lost by the RAF compared with 330 by the Luftwaffe.[19] With their less-experienced pilots such figures appear very creditable – and so they were – but they only told part of the story. All the British planes lost were Hurricanes and Spitfires, whereas in some cases only one in five of the German losses was a fighter plane. In fighter-to-fighter combat, the Germans maintained a clear ascendancy.

The intensity of the fighting soon took its toll, particularly on the RAF. By 19 July the rate of Dowding's losses was already bringing fears that Fighter Command could become extinct within six weeks. Yet contrary to reports received by German intelligence the attrition suffered by the RAF was not for lack of planes; under Beaverbrook's vigorous prompting British fighter production had risen from 155 during the first quarter of 1940 to 340, 563 and 420 planes in successive quarters,[20] levels that exceeded the expectations of the

RAF's Chiefs of Staff by a remarkable 50 per cent. Far more serious were the losses from among Dowding's diminishing pool of experienced pilots, including 80 flight commanders and squadron commanders. Such heavy losses were particularly disastrous for auxiliary pilots, many of whom grew up together in the same neighbourhoods. Of necessity, many of their replacements received only the shortest period of training with little or no practice at firing their guns. Whether the direst predictions were fully justified or not, it seemed unlikely that Dowding's pilots, maintenance crews and support organizations could maintain such a pace for a prolonged period and then go on to fight an expected major battle.[21]

The Luftwaffe was also finding things unexpectedly difficult. Although it succeeded in driving much of the coastal traffic out of the English Channel, major problems were occurring within its air fleets. Its dive-bombers were found to be immensely vulnerable to attacks from British fighters, while its twin-engined Messerschmidts had proved unsuitable escorts for the bombers against attacks by Hurricanes and Spitfires.

The deadly sparring round the coasts was brought to a close when Hitler, in his Operational Directive of 3 August, required the Luftwaffe 'to use all means in its power to mount attacks, first against the flying units, ground organisation and supply installations of the Royal Air Force, then against the air armaments industry'[22] to pave the way for a possible invasion.

German attacks on the RAF's fighter bases were hampered at the outset by the Luftwaffe's inability to distinguish them from aerodromes dedicated to bomber and transport duties. Goering also gave his crews instructions to bomb a wide range of objectives, including the naval installations and convoys attacked earlier. Such large numbers of destinations meant limiting the weight of their attacks on individual targets and against the defending fighters, especially when the defending Hurricanes and Spitfires forced the Luftwaffe into close protection of their bombers. Even so, on 12 August the curtain-raiser attacks on Park's forward aerodromes of Manston, Lympne and Hawkinge, together with six radar stations and naval installations, were undoubtedly successful. The three aerodromes were all hit, and their runways, hangars and offices suffered considerable damage, though determined efforts by all ranks resulted in many of the craters and runways being filled in by the next day. At Ventnor an attack so badly damaged its radar station that Park's radar chain was broken and it was not rectified for almost a fortnight.

These were followed twenty-four hours later by Goering's massive 'Eagle's Day' attack, which, together with others in quick succession, he had vaingloriously promised would overwhelm the British defences within four days. By subjecting a wide range of targets to massed attacks, he hoped to create extensive confusion on the ground and force Dowding's squadrons into a series of air battles where his accomplished fliers could be expected to destroy them. In fact, Park's radar and ops control systems continued to function well and many of the bombers were intercepted short of their targets, although aerodromes at Eastchurch, Odiham, Farnborough, Andover, Middle Wallop and Maidstone were damaged. At the end of 'Eagle's Day', the Luftwaffe had flown 1,000 sorties to Dowding's 700, but although extensive damage had been sustained by aerodromes and naval installations, Park was exceedingly fortunate that most of his fighter aerodromes escaped and Goering himself lost 45 aircraft compared to the RAF's 17.

On 15 August the Luftwaffe sent its planes on an amazing 1,900 sorties across the face of Britain, although Dowding responded with a creditable 1,000.

As before, by far the greatest share of the attacks fell on Park's 11 Group covering London and the south-east, where Lympne airfield was devastated and Hawkinge badly damaged. Following attacks on the coastal radar stations and aero components' factories at Rochester and Eastchurch, the airfields at Middle Wallop, West Malling and Croydon were bombed heavily later in the day. Despite the unequalled number of attacks and the undoubted damage caused, the Luftwaffe failed to break down 11 Group's defences and in the process they lost seventy-five aircraft to Dowding's thirty-four. The heavy losses among their Stuka dive-bombers were also becoming unsustainable.

Unbeknown to the Germans, with the British factories turning out ten or more aircraft a day, Dowding now actually had more interceptors than at the start of Goering's offensive. Although the question of replacement pilots was undoubtedly more serious and their training often short and rudimentary, the situation was far from desperate.

While the battles of 15 August were raging, Goering gathered his most senior commanders at his hunting estate 40 miles from Berlin to enquire into the disappointing outcome of the 'Eagle's Day' attack. Such men might have been far better employed directing the current operations, but instead he upbraided them for their limited successes, while further increasing the tactical restrictions on his best fighters by demanding still greater protection for the bombers, including the Stukas. Finally, in the closing sentence of his address, he made an appalling blunder entirely due to his technical ignorance when he told them that 'it is doubtful whether there is any point in continuing the attacks on radar sites, in view of the fact that not one of those attacked has so far been put out of action'.[23] For Dowding's beleaguered installations, and the Post Office engineers struggling to restore Ventnor, Dover and Rye radar stations to operational capability, this was undoubtedly good news. (Ventnor was, in fact, not fully repaired until the 26th.)

On the 16th the Germans attacked the aerodromes again, mounting over 1,700 sorties. On a day of punishing losses for both sides the RAF, whom Goering hoped was running out of planes, flew 766 sorties, during which they shot down 71 of his aircraft.

Although Goering's four-day assault failed so far to give him the superiority he sought, he was convinced he had hit Park devastatingly hard and could still bring him to his knees in time for the invasion to be mounted. In a further change of tactics he decided to combine the unceasing attacks on 11 Group's airfields – to which the British had to respond – with others on industrial targets, especially those aircraft factories supplying the RAF's replacement planes. This time the daylight attacks would be followed by others at night, and a large number of provincial towns would be hit, giving the defenders no respite. All the Luftwaffe's 109s were concentrated in Kesselring's Air Fleet and moved forward to the Pas de Calais area, and the Stuka dive-bombers withdrawn from daytime use.

On the British side, while Dowding told his staff that defence of their airfields was the greatest priority, his pilots had to continue to avoid fighter-to-fighter combat with the 109s. This was despite pressure from Leigh Mallory at 12 Group to confront the attackers with larger fighter wings. It had now become clear that the battle would be decided by 11 Group's 300 or so Hurricanes and Spitfires, confronting a maximum of 650–700 Messerschmidts working near the limits of their operational ranges, and hobbled by their commitments to escort the bombers.[24]

All-out hostilities resumed on 24 August and continued until 6 September. On 24 August Manston, Hornchurch and North Weald aerodromes were bombed, the former so severely that it had to be evacuated, except for emergency landings. The German system of close support between their bombers and escorts appeared to be working well, for the defenders were not only unable to break up the attacks but they found themselves being forced into the direct fights with the 109s that Goering sought. At one stage Park requested help from nearby 12 Group but it failed to reach him, most probably because of delays in forming up a 'big wing'. The German daylight sweeps were supported by over 100 bombers following up by night, when an attempted attack upon the Thames oil refineries led to London being bombed by mistake. Dowding had little answer to the night raids: the radar sets for his night fighters were not ready, and the ack-ack guns had no equipment to fire at unseen targets.

Meanwhile, Bomber Command (who during the three months that included the Battle of Britain actually lost more aircrew than Fighter Command) decided to send eighty-one Hampden medium bombers on the long and hazardous journey to Berlin, an operation that, despite serious losses, was repeated on subsequent nights.

During the week beginning 26 August the attacks against 11 Group's airfields continued and on the 28th one raid was made by German fighter planes only. The resultant tussle between both sides' fighters developed against Park's wishes, but 11 Group did not come off markedly worse, although on that day the British pilot, Al Deere, was forced to bale out of his Spitfire for the third time in as many weeks.

On 30 August, soon after 11.00 am, 150 bombers with their fighter escorts crossed the Kent coast and in the course of scattered engagements across south-east England, all Park's squadrons were airborne. In the afternoon waves of bombers crossed the British coast at twenty-minute intervals and succeeded in hitting Park's electricity grid, and putting seven vital radar stations out of action.

In spite of their battered airfields, during the 30th the British still flew a remarkable 1,054 sorties, some of the squadrons making 4 sorties each and most at least 2. (Providing a plane was not damaged, it was possible to refuel and rearm it within thirty-five minutes.) The Luftwaffe also made multiple sorties despite the longer approach and return flights involved.

The 31st began with a wave of German fighters again positively inviting combat, followed by bombers and their fighter escorts who approached the Thames estuary. There an attack on Duxford was deflected but Croydon, Biggin Hill and Hornchurch were hit, for the loss of sixty German aircraft.

By 1 September Dowding's pilot casualties were becoming critical, particularly in the case of his leaders, for 'he had lost 11 of his 46 squadron commanders and 39 of his 97 flight commanders killed or wounded'.[25] Some of the replacements had only twenty hours' experience of flying Hurricanes or Spitfires. If the deadly pattern was to continue, both sides seemed sure to lose their best pilots and machines.

Although Dowding felt he had little choice but to respond grimly and safeguard his strength in the hope that the balance would eventually move in his favour, Goering decided that his beloved air force could not continue like this. While on 3 September the Luftwaffe was still pounding the RAF airfields, he held a conference with his air commanders at The Hague. German intelligence reports had put Dowding's strength down to some 300 fighters and the conference decided to bomb the London docks (Hitler still banned them from attacking the city itself), a target that they believed would surely force the English to use their depleted numbers in its defence, thus exposing them to his deadly 109s. On the 4th after more destructive attacks on Park's airfields, the storage tanks at Thames Haven were set on fire and both the Vickers factory at Brooklands (producing Wellington bombers) and that of Short Bros at Rochester (working on Stirling bombers) were hit. Despite exaggerated German hopes, at the end of the day the respective aeroplane losses were about even.

Next day still brought no breakthrough for the attackers, although Dowding was compelled to reclassify his squadrons into ABC, with those graded as B or C either being in no condition to fight in the front line or not at all. In spite of everything, although many of his airfields were flattened and burning and there were heartbreaking gaps among his most experienced fliers, with those left having passed the normal exhaustion levels, the defences still held. In fact, they continued to give almost as well as they received by virtue of their leaders' superior tactics, the high personal qualities of their heterogeneous group of pilots and the speed with which the replacement fliers – if they survived their first near suicidal sorties – adapted to the demands placed upon them. Against them the Luftwaffe, plagued by its leaders' bewildering and contradictory initiatives, was not receiving enough aircraft to make up its losses and when attacking relatively small and well-defended airfields could no longer attack every one in the overwhelming strength required.[26]

On 4 September there came an unexpected intervention from Hitler. The man who had halted Guderman's panzers before Dunkirk made a speech in Berlin during which he promised to respond to the RAF's raids on the German capital by a hundredfold, declaring it was time for an aerial assault on London, to break the morale of the British people in the way earlier raids on Warsaw and Amsterdam had done to the Poles and Dutch. At this time he was strongly supported by Goering and Kesselring, in their conviction that they were close to defeating the RAF, although the more cautious Hugo von Sperrle, commander of Air Fleet 3, still believed the RAF was far from finished. With Hitler now in favour, plans were finally drawn up for a massive raid on London to take place on 7 September.

Park believed that Hitler's decision saved his 11 Group from destruction, although Dowding did not think the position so extreme and that the German attacks were themselves showing signs of slackening.[27] In any event, he looked to the growing likelihood of unfavourable autumn weather promising to relieve things further.[28] Winston Churchill, writing after the war, had no doubt about the significance of the change of tactics. He believed that Fighter Command's 11 Group was indeed coming to the end of its tether and for him Hitler's decision marked the effective end of the invasion threat as well. Churchill believed that 'if any of our cities were to be attacked, the brunt should fall on London ... London was like some huge prehistoric animal capable of enduring

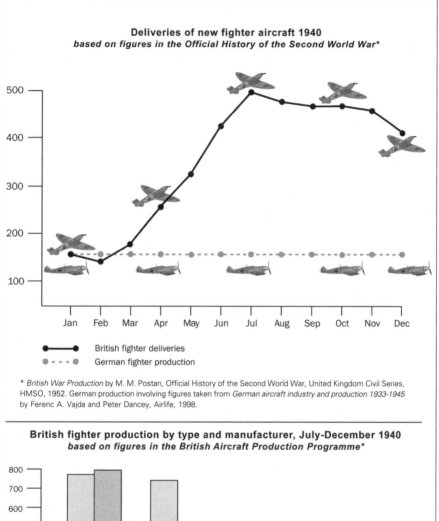

Deliveries of new fighter aircraft 1940
based on figures in the Official History of the Second World War*

● British fighter deliveries
●---● German fighter production

* *British War Production* by M. M. Postan, Official History of the Second World War, United Kingdom Civil Series, HMSO, 1952. German production involving figures taken from *German aircraft industry and production 1933-1945* by Ferenc A. Vajda and Peter Dancey, Airlife, 1998.

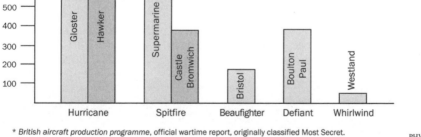

British fighter production by type and manufacturer, July-December 1940
based on figures in the British Aircraft Production Programme*

* *British aircraft production programme*, official wartime report, originally classified Most Secret.

PHV

terrible injuries, mangled and bleeding from many wounds, and yet preserving life and movement'.[29]

Both sides were soon to see the outcome of the revised tactics. At Cap Gris Nez Hermann Goering and Kesselring, Commander of the German Air Fleet 2, stood on the cliffs there awaiting the coming of their air armada with high hopes. The frustrating and costly raids against the RAF air bases were about to take second place to the bombing of London, the British capital and centre of the British Empire. Goering had already boasted that 'my bombers will darken the skies over England' and, following the hum of engines, the two men looked up at 2 waves of bombers numbering about 350 in all, together with their 600 escorting fighters, making up a seemingly irresistible formation covering some 800 square miles of sky, about to cross the Channel. The bombers flew at 16,000ft, with fighters above them in the largest assembly of aircraft yet seen. But however impressive their numbers, they were taking on their largest task to date: unless the Luftwaffe could terrorize London, shatter its ground defences and inflict greater losses than ever before on 11 Group's interceptors committed to defend it, success might still elude them.

Whatever the plans and hopes of both sides, the climax of the protracted battle between the Luftwaffe's bombers and escorts and the RAF's fighters – now directly defending London – was fast approaching, and for ordinary Londoners, as in the previous war, their suffering was about to begin.

Chapter 7

London Blitz, 1940–1 – Ground and Air Defenders

Suddenly, traversing, elevating, madly
It plunges into action, more than eager
For the steel blood of those romantic birds

Gavin Ewart, 'The Bofurs AA Gun'[1]

On 7 September 1940 the armada of planes bound for London marked the opening of the aerial blitz on the city that would continue until 10 May of the following year. In the first instance it involved both day and night bombing by an average of 200 planes during 56 of the next 57 nights.[2] Although other cities were bombed as well, upwards of twice the weight of bombs were dropped on London than all the others put together. This was fully understandable since London represented the ultimate target not only as home to the nation's sovereign and its Parliament but also as its largest manufacturing complex, and its docks that handled a third of the nation's total imports and exports. Whatever the German hopes, after the attacks on the city during the First World War, there were strong reasons for it to have proper air and ground defences this time round. While it was fully understandable in the post-armistice euphoria that these were largely dismantled and the RAF reduced to a bare minimum, it was remarkable that by the time Germany's territorial ambitions became apparent, the ground defences should in many respects be less effective than at the end of the previous war. The desperate race needed to get them ready in time was due as much to negative thinking as to the British tradition of going to war unprepared.

In spite of crises during the early post-war years in the Balkans and the Middle East, and a major confrontation between Britain and its wartime ally, France, for over a decade London's ground defences were limited to a token ack-ack gun brigade and a searchlight battalion. It was not until 1932, when Stanley Baldwin became Prime Minister, that the situation began to turn. Although typical of his generation in believing that bombers would always be able to get through to their targets – unlike the RAF's Hugh Trenchard, who favoured defence through retaliatory bombing – Baldwin believed in the need to strengthen London's own air and ground defences. The latter were duly increased to four brigades (later called regiments), although still supported by only a single searchlight battalion, and they continued to be manned by the Territorial Army. By now the RAF had assumed responsibility for Home Defence and, despite such increases, Air Chief Marshal Salmond remained highly doubtful about the current effectiveness of London's ground defences because 'if there was an immediate declaration of war we could only man 27 per cent of the guns and 22 per cent of the searchlights available'.[3]

Nor was it just manpower, for although in 1935 a rapacious Adolf Hitler had become the German Chancellor, the defensive ring of ack-ack guns being positioned round London was not due for completion until 1946. This date was subsequently advanced to 1940, but manning difficulties persisted. They originated in prolonged recruitment problems within the Territorial Army, particularly during the troubled years immediately before the General Strike of 1929, which had predictable effects upon training and the ability of London's guns to perform their primary task of hitting and destroying attacking aircraft. A low point occurred during a combined exercise with the RAF in 1927 when, although the guns in permanent emplacements fired 2,935 rounds at a 'sitting duck' target flying on a known course, at a known speed and at the best height for shooting, they obtained just 2 actual hits.[4]

During 1934 eight London Territorial Field Units within 5 miles of Charing Cross were converted to ack-ack, a decision far from the liking of many of the men who were thus transferred,[5] but in any case, such personnel were not available for training until January 1936.

By 1936, however, there were indications of technological advances. The first instrument to improve significantly the accuracy of ack-ack guns, by calculating data relating to gun elevations and the fuse lengths needed for ammunition, came into service during that year. In practice, it was slow to arrive, with protracted training being required before its six-man operating teams could become proficient.

Although on 15 December of the previous year the first anti-aircraft division was officially formed with a scheduled strength of 5,200 all ranks, in 1936 it still lacked men and weapons and a proper plan for mobilization. In any case, organizational plans were soon to be revised because of another, most important, technical development – the advent of radar. This would bring rapid improvement in detecting the approach and direction of incoming aircraft, but in the first instance it meant a wholesale relocation of the gun positions. Despite the number of committees, which in the 1930s made sweeping recommendations towards improving the capital's AA defence (that chaired by the commander of Fighter Command, Sir Hugh Dowding, for instance, recommended a doubling of the guns and increasing searchlights by a third), it was not until November 1937, less than two years before the outbreak of the war, that these began to be implemented.

A breakthrough occurred in 1938 following the attendance of the Prime Minister at a meeting of the Committee of Imperial Defence, where it was decided to give AA defences absolute priority over all other forms of war material. The same year also saw the appointment of an outstanding officer, General Sir Federick Pile, as commander of London's 1st AA Division before succeeding General Alan Brooke as Commander in Chief in July 1939 of what had now become Anti-Aircraft Command, where he was destined to remain for the whole duration of the war. An Irish baronet with a marked ability to get on with all types of people, he was well suited to command independently minded territorial soldiers who had struggled for so long with both manpower and weaponry shortages. As a Royal Artillery officer (and previous Assistant Director of Mechanization at the War Office), Pile was also an enthusiast for the scientific advances necessary for his guns and their attendant problems. Pile knew his command would have a high profile, for in London the performance of the AA defences would not only come under the scrutiny of the Army Council but of a Prime Minister with the reputation for wanting to become personally involved and no doubt tour the defences with their commander. From the moment he arrived Pile made it his first priority to establish a good relationship – one that was to develop into genuine friendship – with his outstanding ally, London's aerial commander Hugh Dowding of Fighter Command. Whatever Pile's un-questionable abilities, the limited period available to him before the outbreak of the war was not nearly long enough to solve many of the outstanding problems.

This became apparent with the conscripts mobilized by the 1939 Militia Act and drafted into the Ack-Ack who left much to be desired. Many represented the leftovers after the field formations had taken their pick, and Pile found that in a fairly typical section of twenty-five men who reached him before Christmas 1939 'one had a withered arm, one was mentally deficient, one had a glass eye that fell out whenever he doubled to the guns, and two were in the advanced and more obvious stages of venereal disease'.[6] Some weeding out was clearly required, although extra recruits were still urgently needed for, in 1938 prior to the Ack-Ack's rapid expansion, it had a 50 per cent shortage in officers and numbers were not much better for the gunners.[7]

The shortcomings were not limited to manpower: his guns were still a hotchpotch, including 3in relics from the previous war incapable of reaching the height ceilings of modern aircraft, while the much needed 3.7in guns arrived only slowly, as did the still heavier 4.5in versions being sent by the Royal Navy. As a result, there was little time to train with the new equipment. There were teething troubles with the solid-fuel rocket systems designed to counter low flying aircraft, and there were also still too few of the excellent Bofurs 40mm light AA guns capable of firing 2lb explosive shells at the rate of 120 rounds a minute. In their absence, .303 machine guns had to be used. Some of the guns which had been received still needed to find a site, for although war was imminent some local authorities continued to object to emplacements being situated in their parks, and local farmers and landowners were apparently far from helpful.[8] Searchlights, particularly those with the new, more powerful 150cm light beams, were still below strength and the London balloon barrage had only been re-established in 1937.

Following the declaration of war, the eight-month 'phoney' period before Britain was attacked appeared to give Pile's defenders a precious breathing space to 'shake down, to obtain missing parts of equipment, practise the necessary plotting and control with their operation rooms and perfect drills and procedures'.[9] However, the combination of a particularly cold winter and no Germans to fire at brought serious morale problems. As Pile remarked, 'to spend all the grey hours of daylight on the freezing roof of a waterworks with no off-duty shelter other than a tarpaulin was a job which, lacking any excitement or action, or even the threat of action, quickly palled'.[10] After threatening to stand down any units without adequate accommodation, civilian contractors were engaged to provide Nissen or wooden huts, and self-help programmes by the units themselves, assisted by the Royal Engineers, led to marked improvements, although for many gun crews conditions remained far from comfortable.

Ironically, after awaiting action for so long, the Luftwaffe's first daylight attack on 7 September, rapidly followed by another that same evening and more on successive days and nights, soon caused Pile and his gun crews to look back with longing to the previous period of inactivity. The strain of repeated raids on under strength batteries, more often than not manned by inexperienced recruits, was immense. 'Somehow rest and sleep had to be fitted in with manning, maintenance, repair tasks, the boiling out of gun barrels and the endless labour of unloading, checking and stacking of ammunition ready for use.'[11]

Within seventy-two hours artillery pieces from elsewhere in the country brought a doubling of London's guns. Some of these were equipped with early radar gun-laying equipment but, because of their crews' inexperience in night shooting, this did not bring much increase in the rate of fire or in the number of hits claimed. Pile quickly realized that in the face of such heavy attacks what Londoners needed to hear above all was the sound of their own guns firing. On 10 September he assembled his gun commanders in the Territorial Drill Hall on the Brompton Road and told them of his changed plans. Henceforth, search-lights would be temporarily extinguished and fighters banned from the inner artillery zone, following which all guns were to fire every possible round they could on approximate bearings and elevations. Rough and ready as it was, this soon improved matters, for the resultant barrage not only brought strong approval from Londoners but it caused the German aircraft to increase their height, with some even turning away before entering the inner artillery zone.

On the debit side, over 260,000 rounds of ammunition were expended during September, at which rate it was estimated that more than 15,000 rounds had been required to damage a single aircraft. This, however, was hardly the most important consideration at the time, for the period 7–15 September saw the Luftwaffe mount its largest number of daylight attacks on London – there were thirty-eight major ones from 7 September to 9 October[12] – by which it hoped to force the RAF fighters to commit themselves to the city's defence in disadvantageous conditions. In fact, 15 September proved the turning point of the air battle. Understandably, this would have been less apparent to the gun crews who, after repeated daylight alarms, had to turn out at night to help sustain Pile's barrage and who, by the 15th, were exhausted. On the ninth day of the battle they were finally given some relief by recruits who, for the most part, had received only a few hours training themselves. Although by late September the numbers of daytime raids diminished, the defenders were given no respite since the night-time attacks increased proportionately, bringing with them different problems.

While Pile's ground detachments were doing their best in most demand-ing circumstances, in the skies overhead Park's fighters were locked in all-out combat with Goering's air fleets and their massed escorts. Although Park's early warning system gave him time to muster his squadrons, as luck had it, on the first day of the Blitz he was away from his headquarters visiting Dowding at Bentley Priory. Park's Group Controller was more than capable of co-ordinating the defence forces, but the pattern of the radar tracks gave him no clear message and at 4.00 pm, following reports of a large formation approaching, he assumed that, as with earlier attacks, they intended to strike at the airfields. When it became clear that London was the most likely target, all available fighter squadrons were airborne, but the operations room sent them too far north and most of the bombers succeeded in reaching the capital without much opposition. Things were different when they turned for home and the two sides' final losses were relatively even, with thirty-nine German bombers lost to thirty-one British fighters – but the damage suffered by London during the half-hour raid proved immense.

Scarcely had General Kesselring's attackers landed when a further wave of 250 bombers from Sperrle's Third Air Fleet were warming up for a night raid on the wounded capital, one that would last until morning and involved dropping not only high-explosive bombs but 13,000 incendiaries. Whatever the eventual outcome, London was to pay a high price for the sparing of the RAF's fighter bases.

The second day of the Blitz was relatively quiet because of indifferent weather, although there was another night raid by 200 bombers.[13] On 9 September 200 of Kesselring's bombers mounted a fresh daylight attack, and this time the aerial defences were more effective. The fighters, working as paired squadrons, succeeded in meeting them nearer the coast and the first wave of bombers was compelled to drop their loads on Canterbury and other towns short of the capital, while the second scattered their bombs widely across the city. Although there were rumours within the German Embassy in Washington to the effect that the heart of London resembled an earthquake zone, this was far from the case.

As in earlier exchanges, 12 Group's Duxford wing, flying south to join in the aerial battles, failed to cover 11 Group's airfields, but with London now the target this was of less importance, freeing it to join in the aerial battles close to the city where, although it claimed nineteen aircraft destroyed, none were subsequently confirmed by German records of this engagement.[14] Even so, in the exchanges the Luftwaffe lost twenty-seven aircraft to fighter command's twenty-one and it was obvious that whatever effect the bombing might be having on London the Germans were still far from achieving genuine air superiority.

On 11 September co-ordinated attacks were mounted by both German air fleets, when the RAF opposition was not particularly effective and more losses were inflicted on the defenders than the enemy. Even so, the continuing large numbers of fighters still available to move against them, including ones from 10 and 12 Groups, were both unexpected and dispiriting. Kesselring recognized this with an instruction to his pilots that, 'In the event of formation leaders meeting heavy opposition they are now permitted to disengage'.[15]

During a conference with Goering the day before, Hitler, despite being heartened by the uneven performance of the RAF defenders, realized that the air war had still not swung in Goering's favour, although German intelligence reports led him to believe that if only the Luftwaffe could enjoy a few more consecutive days of fine weather it might well succeed. Consequently, it was decided to wait until 17 September before sending out preliminary orders for the invasion of Britain – which in practice meant there could be no launching before 27 September. If this date were missed, the chance might well be lost, for the next favourable tide was not until 8 October when the days were shortening and the weather much more likely to be uncertain.

Goering knew he had to launch another enormous daylight assault on London, in the course of which he must devastate the city and knock 11 Group's fighters out of the sky, before he could follow up with what would then be un-stoppable attacks. After two relatively quiet days when single aircraft had roved deeper into Britain to bomb Harrogate, Banbury and Reading, on 14 September a medium raid involving some fifty planes was made on the London suburbs, while other aircraft struck Eastbourne and Brighton. Such relatively light activity resulted from the build up for a rerun of the previous 'Eagle's Day' offensive against the RAF – only this time against London.

The 15 September is generally accepted as the climax of the Battle of Britain, although this time the Luftwaffe could no longer mobilize the numbers of planes used during the earlier 'Eagle's Day' offensive. Weeks of the utmost strain had brought Kesselring's forces down to not much above half their establishment – and markedly reduced their pilots' confidence in the expected outcome. Fighter ace Adolf Galland later described their state of mind at this time, 'Failure to achieve any notable success; constantly changing orders, betraying lack of purpose and obvious misjudgement of the situation by the Command, and unjustified accusations had a most demoralising effect on its fighter pilots, who were already overtaxed by physical and mental strain.'[16]

Such diminished numbers also gave the attackers far less opportunity for diversionary attacks: Sperrle was reduced to scraping together a few aircraft to raid Portland and sending his fighter-bombers to raid the Supermarine factory at Eastleigh. These aside, the day's battle promised to be a headlong clash between the rival air forces.

On the British side, 11 Group was now in an undoubtedly stronger position since its airfields were no longer under attack and new aircraft had replaced its losses, so more concentrated sorties were possible. With an inland target like London, Park's early warning system gave his operations rooms ample time to scramble the defending squadrons who could now work in tandem, with 10 and 12 Groups able to shoulder a share of the responsibilities. As before, Kesselring's attack was made in two waves. The first of 100 bombers, with some 400 fighter escorts, crossed the coast at 11.30 am. The weather was clear and bright and before reaching London it had to run the gauntlet of five pairs of squadrons lying across its path before 12 Group's Duxford wing, operating closer still to the capital, could become involved. This time the defenders succeeded in breaking up the bomber formation before it reached the capital, although London still suffered from random bombing, and by 12.30 pm the attack was over.

That morning, Winston and Mrs Churchill were spectators in Park's operations room as he despatched his last four squadrons in pursuit. As Churchill described it, at this point he asked Park how many squadrons were left, to which he received the grave reply 'none'. While Park was undoubtedly correct, and he was not a man to milk the drama, it was likely that some of his planes being refuelled on the ground had a good chance of taking off and intercepting new raiders crossing the coast. In any case, it was an impressive demonstration of Fighter Command's efficiency at marshalling all its aircraft, providing, of course, they proved good enough.

In fact, Kesselring was unable to mount his second attack until his fighters had re-crossed the Channel to refuel and rearm, thus giving Park's Hurricane and Spitfire pilots – who were that much closer to their bases – time not only to refuel and rearm, but even take a hurried meal, before rising to meet it. The attack came at about 2.00 pm and it was once more in two formations. The first group of bombers were preceded by high-flying fighters with instructions to seek out the defenders to clear them from the sky. The all-out tussle between both sides' fighters that Goering and Kesselring had long sought took place over Dartford. This time they found the outcome bitterly disappointing for Dowding's squadrons were not only stronger than ever, but fully capable of holding their own. Although such combats enabled around seventy bombers to get through to London, they caused far less damage than on the 7th. They were then caught by the late-arriving Duxford wing which caused them significant, if far less, casualties than it claimed. At the end of the day, the figures spoke for themselves: the Luftwaffe lost fifty-six aircraft to Dowding's twenty-seven fighters, and with it any real opportunity to destroy Fighter Command and establish the air superiority required for an invasion. Henceforth, although the air fighting continued, the weather would deteriorate and, as Dowding had expected, on 17 September the British intercepted a German signal 'ordering the dismantling of German invasion air transport facilities in Holland'.

The decision to attack London proved the turning point for German hopes. By drawing off the bombs that could have disabled Fighter Command's aerodromes and radar installations it made sure that the heterogeneous, if fully committed, group of young men in their Hurricanes and Spitfires, under cool and analytic commanders like Dowding and Park, not only survived but prevailed against a magnificent Luftwaffe indifferently led by Hermann Goering and unable to make good its losses.

The last of the massed daylight raids on London took place on 30 September, although October saw frequent and heavy night-time bombing that would continue until May 1941, with notably destructive raids coming at the end of 1940 and on 10/11 May 1941. There would still be daylight bombing but it was now carried out by small formations of fighter-bombers sometimes undertaking up to 1,000 daytime sorties.[17] These were countered by RAF fighters mounting standing patrols to protect the capital, while the response to the regular nightly attacks on London depended on its night fighters – Blenheims, Defiants and Hurricanes, to be joined later by Beaufighters as they entered service. During the latter months of 1940 these aircraft were not particularly successful, with low rates of interception resulting from major difficulties with their inboard radars and because searchlights still awaited their radar control gear. As a result, the German losses were light, just sixty-six aircraft, representing 1 per cent of the total sorties made.

London paid a high price for the frustration of German invasion hopes. Night after night, the uneven wail of the sirens would be heard, followed by the sound of anti-aircraft guns opening up, if to relatively little effect. On the night of 15/16 October, for instance, the Luftwaffe mounted a major attack by 235 planes, of which the guns reputedly destroyed 2 for an expenditure of 8,326 rounds. General Pile pointed out that this was, in fact, their best night achievement, which illustrated 'just how far we were falling short of what was required of us'.[18] As well as the difficulties experienced by the guns, bad weather often prevented the RAF's interceptors leaving the ground when the Germans had the ability to bomb from height, using radio beams, codenamed, 'Knickebein', or 'crooked leg', by which their pilots could listen to a continuous signal from a Knickebein transmitter in France to keep them on course. By September the RAF were able to jam the Knickebein transmissions, although by then an improved system, called X-GERAT, of intersecting beams enabled the German bombers to hit their targets within an accuracy of 120yd before this was also jammed.

The fact remained that during the long winter months from October 1940 to May 1941 Londoners were subject to near nightly bombing from German aircraft which, for the most part, survived to set off again a few hours later. Such a favourable situation had never been achieved by the Zeppelins of the First World War, particularly after the British acquired explosive ammunition, and the losses of their far fewer Gotha bombers, whether through a combination of defensive actions and mechanical failures, had been proportionately heavier.

Under Pile's lead things gradually improved for the ground defenders, and during the final raid of the London Blitz on 10/11 May 1941 the Luftwaffe lost a devastating 8 per cent of its planes. The night fighters' techniques also improved, although it was not until the delivery of the Mosquito towards the end of the Blitz that their capabilities would be transformed. With such defensive limitations, during the 1940/41 Blitz there was widespread forbearance on the part of Londoners with regard to the regular raids, in the course of which they went on with their lives as best they could, unlike the previous war when there were feelings of shock and outrage if the city's defences were penetrated.

From June they were relieved, as the Luftwaffe switched the major part of its forces to the Eastern Front in support of Hitler's invasion of the Soviet Union. Although further manned bombing raids would be mounted on the capital and elsewhere from time to time, including the one during the spring of 1944 that became known as the 'Little Blitz', there would never be the same high hopes on the part of the attackers for a forthcoming invasion, or for them to bring the war to an end in Germany's favour. It would take the German unmanned V weapons late in the war to revive such hopes and, in the case of the V1s, would see London's air and ground defenders come into their own. Meanwhile, with London thus spared – if only in the short term, the RAF's interest returned to Bomber Command and its traditional policy of defeating Germany through strategic bombing. Although during 1942 and 1943 such bombing was the only means by which attacks could be made against the German home-land the cost was enormous: 56,000 skilled aircrew and their machines would be lost when, together with the US Seventh Air Force, they attempted to break the will of the German people. German air and ground defences remained formidable and, in any case, London had already convincingly shown how difficult this might prove to be.[19]

Whatever such offensive plans, as the Official History of the air war observed, 'The first great victory of the Royal Air Force which had been born of the desire to attack, came, not from the offensive but from a glorious defence in the Battle of Britain'.[20] Such defence of both Britain and London was carried out by a comparatively small number of young men in their Hurricanes and Spitfires during 1940, who met and checked the hitherto all-conquering Luftwaffe and whose total casualties were to be exceeded in one tragic raid on Germany by Bomber Command.[21]

Whether they were inspired here by the traditions that Trenchard worked so hard to create or were motivated, in the case of New Zealanders, Australians and South Africans, by their loyalty to the home country, by Americans and Irishmen impatient with their country's neutrality or Polish and Czech pilots driven by a hatred of their German conquerors, they not only brought about the first German defeat of the Second World War but succeeded in prevent-ing the German invasion of the British homeland. In their campaign's final stages, when London acted as a massive decoy to spare their airfields, they were finally able to turn their full strength against the German attackers. Whatever their background, such men knew they had to win and were aware of what they had achieved. As George Bennions, one of their number who was badly burned and blinded in one eye, maintained afterwards, we 'would have fought on and on until there was nothing left',[22] while Peter Townsend, who commanded 85 Squadron, took a wider view when he wrote, 'Our battle was a small one but on its outcome depended the fate of the western world'.[23] None of them doubted the part played by their planes, which reached them just in time, and the particular regard aroused by the Spitfire, that most beautiful of planes, can be seen in Patrick Bishop's affectionate and extravagant description of its engine notes, 'like the note of a grand piano after a bass key has been struck, fading and swelling as if it is trying to tell us something, the most poignant and romantic sound on earth'.[24]

In their moment of success one could not expect such men to acknowledge greatly the supporting role played by their complementary defenders, the sweating, exhausted gun crews, and even less by London's unlikely civilian heroes. Such men and women, young and old, from widely different backgrounds, universally proud of their young fliers, who carried on as best they could in their Leviathan-like city, and whose constancy proved fundamental. Along with such highly dedicated air and land forces Londoners would come to owe an additional and most significant debt to their 'so-called' civil defenders.

Chapter 8

The London Blitz, 1940–1 – Civil Defenders

'That 'itler – Giving us the all-clear when we was settled. <u>Now</u> what are we going to do?'

Stepney woman in a shelter during the London Blitz[1]

When Winston Churchill wrote after the war that Londoners 'took all they got and could have taken more' he already knew of the contributions made to the capital's defence, not only by the men and women of the armed services but also by London's citizen army engaged on so-called Civil Defence. These numbered over ½ million and ranged from the ubiquitous air-raid wardens to those in the more specialist roles of fire fighters, ambulance and first-aid, rescue and demolition and bomb reconnaissance units that proved so important in helping London withstand heavy and continual air bombardment. While in the previous war special constables had been recruited to help maintain public order, particularly during air raids, with the increased levels of destruction expected this time, more and different officials were plainly needed.

Recognizing this took longer than might have been expected, although, as early as 1922 during a serious crisis with France, London was already seen as the key target in any future war. At the time, however, the will to take any practical precautions was lacking. This was also the case two years later when, although the Committee of Imperial Defence established a Civil Defence sub-committee on Air Raid Precautions, the cataclysmic expectations regarding future air bombardment brought grave doubts about whether such measures could really be expected to make that much difference. The situation following an air raid as described by Lord Thompson, Secretary of State in the Labour government of 1924, was unbelievably pessimistic: 'Both victors and vanquished would be left with ruined cities, widespread distress among the masses of the people, hospitals filled with the maimed and the mutilated of all ages and both sexes, asylums crowded with unfortunate human beings whom terror made insane.'[2]

Such a scenario was quite in accordance with the towering estimates of casualties by early air theorists such as Emilio Douhet and Britain's Hugh Trenchard in their tendency to emphasize the value of their new arm. In the case of London these were put at 200,000 a week, of which 66,000 would be fatal – equal to the unprecedented losses at the opening of the Battle of the Somme in 1916, but occurring every week. While the Air Raid Precautions Committee undoubtedly discussed a range of possible initiatives, including the best ways of warning about the coming raids and protecting the civilian population by treating the injured, minimizing or preventing damage to buildings, maintaining public services and, if necessary, moving the seat of government from the capital, no meaningful action occurred for about twelve years. It was not until 1934 that Stanley Baldwin's attempts to strengthen the land defences brought £100,000 in the 1935–6 Home Office estimates for ARP services, thus marking the birth of Civil Defence, or at least the first modest advance towards it. In that year cinema newsreels showed German bombing attacks on Guernica, the small town in northern Spain where in one raid its centre was devastated, but shortly before the Munich crisis the earlier fatalistic attitudes were giving way to a realization (as yet still far from unanimous) that it was possible things could be done to help withstand devastating air attacks. By late 1938 the Labour Party, now in opposition, revised Lord Thompson's earlier stance and declared that air-raid precautions must now take equal importance with the three defence departments and be made thoroughly efficient, and censored the government on its unpreparedness.[3]

As a result, a senior Cabinet figure in the person of Sir John Anderson, the Lord Privy Seal, was appointed Minister of Civilian Defence with a brief to hasten defence measures over the whole Home Front and to extend air-raid protection. In April 1939 Commissioners were appointed for Civil Defence regions across Britain, the boundaries of which were almost exactly the same as those under Cromwell's Inspectors General almost 300 years before. London, with its 100 local authorities, was given 2 Regional Commissioners under a Chief Administrative officer, Mr Harold Scott. Most of the Commissioners were, in fact, retired officers of the fighting services who fully recognized the urgency of the situation and by 1939 London's defence arrangements included a so-called Regional War Headquarters at the Geological Museum in South Kensington. Across the Greater London region locations for Chief Wardens' Posts had already been selected and equipped and London's Ambulance Service, including its mobile first-aid units, was reorganized and the responsibilities for Rescue and Demolition Parties decided. In the case of the Fire Service, the Chief Officer of the London Fire Brigade was scheduled to become the capital's Regional Fire Officer in time of war. Such arrangements apparently went so well that on 30 August 1939 *The Times* felt able to observe that all the ARP preparations had eliminated the factor of surprise against air attacks.[4]

As if to confirm this, the very next day an order went out to evacuate the young and most vulnerable from London to safer locations. As a consequence, thousands of school children accompanied by their teachers, all carrying gas masks with large cardboard labels around their necks giving their names and those of their schools, were shepherded onto trains at the London termini for dispersal to safer regions. Whatever their other emotions, the watching parents could be in no doubt that their city was about to be besieged. That night Germany broadcast an ultimatum of war to Poland and the next day its Panzers and dive-bombers attacked.

For the vast majority of Londoners who remained in the city there were other signs of the anticipated attacks, including buttresses of sandbags around public buildings and war rooms. For individual householders with gardens the government had produced prefabricated 'Anderson' air-raid shelters. These consisted of fourteen pieces of corrugated steel (plus a spanner) which, when assembled, took on the form of a small hut; this, when dug into soil to a depth of 3–4ft and given a covering of at least 15in of earth, was reckoned to give protection against anything but a direct hit. Such shelters were not spacious, just 6ft high, 4ft 6in wide and 6ft 6in long, but, although damp and prone to flooding after rain, they were considered suitable for four people, or six at a pinch. These cost householders £6 14s, although to families with an income of less than £250 a year they were supplied free of charge. (Buyers were assured that unlike ordinary dwellings they were entirely free of rates!) The general public, local authorities and employers were required to build or adapt buildings into surface air-raid shelters,[5] for with labour short and the costs likely to be high, no attempts were made to provide any underground. For those seeking deep protection it was decided to make the London Underground available, as in the last war.

In the case of the officials concerned with the protection of the public, while in the previous war these had been special constables who ensured precautions were taken in the event of raids, this responsibility was now assumed by the less authoritarian air-raid wardens (based on the German idea of road wardens) who would make up a third of all Civil Defence officials. Their job description required that 'each should be a responsible member of the public chosen to be a leader and adviser of his neighbours in a small area, a street or group of streets in which he is known and respected'.[6] The wardens' brief was a wide one, namely to provide leadership and advice by supervising air-raid shelters, issuing gas masks, if necessary, reporting incidents, dealing with light incendiary bombs and checking blackout precautions.

By the end of 1938 some 1,140,000 men and women from across the country (more than twice the combined strength of the three fighting services at this time), ½ million of whom were in London, undertook 'to give some of their leisure time to defend their homes'. With so many of the capital's citizens occupied in this way, and with such blatant Nazi aggression, there appeared to be far greater unanimity over the decision to go to war than in 1914. By the time the Blitz started the younger wardens had been conscripted into the armed services, but there were still 10 middle-aged officials (1 in 6 of whom were women) to every square mile of the city: 16,000 senior wardens, employed full time, were paid £3 a week (women £2 a week) and were supported by approximately 200,000 part-timers. Wardens had a silver ARP badge together with an armband, a tin hat (those of senior officers were painted white), a gas mask (in a cardboard box), a rattle, a torch with a cowl pointing towards the ground and, in some cases, a stirrup pump. Apart from their responsibilities for public air-raid shelters they were expected to give warnings about the presence of unexploded bombs, carry out minor rescue work and if elderly or frail residents were in danger areas, help them from their homes. Chief Wardens worked with their opposite numbers in the Metropolitan Police, but following a bombing attack they were expected to defer to specialists such as those concerned with Rescue and Demolition, and to the London Fire and Ambulance Services.

From March 1938 arrangements were made for the prestigious London Fire Service to be assisted by an Auxiliary Service, 30,000 strong, with 2,800 pumps of its own. Upon the opening of hostilities the auxiliaries were scheduled to provide relief for the regular service to keep the stations open on a twenty-four hour basis.[7] Predictable difficulties were soon experienced between the regular firemen and the partially trained auxiliaries with their one uniform and pay of just £3 a week, whose promotion at the beginning of the war had not been entirely satisfactory and whose service was still not fully recruited. In 1940, among other attempts to improve matters, a scheme of unification was devised where every man, whether a regular or auxiliary, considered suitable as an officer would receive the same pay and service conditions. In practice, this meant that many regular firemen came to be promoted and posted to the auxiliary service. With the opening of the Blitz earlier animosities were quickly forgotten and the firemen united in the common cause. When blackened and weary men, whether auxiliaries or regulars, finally returned to their stations people in the streets stood and cheered them for their efforts.

In the case of the London Ambulance Service, whose drivers were mainly women volunteers, its head also assumed responsibility for the new mobile First Aid Parties. These were assigned to work with the rescue teams and the authorities were uncertain how such (female) shop assistants or members of the clerical professions (thought of as 'cissies') would work with builders, artisans and labourers (thought of as 'toughies'); in fact, amid the debris of buildings they complemented each other well.

Following the bombing raids in September 1940, another large civilian defence body was established, namely that of 'Fire Watchers'. This was a direct response to the need for defences against thousands of incendiary bombs which, if found, could be dowsed quite quickly, but if left were likely to cause great conflagrations. Although all major employers were required to have their own representatives on patrol in their premises after working hours, following the firestorm raid on the City of London during late December 1940 the numbers engaged on such tasks were massively increased and their duties regularized.

Whatever Civil Defence arrangements were in place and however many volunteers were embodied, the initiative understandably lay with the attacking Luftwaffe. As one warden who served in London during the whole war observed, 'Civil Defence was essentially a waiting game'.[8] It was also difficult for such volunteers, for while the professional services, the police, ambulance, fire and the rest knew what was expected of them, the widespread and less-definable duties of the wardens who, in the radical areas of London such as Poplar were actually elected by the local people,[9] were less clearly defined. They were required to act as guardians, social workers and managers of the street or streets under their authority, and to demonstrate a marked sense of obligation for their fellows. Many, of course, were not able to live up to the expectations put upon them but, unlike Captain Mainwaring's bête noir Warden Hodges, they not only caused amusement on occasion but also earned a degree of respect.

While in some respects less arduous, the Fire Watchers' responsibilities were by no means easy. After a full day's work they had to spend hours on uncomfortable rooftops in all weathers, staying awake and alert, and when the bombs fell, sometimes after a lengthy interval of complete inactivity, they needed to extinguish them with the utmost speed.

* * *

Neither their training nor the earlier light raids could fully prepare such officials for the opening of the Blitz. This commenced at 4.14 pm on Saturday 7 September 1940, when some 320 German bombers, supported by 600 fighters, using the Thames as a pathway, bombed Woolwich Arsenal, Beckton Gas Works, the London docks, West Ham power station and then the City, Westminster and Kensington.[10]

In the raid an area of about 1½ miles between North Woolwich Road and the Thames was almost completely destroyed, causing the London Fire Officer at Pageants Wharf to ring in to his superiors with the message 'Send all the bloody pumps you've got. The whole bloody world's on fire.'[11] The neighbouring area of Silvertown and its factories – which had been a target in the First World War – was surrounded by fires and its population had to be evacuated by boats. The reactions of 18-year-old Len Jones, who was living in Poplar at the time, reveal the intensity of the largest raid ever made at this time, together with the extent of the damage caused:

> The suction from the compression pulled you and pushed you, and the whole of this atmosphere was turbulating so hard that, after an explosion of a nearby bomb, you could actually feel your eyeballs being sucked out ... I couldn't get my breath, the smoke was like acid and everything round me was black and yellow. And these bombers just kept on and on, the whole road was moving, rising and falling.[12]

The raid occurred as families were having their tea and by 5.45 pm, when the German bombers headed for home, the Woolwich Arsenal and the nearby Siemens Electric works had suffered severe damage, although it was the massive docks – Surrey Commercial 2,600ft long and 450ft wide, West India, Millwall and the huge Royal Victoria and Albert Dock, an amazing 1¾ miles long, with imposing five-storey warehouses alongside – that took the main brunt of the attacks. At Millwall docks 200 acres of timber, including 250 different varieties of wood, were aflame. Oil storage tanks were split open and huge clouds of black smoke billowed and spiralled up into the clear blue sky. The docks looked as if they had been reduced to one great inferno: the rum quay of the West India dock buildings was alight from end to end, with blazing spirit gushing over it. From damaged spice warehouses the air was heavy with pepper, cinnamon and nutmeg, while a short distance away an army of rats ran from the Silvertown soap works.[13]

The densely populated area of flats and tenement houses bordering the docks also suffered very heavily, particularly Stepney where 200,000 people of all races lived, packed together, with 12 to a flat on average.[14] With such a raid the London Home Front had become a genuine battleground and, if any confirmation were needed, at 8.10 pm a second wave of 250 bombers, with their accompanying fighters, came to extend the damage. While the German Heinkel and Dornier planes were only medium-sized compared with the British Lancasters and American Flying Fortresses later in the war, they succeeded in dropping a further 300 tons of high explosives, accompanied by thousands of incendiary bombs. The fires made it easy for them to identify their main targets, including the West India Docks where huge casks of rum had ignited, the flames from which could be seen for 30 miles around.

As was to be expected, human reactions varied widely. While sheltering in a church crypt during the first raid, Jim Wolveridge's sister Lily had a fit of hysterics, but during the second one, when things could hardly have got much worse, there was an accordion player in the same crypt, with whom Jim and the others sang 'Roll out the Barrel, We'll have a Barrel of Fun – and the nearer the bombs fell the louder we sang'.[15]

Such stout defiance was far from the only emotion, for Poplar was so devastated in this initial raid that later that Saturday night 'scores of people' moved to the West End (which was considered safer) or into the Essex countryside (where many had relatives) and 'Pony carts, hand-drawn barrows, perambulators and cycles with heavily laden carriers, all rolled out of the borough in a steady stream'.[16]

The docks and their boroughs remained prime targets for the Luftwaffe and over the coming weeks two men in particular, Poplar-born Chief Warden E H Smith and his Irish deputy Cotter proved outstanding in helping to keep people's spirits up.[17] On that first night of 7 September there were 9 con-flagrations,[18] 59 large fires and nearly 1,000 lesser ones. To help combat them, pumps were sent from all across the city to the Docklands, where by the morning 450 people had died and 1,600 were seriously injured. When other Londoners emerged into the daylight to take stock, they included three eminent American reporters, Ben Robertson, Ed Murrow and Vincent Sheean, who had spent the night in a haystack beside a turnip field from where they drove back through the East End to the centre of London. In Fleet Street they wired their editors that 'the Battle of London had started and on that first Sunday it seemed to all of us like the end of civilization'.[19]

Had they slept in a haystack to the north or west of London, while they were bound to be aware of the massive fires in Docklands and the East End their locality was likely to have escaped relatively lightly. Whatever terrible damage had been sustained the sheer size of London, with its conurbation stretching along a 15-mile radius from central London, would always present a daunting target for the Luftwaffe. Unless a succession of targets was hit simultaneously the majority of its 8 million population was likely to be unharmed, while the very size of its Civil Defence services enabled them to deploy officials from less affected areas to the main sites of the raids.

On the morning of Monday 9 September 1940, following a second raid by a further 200 German bombers, most Londoners still had a reasonable chance of reaching their workplaces. Blocked roads, the dislocation of their trains and buses and diversions caused by unexploded bombs doubtless gave rise to unexpected experiences which they compared with their fellow travellers in a way that belied their normal reserve. Life was not easy under such circumstances: their return journeys would also have met with difficulties and, when home at last, they faced a night in their shelters, followed by fresh problems getting to work the next day.

So began a nine-month siege, the like of which had never yet been experienced by any other city. Londoners had to adapt to a pattern of life akin in some ways to being under siege from land forces. Instead of the shelling from surrounding enemy land batteries to be answered by the defenders' own fire, the wailing of the sirens would be followed by the drone of aero engines, a rushing noise and then the exploding of bombs, answered by the boom of the ack-ack counter batteries. In such circumstances life took on a new sense of impermanence, with priorities placed on short-term goals, such as getting to work or hoping to find one's house still standing after returning from work. For many there were also the extra duties involved in assisting their fellow citizens when under attack.

The raids continued incessantly through the rest of September and then during a full moon – 'bombers' moon – on 15 October came a particularly heavy raid with over 400 bombers dropping more than 2,000 tons of bombs, causing 430 deaths and seriously injuring 900 more. In fact, there was only one night in October without a raid, although sometimes the weight of the bombing dropped when the Luftwaffe targeted provincial cities as well. In December the tempo again rose sharply. On the 8th between 300 and 400 bombers dropped thousands of incendiaries over a wide area starting a record 1,316 fires, killing 250 people and injuring 600. Then, after an uncharacteristic lull, on 29 December it was the turn of the City of London to suffer a massive raid.

By now the Civil Defence services had experienced four months of raids and it was apparent that certain of their plans had been based on massive miscalculations. Instead of an expected 600 tons of bombs a day, which would have had at least 140,000 tons of bombs falling on London, during the Blitz the actual tonnage in the autumn of 1940 and the first 5 months of 1941 was not much above 18,000 tons.[20] Such overestimation was even more marked with the expected casualties (including those from gas attacks), which had been put at 3,000 deaths and 12,000 seriously injured every day, even higher than the estimates of the early air theorists. This would have brought 720,000 deaths and 2,880,000 wounded during the London Blitz, not to mention cases of panic and hysteria resulting from a disorderly flight from the city. Working on such figures it was expected that some 100,000 hospital patients would have to make room for air-raid casualties.[21] In fact, during the London Blitz there were 20,083 deaths and 26,019 seriously injured[22] – lower figures not only due to the much lighter weight of bombs actually dropped, but the use of public and private air-raid shelters and Tube stations. While all this was excellent, the dead would have needed few resources beyond being placed in mortuaries; but although far fewer bombs were dropped, the increased power of the high explosive caused much more damage than had been anticipated. To rescue those civilians who were alive but trapped in buildings, far more manpower and resources were required – including heavy lifting gear – than had been planned for.

Although by late November 1940 it was considered possible to dispense with up to 50 per cent of the London stretcher parties without ill effects, the strain placed on the rescue parties had already been extreme and prolonged. Unexpected difficulties had arisen when attacks occurred during darkness. Not only did the rescuers soon suffer from persistent loss of sleep, they also needed emergency lighting equipment to carry out their work. Hand torches and lamps proved ineffective and in some cases tarpaulin screens were erected over the debris with arc lights or the screened headlamps of cars playing on the scene.

Another unexpected feature of the actual attacks was the number of un-exploded bombs or unexploded parachute mines. Some of these had timed fuses and were not constructed to explode immediately, but others (with percussion fuses) failed to explode when their parachutes were snagged in trees or on sides of buildings, thus preventing them from striking the ground. These posed one of the largest threats to normal activities by immobilizing railway junctions, blocking main roads, preventing factories from operating, making it necessary to evacuate large numbers of citizens from their homes. In such a situation priorities had to be set for blowing them up. Bomb-disposal work was tradi-tionally carried out by naval personnel, and although some 7,000 were initially employed on this task countrywide it was not enough, and for many weeks up to 3,000 unexploded bombs remained to be dealt with, the majority in London.

The immediate results of the heavy destruction of individual homes and the need for families to be evacuated because of unexploded bombs also brought a requirement for temporary shelter and care, including feeding, on an undreamt of scale. The accommodation provided was often lacking in any structural protection, adequate sanitation, blankets, clothing or feeding arrangements. By the end of September 1940 London had a rest centre population of 25,000, of which 14,000 were in desperately overcrowded premises run by the London County Council. As a result voluntary bodies such as the St Martin-in-the-Fields Association and the Central Hall, Westminster, stepped in to help provide additional shelter, food and other assistance for those who had been bombed out. In accordance with a tradition started in the seventeenth century, the Lord Mayor opened a Mansion House fund for clothing and other essentials to help those placed in need by the Blitz. This was distributed by the Women's Voluntary Service and by the end of the war it had raised over £4,700,000.

In addition to temporary accommodation, during the winter of 1941 an unexpected need arose to feed people following the raids. This included those accustomed to spending long periods in air-raid shelters, together with emergency workers and victims immediately after a raid, all of whom urgently needed hot drinks and snacks;[23] other Londoners required canteens providing full meals. Together with the British restaurants, many of these came to be run by the WVS and YMCA.

The rest centres were, of course, no more than staging posts through which homeless people could hopefully progress to good temporary accommodation before returning to their own homes. During the 9 months of the Blitz 200,000 Londoners passed through them,[24] although no less than 1,400,000 others (out of 2,250,000 people countrywide) coped in some other way because, whether for a short or longer period, 1 in 6 Londoners were bombed out of their homes.

Another unexpected result was that with the continuous bombing houses were damaged at a rate that far outstripped repairs, and the rest centres – akin to casualty clearing stations on a battlefield – were in real danger of damming up. Ideally, the disruption brought about by one night's raid needed to be dealt with within twelve hours, but although by October new rest centres were established the existing ones suffered damage and the overcrowding, if anything, became worse. By the middle of the month some 250,000 Londoners had been made homeless: 'Of these some had been evacuated or had moved away, others were sleeping in tubes and shelters, about a tenth were in crowded rest centres and the larger balance were lodging with friends and relatives or were starting a new home.'[25]

The two greatest problems were the slow rate of repairs and the personal crises caused by the loss of money, clothing and furniture from bombed-out buildings. Fortunately, during the summer of 1940 a scheme had been announced to compensate people of limited means for their household furniture and personal clothing, which was later extended to all householders who had lost their homes through enemy action. Arrangements were also made to insure every class of property against war damage (thereby removing one of the householders' greatest fears over the bombing).

Winston Churchill, whose detailed directives and pointed memoranda helped to keep things moving, emphasized that generosity must be the dominant role in the treatment of bombed and homeless Londoners, and that information about all the services provided should be clearly disseminated. This was done through the Citizens Advice Bureau, which, like so many other special services, was run by civilian volunteers. The Prime Minister ensured that the numbers of bomb-disposal teams were increased before turning his attention to the question of the emergency building repairs. There was a shortage of labour as a result of many builders being called up and, although the repairs were the responsibility of local authorities who in times of crisis could ask for central assistance, military works and installations always took first priority.

To tackle this, by the end of December 1940 the Ministry of Works had established a special repair service with its own squads of men who could be despatched to the most heavily damaged areas. This transformed the situation and those concerned earned a generous tribute from the official historian of the wartime buildings and works: 'It was a much diminished and ageing labour force on whom, at the height of the war, fell the heaviest burdens of the building programme. Under conditions of great hardship, often of considerable danger, these men, of whom many were elderly or unfit, or both, fulfilled exacting tasks.'[26]

Whatever the personal costs to the artisans involved the repairs now accelerated, and even with the heavy German raids during the first half of 1941 the rest centres did not become overwhelmed. While of immense benefit, such repairs were by no means lavish and several million people in London (including the author as a boy) were compelled to live in their damaged homes for some years, for in January 1941 the average spent on making them wind and weatherproof varied between just £8 and £9 each,[27] and windows were routinely covered with felt rather than opaque material. At least these were better to live in than rest centres, shelters or other people's homes.

Four years after the apocalyptic expectations of demoralized, panic-stricken citizens fleeing from the cities and dying in their tens of thousands, by the end of 1940 a viable programme for Civil Defence and the repair of damaged property had been instituted both for London and elsewhere, demonstrating the typical 'bulldog' character of the British.

With such support the capital showed itself to be capable of withstanding the nightly bombings, which during September and October 1940 resulted in 13,000 fires and the consequent damage that accompanied them. However, with Londoners' chances of being killed by bombing standing at 400 to 1 (although it was higher in a target area) what had become primarily terror raids fell far short of achieving their purpose, particularly when ¼ million of the capital's citizens were committed to undertaking responsible tasks on behalf of their fellow men.[28] Even so, the situation could have swiftly changed for the worse if by hitting Parliament or Buckingham Palace the bombers had killed the country's leaders, or alternatively created a conflagration that would destroy the city's financial and commercial districts or any of its major industrial centres, such as Woolwich's Royal Arsenal or Enfield's Small Arms production lines.

For those who experienced the Blitz day-by-day the position might have appeared less favourable. The loss of sleep combined with the extra burdens on everyday existence, such as constantly airing the bedding for use in the garden shelters, together with the sight of many prestigious buildings and ordinary houses destroyed, strained nerves to the limit. As if this were not enough, on 29 December 1940, a firestorm raid on the City's Square Mile brought immense destruction which approached that during the Great Fire of 1666.

Londoners also read reports of the Luftwaffe's attacks on provincial towns and cities in further attempts to cripple the country's industrial ability. The ports of Plymouth, Portsmouth, Southampton, Bristol and Liverpool were heavily attacked, so too were industrial centres like Birmingham, Sheffield, Manchester, Leicester and, of course, Coventry. The destruction of Coventry's city centre during an eleven-hour raid from 7.00 pm on 14 November to dawn on the 15th, resulting in 568 deaths, the destruction of its cathedral and damage to three-quarters of its central housing stock, brought comparisons with Guernica. Although the provinces endured far fewer raids than London, their smaller size made the damage comparatively more extensive and in general their civil defences were less proficient. But in all cases, following the numbing shock of the heartbreaking desolation there was widespread determination to return their factories into production and restore some degree of normality.

At the end of 1940 the City of London experienced a raid equivalent in destructiveness to any of these in the provinces, including that in Coventry. It not only demonstrated the Luftwaffe's improved bombing techniques but it was made far worse by the fact that, with no previous raids during the run up to Christmas and over the holiday season, many of the City of London's small businesses were locked up as their proprietors and employees took a festive break until Monday 30 December.

Not so the Luftwaffe and its crack Pathfinder force, Kampfgruppe 100, now equipped with its airborne radio transmitters following X-GERAT radio beams to within 120yd of their targets. On Sunday 29 December, when the tide in the Thames was exceptionally low, ten Pathfinder planes targeted the heart of the British Empire's financial and commercial operations, where towering buildings and narrow, winding streets made it easy for fires to spread and very difficult for fire appliances to combat them. At 6.00 pm a yellow warning (signalling approaching aircraft) was relayed from Southern Command 'to the city's civil defenders, ARP, First Aid Posts, Stretcher Parties, Heavy Rescue depots and key points around the Square Mile'.[29] With the warning changing to red, the air-raid sirens sounded and at 6.12 pm the anti-aircraft guns began firing, as their accompanying searchlights probed the sky. Prefaced by signal flares, Kampfgruppe's 10 aircraft dropped incendiaries at a rate of 300 a minute up to a total of 10,000. A further 90 bombers followed, guided by the fires now blazing in the intended target area, dropping both high-explosive bombs and fresh showers of incendiaries, 1 in every 10 of which was primed to explode after a short period.

Although the City's larger concerns had their own dedicated bands of fire watchers – none more efficient than the watch at St Paul's which included middle-aged architects, thousands of buildings (with less than thirty employees) were not guarded at all and were targets for the tens of thousands of incendiaries raining down. Within half an hour fires were spreading over 135 acres, more than a fifth of the Square Mile.[30] By 8.00 pm 300 of London's 2,000 fire pumps were concentrated on this small area but, with the fires growing in intensity, the hot currents rising from ground level created a partial vacuum subsequently filled by a mighty wind that created a firestorm.

The destruction was heavy, rapid and widespread and it included the Mansion House, the City's headquarters. That night there were many remarkable actions on the part of firemen and wardens, but none more praiseworthy than those of the St Paul's fire watch, who successfully extinguished every incendiary that fell on the cathedral, including one that started a fire high up in its dome. Such brave and dedicated men enabled *Daily Mail* photographer Herbert Mason to produce the iconic image of the cathedral's famous dome silhouetted against the flames and smoke of blazing buildings on every side. Even so, for officials standing on the Bank of England roof 'the whole of London seemed alight. We were hemmed in by a wall of flame in every direction. It was not just big fires just here and there but a continuous sheet of flame all around us.'[31]

At approximately a quarter to midnight, while the fires still raged, there came the welcome sound of the 'all clear'. The weather had closed in and there would be no further German sorties that night to extend the conflagrations. However, the city faced further disaster with the firemen handicapped by a lack of water: the city's hydrants could not feed the multitude of hoses in use and the low level of the Thames prevented additional river water being taken; in places it was decided to let the fires burn. By morning the area of the Square Mile consumed by fire was not much less than in 1666, but without the labours of the contemporary fire and demolition services it would certainly have been even larger. A further raid that night must surely have completed the city's devastation.

With Fleet Street so close, there were many journalists to witness and marvel at the phlegm and indomitable reactions of ordinary people. The American journalist (Bill) White watched a group of the city's caretakers and cleaners who had already been moved from two shelters that night, and were on their way to a third: there they stood patiently in line holding their shabby bedding, some of which the wardens carried for them.[32] Next morning British journalist Ritchie Calder heard the familiar thud of the morning papers on his doormat – among them was the *Daily Telegraph* whose building had been hit and was still smoking.[33]

There was no question of London succumbing, but five rail termini had been hit and sixteen Underground stations were closed. Elsewhere, however, the skyline was still the same. By Tuesday, all across the Square Mile ropes that blocked off ruined buildings were festooned with notes informing postmen and visitors where they could find the firms' new locations. In some cases, there were offers to meet outstanding accounts if the copies of relevant invoices could be sent to them, as theirs had been lost.

A fortnight later on 15 January 1941 Herbert Morrison showed the government's determination that everything should be done to prevent other London districts – or other cities – from suffering the same fate as the City. In his famous broadcast 'Britain shall not burn' he announced compulsion for what was now to be the Fire Guard – Churchill's 'Jim Crows'.[34] Men between 16 and 60 were required to register for fire watching for up to forty-eight hours each month, while women and youths were 'encouraged' to do the same.[35]

This was timely for during the first five months of 1941 both London and the provinces continued to feel the power of the German Luftwaffe. Heavy raids were mounted across the face of Britain, which typically made Churchill conclude that the German leaders were baffled about how best to proceed. 'He was sure they would have done much better to have stuck to one thing at a time and pressed it to a conclusion.'[36] But the fact was that, however energetically used, the Luftwaffe's 600 medium bombers were unlikely to cause severe interruption to wartime production or port facilities throughout Britain for long, although there were times when, despite their civil defences, on the morning following a particularly costly and destructive raid some provincial cities were heavily shaken.

It was certainly not for want of trying by the Luftwaffe: from its bases along the European coast it mounted repeated attacks on both London and what they considered were prime targets in the provinces. During the early part of 1941 the coastal cities again came under attack. With its naval installations, the raids on Plymouth reached a total of 57, resulting in 1,172 civilians being killed and 2,177 severely injured. During an attack by 300 German planes on the night of

20/21 March 1941 the centre of the city stretching for 600yd from its Guildhall was reduced to a brick-pitted desert. Early in the same year 300 German bombers also attacked Portsmouth, inflicting extensive damage on its central region, while on 16 March Bristol suffered a fire blitz in which 257 people died and 391 were seriously injured, during the course of which its old town, including fine old Regency buildings and its famous medieval half-timbered Dutch House, was destroyed.[37] Apart from numerous attacks on Glasgow itself, during 13 and 14 March 1941 its port of Clydebank (population 50,000) was devastated with only 8 civilian homes left undamaged out of 12,000, while further south Merseyside endured 68 aerial attacks of which 8 were major: following raids on 7 successive nights during May 1941 its docks were close to being disabled.

Cardiff, Swansea, Dover, Great Yarmouth and Belfast were also attacked, with a largely unprepared Belfast suffering some 900 casualties during a raid on 15/16 April, while Dover faced additional attacks from long-range heavy artillery. Yarmouth lay on the route for both London and the Midlands and was therefore bombed no less than 96 times, with 102 people killed and 329 injured in its worst raid during 1941. At Hull the raids on 2 consecutive nights killed 450 people, seriously injured 300 and destroyed almost 10 per cent of its housing stock.[38]

Of the inland cities, Birmingham was again bombed in 1941 when in all 2,000 people were killed and 3,000 seriously injured. Manchester also experienced major raids, as did Coventry and Nottingham. Although port facilities and factories were bombed during such raids, the main intention was to destroy a city's nucleus in accordance with Hitler's promise to raze British cities to the ground.

Despite the heartbreaking consequences of such raids upon provincial targets, none experienced the continuous pounding of London over a full nine months. On 8/9 March there was a raid by 150 bombers followed by one involving 300 bombers on the 19th, the heaviest raid of the year so far. On 16 and 19 April, 350 bombers dropped even larger bombs over central London, killing some 1,000 people and injuring 2,000 more on each occasion. Finally, on 10 May the Luftwaffe mounted a massive raid across the face of the capital that confirmed it as both the outstanding and chief target for Hitler's Luftwaffe.[39]

The pattern of the attack on the night of 10/11 May was familiar, although the numbers of bombers were heavier than ever before. Starting with eleven Heinkel 'fire raisers' of Kampfgruppe 100, the area from West Ham to the West End was soon 'bubbling (with fire) like a pot of boiling tomato soup'.[40]

Over 2,000 fires were started during London's worst raid of the war and the notable buildings destroyed or heavily damaged at that time included the

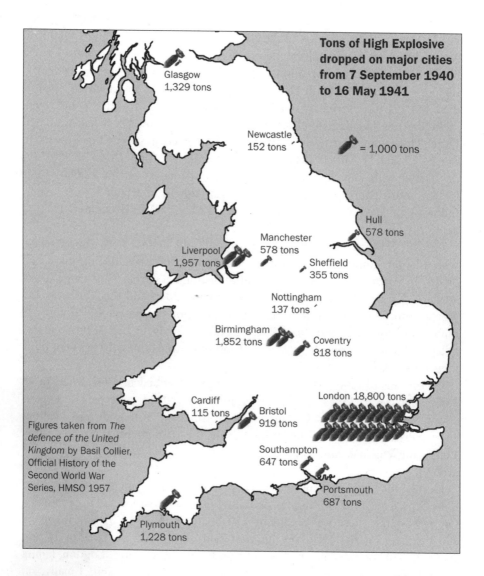

Tons of High Explosive dropped on major cities from 7 September 1940 to 16 May 1941

Glasgow 1,329 tons

Newcastle 152 tons

= 1,000 tons

Hull 578 tons

Manchester 578 tons

Liverpool 1,957 tons

Sheffield 355 tons

Nottingham 137 tons

Birmimgham 1,852 tons

Coventry 818 tons

Cardiff 115 tons

London 18,800 tons

Bristol 919 tons

Figures taken from *The defence of the United Kingdom* by Basil Collier, Official History of the Second World War Series, HMSO 1957

Southampton 647 tons

Portsmouth 687 tons

Plymouth 1,228 tons

Chamber of the House of Commons, Westminster Abbey, St James's Palace, the London Museum, the Queen's Concert Hall, the Public Record Office, the British Museum, the Mansion House, the Guildhall Art Library and the Tower of London. Many city churches and livery halls were damaged or destroyed and all but one of the main-line railway stations were blocked. On the following morning 150,000 families were without gas or electricity, 2,000 acres of the city were without water and 959 roads closed. Yet with the capital's noted resilience and honed by its experiences over the previous nine months, by Sunday

The caption on the postcard reflects Londoners' initial reactions of fear and anger towards such raiders. (*Author's Collection*)

THE LOW DOWN THING THAT PLAYS THE LOW DOWN GAME.

London is watching. With London's improving defences the mood begins to lift. (*Author's Collection*)

London is watching:—"All's Well!"

(*Left*) The strafer strafed. Little sympathy was shown by most Londoners towards the German aircrews who suffered horrific deaths in their blazing craft. (*Author's Collection*)

(*Right*) Lieutenant William Leefe Robinson, who was awarded the Victoria Cross for being the first British airman to shoot down a Zeppelin over London. (*Author's Collection*)

"THE STRAFER STRAFED"
SOMEWHERE IN ESSEX. SEPT. 24th. 1916.

A rare image of the skeletal remains of a No. 8 bus following a Zeppelin raid in which the driver, conductor and two passengers were killed outright. (*Author's Collection*)

This photograph illustrates the massive wingspan of the Gotha bombers that raided London and other locations in Britain. (*Digital image by Paul Vickers from a model in the FAST Museum, Farnborough, Hampshire*)

The unmistakable profile of Supermarine Spitfires, the sleekes and most potent British fighters operating during the Battle of Britain. (*Pen and Sword Historical Collection*)

Hawker Hurricanes, more rugged and easier to build than Spitfires, shouldered the bulk of the fighting against the German assaults during 1940. (*Pen and Sword Historical Collection*)

A Messerschmidt Bf 109, the Luftwaffe's outstanding fighter plane whose performance at high altitude was superior to both Spitfires and Hurricanes.
(*Pen and Sword Historical Collection*)

A German Messerschmidt Bf 110, which was somewhat slower and less manoeuvrable than either the Spitfire or Hurricane.
(*Pen and Sword Historical Collection*)

The Dornier Do 17 medium bomber was obsolescent by 1939 but still made up a quarter of the bomber units deployed against Britain during 1940.
(*Pen and Sword Historical Collection*)

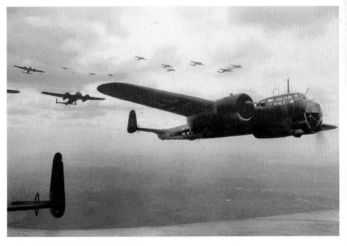

The Heinkel He 111 carried almost twice the Dornier's bombload but was also vulnerable to the defending British fighters.
(*Pen and Sword Historical Collection*)

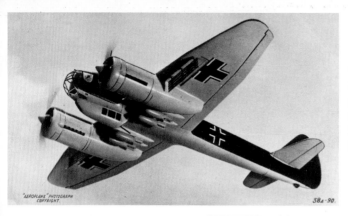

The Junkers Ju 88, an outstanding German bomber, which was both fast and durable and represented a difficult target for the RAF interceptors guarding London. (*Author's Collection*)

After erecting their Anderson air-raid shelter, complete with its earth covering, a London family relaxes in the sun. (*Author's Collection*)

Death and devastation – shattered buildings along with a recent victim of the raids. (*Author's Collection*)

'Are we downhearted?' London children sitting it out on debris from a previous raid. (*Author's Collection*)

'How do I look?' A wartime evacuee puts on his gas mask for his new foster parents. (*Author's Collection*)

Preserving the city's heritage – statues in Trafalgar Square covered up for the duration of the war. (*Author's Collection*)

This photograph of St Paul's Cathedral from Paternoster Row shows the extent of ruined buildings close by. (*Author's Collection*)

London's rail system under attack – the remains of Moorgate station following a raid. (*Author's Collection*)

Cut-price breakfasts – business as usual in the East End. (*Author's Collection*)

Officials inspect the damage caused to All Hallows, the Guild church of Toc H. (*Author's Collection*)

Changed perspectives – High Holborn following the Blitz. (*Author's Collection*)

A V1 flying bomb plummets to earth.
(Pen and Sword Historical Collection)

'Open-plan' buildings, looking towards the city from New Bridge Street. *(Author's Collection)*

Justice prevails – the Old Bailey stands tall amid the ruins. *(Author's Collection)*

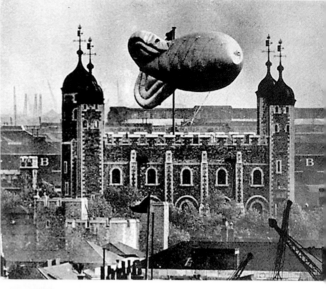

(*Top left*) After being bombed up, a V2 rocket is fuelled for launching. (*Author's Collection*)

(*Top right*) Neither London's ancient fortress nor barrage balloons could offer any defence from rocket attacks. (*Author's Collection*)

(*Left*) The result of the IRA's 'bombing spectacular' against the City's Baltic Exchange. (*By courtesy of Getty Images*)

(*Below*) The London bus destroyed after the al-Qaeda attack in Tavistock Place, July 2005. (*By courtesy of Getty Images*)

lunchtime conditions were already returning to some normality. Beethoven's *Coriolan Overture*, for instance, due to be performed at the bombed out Queen's Hall, was switched to the Royal Academy of Music, and although the musicians were denied their usual final practice they started promptly at 3.00 pm.

Elsewhere Londoners found other recreations. On Sunday afternoon, in the same way that people in previous centuries had watched public executions, 'Blitz trippers' arrived from the suburbs to stare at the ruined and still smoking buildings. In the East End, in spite of the Home Guard being deployed to prevent such practices, some of the damaged shops were plundered and there were reports of bombed-out pubs having their contents drunk dry. The vast majority of people were, however, just happy to be alive and able to go about their domestic tasks. On the Monday morning, while Londoners struggled to work, an emergency meeting was held in the Imperial War Museum to discuss which actions could be taken in the event of further comparable raids. No new initiatives were considered necessary, but it was concluded that if four more similar attacks occurred the effects could be disastrous for the capital's water system. Some of those travelling to work were able to use their normal termini since Euston, King's Cross, Liverpool Street and Paddington stations had reopened, although Victoria and Waterloo were not to do so for a further week. Others would have met different problems as 30 miles of London Underground's track was destroyed and there were no buses in the City.

People were further impeded by 162 unexploded bombs. A parachute mine suspended above the stage of the Palladium had been defused on Sunday and when the stars, including Vera Lynn, arrived on the Monday they divided up sections of the parachute which still hung there.[41] At Westminster, MPs retrieved what they could from the wrecked Commons Chamber and the Dean of bomb-damaged Westminster Abbey, Dr Paul de Labilliere, regretted that, like many others, he had no clothes other than those he stood up in.[42] Damage to gasholders and supply pipes impeded production in some factories, including the Royal Arsenal which was throttled by a lack of supplies.

The raid caused the rest centres to be under siege again, with 1,100 houses damaged beyond repair and 12,374 people rendered homeless. The mortuaries and hospitals had to cope with 1,436 deaths and 1,800 serious injuries – figures that were not released to the press.

On that Monday as the city and its emergency services were shaking off the worst effects of its most serious raid the authorities were anxiously awaiting the next. Unbeknown to them, the raid of 10 May marked the last of the initial German Blitz, although 8 days later 111 bombers attacked Birmingham. Hitler's mind was on new conquests, and on 21 June 1941 with his invasion of Russia the Luftwaffe was redeployed to the Eastern Front.

Battered and bruised from prolonged aerial attack, London was reprieved, although as long as it remained the pre-eminent symbol of the free world only the most naive of its civil defenders could believe that Hitler had done with it yet.

Chapter 9

The London Blitz, 1940–1 – Home Morale

Things blew up and things blew down
Seemed a blink-in' shame – Blooming fire and flame
Blimey what a game. But who stood up and saved the town. When
London Bridge was falling down – MISTER BROWN OF LONDON
TOWN – OI – MISTER BROWN

Second World War song[1]

Unlike with the previous war there is no shortage of material relating to civilian morale during the London Blitz, or for that matter during subsequent attacks on the capital. In fact, two massive studies were undertaken. As a result of official apprehension at the beginning of the war regarding the reaction of ordinary people – particularly in London – to mass bombing, the Ministry of Information formed a Home Intelligence Section specifically to chart people's reactions both to the bombing and the defence measures undertaken. This would be done by consulting the BBC's Listeners' Research Unit, Gallup polls, postal censorship (examining up to 200,000 letters a week) and information obtained from eavesdropping on telephone calls.

The Home Intelligence Unit produced daily reports from 18 May until the end of September 1940 when, after people's seemingly stalwart response, they were then reduced to weekly bulletins. The other study was by the so-called Mass Observation Unit, a privately sponsored social reporting organization, largely inspired by the London anthropologist Tom Harrisson, which focused chiefly on people's states of mind. It assembled a nationwide panel of 1,500 voluntary observers plus a smaller group of full-timers, mostly drawn from the middle class, who monitored civilian morale both through interviews and by sitting in on civilian activities, whether in air-raid shelters or shops. With their underlying patriotism and frequently left wing views it is fair to say that their approach was impressionistic rather than scientific, and by accepting a commission from Home Intelligence much of their work was for the government. As Tom Harrisson self-importantly put it, they were committed to ascertain the facts as accurately as possible, develop and improve the methods for ascertaining these facts, and disseminate the ascertained facts as widely as possible.[2] In fact, this ramshackle, triumphantly unscientific organization collected a rich vein of information about how people felt and acted at the time.

The vast body of evidence from both sources has been extensively worked over during the last sixty years, and the first researchers came to most positive conclusions. Professor Richard Titmuss, who had full access to the Ministry of Information records for his *Official Volume on Problems of Social Policy, History of the Second World War*, maintained that not only did home morale not break down during the Blitz, but that the air raids on London actually strengthened social solidarity: 'There are sensations of a new visibility, of paradoxical freedom, and of a rather bawdy life-for-today philosophy ... an unsettling vista of smiles to reflect that it had needed to disinter the state of everyday comradeship'.[3] He was soon supported by Constantine FitzGibbon,[4] whose personal reminiscences highlighted the shared dangers and who also felt the Blitz weakened class prejudices and showed the 'extraordinary adaptability, not always rational but nevertheless effective, of the inhabitants of a great city'.[5]

This view went generally unchallenged until Angus Calder undertook a broader and less-idealistic approach to people's behaviour,[6] which in turn was taken a step further by Tom Harrisson. His *Living Through the Blitz* drew heavily on the individual interviews conducted by his observers which sometimes revealed the extreme difficulties, and indeed terrors, of people not always supported by their local authorities as they should have been. He still concluded that they did not let their soldiers or their leaders down – indeed not infrequently they propped their leaders up, in a situation where leadership at the local level was lacking.[7]

A rising tide of criticism with regard to the public arrangements followed with Angus Calder's *The Myth of the Blitz*, in which he maintained that 'the Blitz supported a myth of British or English moral pre-eminence, buttressed by British unity'[8] that gained a similar aura to the evacuation of British troops from Dunkirk.

Around the same time Clive Ponting's *1940 Myth and Reality*[9] went furthest of all, maintaining that the official version of the Blitz was nothing less than lies and the work of government propagandists. In 2002 came the inevitable re-correction with Robert Mackay's *Half the Battle, Civilian Morale in Britain during the Second World War*, which stated that during the Blitz people did carry on with few of them succumbing to apathy or despair and many acting beyond the call of duty.[10]

The present author is convinced that the majority of Londoners did in fact carry on during the bombing onslaught, although many were far from attaining the noble reactions ascribed to them at that time. Worthy of consideration is how far this might have been due to Londoners' personal ties with their great city, which in practical terms generally came through the facilities made available to them in their boroughs. Despite the limitations of a single chapter in giving an adequate account, the authentic and compelling evidence from the surveys makes this feasible.

No such attempt can ignore the findings of Richard Titmuss, whose official study of social policy at this time included the decision made to evacuate the most vulnerable – the children, the handicapped and the elderly – before the bombing began. Whatever the outcome of later initiatives designed to help Londoners cope with the anticipated raids, the one concerning evacuation undoubtedly failed. The pull of the city on Londoners and their families meant that, despite most energetic attempts on the government's behalf, only half of those eligible decided to leave the city. In practice the scheme was not helped by the fact that by 31 August 1939, when the order for evacuation came, arrangements within the rural areas for accepting what were still undoubtedly large numbers were quite inadequate.

The process itself was also not well handled. After travelling with their teachers in crowded trains, sometimes without lavatories and with their drinking water limited to what they carried, the older children were more than likely to have arrived in a dirty and unco-operative state. They were then lined up for inspection and selection. The author remembers being told to keep quiet and stand still while the householders took their pick in a situation that Titmuss described as 'scenes reminiscent of a cross between an early Roman slave market and Selfridges bargain basement'.[11] The hosts were to be paid 10*s* and 6*d* for a child's upkeep, and at just 7 he remembers being one of the last to be picked up as larger boys and girls who could lend a hand in the home or farm were taken first.

Following such a journey the shock for some mothers with still younger children was such that they did not wait, and by the time the last trainloads of evacuees were arriving, small groups of mothers and children had moved to opposite platforms to return home. While there were a proportion of successful billetings, it all too easily became a personal tragedy when the majority of evacuees who came from the poorer areas of London found themselves placed with proud and critical middle-class families, quite apart from the rivalries and misunderstandings between the urban working class from London and their rural working class hosts. One girl evacuee recalled the occasion when she and her mother went into a shop with their ration books only to be told, 'Oh, you come from London, we haven't got any rations for you London folks'.[12]

One of the most publicized problems of the evacuation was that after a long period in a crowded carriage many of the children had their heads crawling with vermin. As Richard Titmuss observed, 'the louse is not a political creature; it cannot distinguish between the salt of the earth and the scum of the earth'.[13] The infestation of children arriving from London ranged from 8 to 35 per cent, with still higher proportions for other cities.

The process of evacuation which removed children from their families in such a draconian way deserved to fail for reasons of its utter insensitivity if nothing else, but it was guaranteed to do so because of the extent the adults and children involved missed their home surroundings and their city's communal activities. By the end of September 1939 22 per cent had returned, and by January 1940 over 80 per cent decided to face the bombs rather than remain in what so many viewed as an alien environment.

This sense of alienation was also felt among the elderly, even when fleeing from heavy bombing. One such lady was a Miss Q, aged 70, deaf, quite toothless, not very clean, living in a basement of an empty house in a much bombed area. Determined to take with her a cot, a feather bed and two large trunks, besides the usual complement of parcels, cases and carriers, the arrangements for the transport of her and her luggage at both ends of the journey were not altogether easy, and the storage of her London furniture was another problem that the Ministry of Health had to deal with. In the event she stayed one month, borrowed money from all her neighbours and returned to London because she 'couldn't seem to take to a place where there wasn't no Picture House nor no evening paper neither'.[14]

Those grandparents and parents who returned voluntarily to 'the smoke' and the Blitz had good reasons to carry on. Not so all Londoners. A report for Mass Observation about preparations for the forthcoming raids gave the impression that, far from panicking when a selection of Londoners took part in a question and answer session led by a warden about their actions when coming upon an incendiary bomb, only a third showed they knew what to do. Their responses were not only laid back but deliberately mischievous. Their commonest response was acceptable, namely 'throw the bomb into water' or 'throw water over the bomb'. But others included,

Stand up by a brick wall
Lay on it
Leave it to a warden
Flip a coat over it, or throw it into a sewer or anywhere there is water

Pick it up and run it in water
Sit back and hold tight
Leave it where it was and run
Put on your gas mask[15]

However admirable his instructions about dealing with incendiaries (and whatever the marginal attention paid), a warden's other responsibilities, including that of telling people that they had a light showing, brought him the level of respect accorded to today's traffic wardens. One warden patrolling the neighbourhood of World's End, Chelsea, for blackout failures, for instance, found himself 'struck by an accurately thrown boot'.[16] While not deserving such treatment, wardens, like other Londoners, varied widely. One full-time warden in Kilburn was reported as saying to another, 'They started off this service with the idea that it was a kind of muck heap for anyone they didn't want in the army. Can you tell me of four wardens at our post, bar you and me, who can run fifty yards without conking out?'[17]

After the younger men had been conscripted, the remainder, including women, tended to be more committed and there were undoubtedly fine wardens. When, for instance, the huge Tilbury air-raid shelter received a direct hit and was plunged into gloom, 'a single warden standing at the top of a narrow passage was able to control about three thousand people, who calmly and coolly groped their way through the darkness as he ordered'.[18]

Preparations for the anticipated Blitz and the codes of conduct in air-raid shelters differed widely from borough to borough. A representative from Mass Observation reported on the Tilbury Docks shelter in a much-bombed and undeniably poor quarter of London. He wrote of mothers and small children coming to the shelter every day, a few arriving as early as 9.00 am, with the queue becoming fairly long by 2.00 pm for the shelter's opening an hour later. With its relatively large capacity and the high demands made upon it, regulations became necessary. The official ones required by the Port of London Authority police, who controlled affairs until 10.00 pm at night, appeared to be a restriction on trading in the shelter and forbidding the sale of the communist *Daily Worker*.

Much more numerous were the unwritten laws which, as the observer noted, evolved out of necessity. Every passageway for instance, had to be kept clear, and it was an unpardonable crime to tread on anyone's blanket. Although those entering the shelter could reserve a 'place' for others, there was a limit to the amount of space that could be held back in this way. Music/storytelling was to cease at 10.00 pm in the main part of the shelter and by 12.00 pm in the space by the back entrance. Although the police banned smoking, it was an unwritten law that smoking could take place at the back entrance. After 10.00 pm public order was in the hands of the shelter marshals, either self-appointed or soldiers on leave who were allowed to take on such responsibilities.

At Tilbury these proved more trouble than they were worth. One shouted loudly all the time and issued the most unnecessary instructions, such as 'Don't tread on that woman's foot. Don't keep bashing into each other.' He continually argued with overwrought women, being himself highly strung and easily unnerved. One soldier, not yet 21, adopted a most domineering attitude, wandering round the shelter shouting 'Pass along there' and 'Break it up you blighters' even when there was nothing to pass along or break up. This particular young man accepted bribes of sixpences from people to find them good places. Such 'little Hitlers' held watches in their hands as they listened in to private concerts being played on portable radios. On the stroke of ten they triumphantly shouted 'Quiet please'. Despite such petty officials, if arguments occurred after 10.00 pm they were usually quickly taken in hand by the shelter's fellow sleepers.[19] Despite such annoyances, providing the noise made by the raiders and the answering guns was not too great, most achieved a reasonable night's rest.

The community frequenting the Tilbury Docks shelter contrasted with that at the Vale of Health on Hampstead Heath. On 25 August 1940 a Mass Observation observer was shown round by the post warden there, who explained that it was the first of the Hampstead districts to think of a 'Housewives service' prior to official arrangements being set in place. This was to operate in the event of a raid suddenly cutting the community off from its normal food and other supplies. The response was apparently tremendous, every one of its seventy resident families agreeing to take some part (including the inhabitants of the caravan down by the fair ground). All housewives with refrigerators arranged to maintain an extra quart of milk every day, so that children and babies would not suffer during the day or two while new methods of supply were being devised. For similar reasons home baking of bread had been planned: two housewives each laid in large stocks of flour and guaranteed to produce thirty loaves of bread at six hours' notice.[20] The observer went on to detail the stretchers and other equipment at the First Aid Post which had been hand-made by the senior warden on his own initiative and in his own time, while also carrying on a strenuous job.

The Londoners who used the official public shelter near the Ritz Hotel in Piccadilly came from yet another social background. Apparently it was remarkably well appointed, and not split into different rooms but formed by a labyrinth of passages with benches lining the walls. There were electric lights at intervals, closets, stone bottles of water and cardboard drinking cups. The observer said that the numbers here were difficult to estimate, probably about 200: of these about half conversed (with him) and 12 per cent were eating or sucking something, 11 per cent read the papers, 4 per cent read books, 2 per cent knitted, 2 per cent smoked (no official forbade this), 4 per cent were couples holding hands and physically comforting each other, and 10 per cent were children. The final 4 per cent were dogs (no ban was enforced here). On the question of morale, the observer said that no defeatist talk was heard and no one showed any obvious signs of distress, but a certain amount of tension was revealed in an abnormal amount of talk to strangers![21]

The shelters much varied in size, one huge cellar in Stepney nightly housed 10,000 people in notable squalor. In many of the shelters the regular users came together and developed codes of conduct, including cleaning rotas and emptying lavatory buckets.

There were, of course, limits to what such voluntary committees could achieve without support from their local authorities. Due largely to the efforts of Herbert Morrison, in February 1941, during a lull in the raids, facilities were much improved with bunk beds and toilets, while canteens were established on the large Tube stations. As always, Londoners succeeded in developing some form of community spirit whatever the facilities. In the case of the extensive Chiselhurst caves, these were comparatively lavish: bunk beds, canteens, a children's chapel and a cave hospital were among the amenities provided,[22] and the level of organization was acknowledged to have been astonishing.

Other boroughs also showed undoubted imagination. In the Bermondsey shelters the borough council set up a range of evening classes. In some shelters you could go in any night of the week and find, for example, a dressmaking group in one corner and a drama group in another, preparing for a play which subsequently the rest of the shelterers would watch.[23] St Pancras set up travelling libraries for people in rest centres, shelters, billets or even ARP units.

Compared with the First World War the raids brought no such comparable terror. That war had shown the way and as Tom Harrisson observed (after the Great Depression) 'the need to work for money linked to the habit of working (and the fear of not having a job) proved far more powerful than the prophets ever assumed'.[24] Londoners needed to keep going to get to work. People also seemed to have powerful safety valves when under great strain and often seemed most concerned with the trivia of survival than anything else. Grace Foakes was with her family in their Anderson shelter when a bomb hit their home. When neighbours dug them out of their shelter she saw 'just a pile of rubble where our bungalow had stood ... I had planted rows of spinach in the garden ... although we had lost everything we possessed the thing I mourned for most was my precious spinach!'[25]

In October 1940 one of the Mass Observation observers was stopped by a policeman at a place with a rope across the road. She told him that she had a friend with a flat there and found she was crying as she thought of T and B and T's mother and hoping they were safe, but then 'of her lovely room full of all the books they had collected, both of them for years, and their nice little flat'.[26]

In Croydon an observer noted that the complaints were not that bombs were dropped, but that their local officials were negligent in not warning them beforehand, and wardens were always favourite butts. People also appeared to react most strongly against anything that went against the habitual rhythms of their life. As observer P V Smith noted, 'We have had many warnings and raids since the war, but the effects on most people appear to have made them worry about their food more than anything else. Bombs of various types have been dropped nearby, but the worry about them is negligible in comparison with the worry about sleep'.[27]

While inhabitants of a great international city were fully aware of its supporting infrastructure, their routines were essentially parochial. Many people were, in fact, too busy, too tired and too concerned with their everyday existence to devote much energy to wider issues beyond the single, unbreakable custom of listening to Winston Churchill on their radios, and therefore people appeared to take the raids very calmly. One observer was somewhat surprised to report that during a raid his subject continued to sit in his kitchen with a friend, and at Dulwich Tennis Club, after watching an aerial dogfight over Croydon, members decided to play another half set before the inevitable warning went.[28]

Another observer described being with a family in North London during an air raid where 'we talk about all sorts of non-air raid things. About our mutual landlord; the damp in the walls, the state of the gutters, the last tenants, and the possibility of planting vegetables in the garden'.[29] In another public shelter most time was spent in doing the *Daily Mirror* crossword, talking to other tenants, cuddling and petting kittens, sometimes with needlework, and only occasionally by listening to the news on a wireless. After hearing the BBC news, vain attempts were made to tune in to Hitler's Lord Haw-Haw. If one was unlucky some time would be taken up by the shelter bores, in this case an opinionated drapery salesman who, after reading the paper and playing chess with other members, held forth on almost any subject – 'last night on deep sea fishing, or Jews or inflation or the position of America, or the care of the stirrup pump or the advantage of communal feeding or the best way of getting rid of mice ...'.[30] Not that much attention was paid to his ideas.

In another shelter the majority thought very little about the news, with some not even remembering the headlines of the day's papers, even if they included some mention of the RAF's bombing of Germany. Most of them in that particular shelter had not been outside London since the beginning of the war, although middle-class Londoners apparently tended to have had at least a few days away.[31] Most observers at this time believed that the Blitz had affected public morale very little and that, however they went about proving it, people possessed a courage they did not realize they had. In any case, the bombing was a nightly occurrence. Observer Frank Edwards interviewed a man who told him that 'we awoke this morning to find that no alert had sounded all night and this is the first bombless night in fifty-seven nights, which I think is an occasion to chalk up'.[32] One girl explained her relative calmness in the following way: 'It's a funny thing but I live from one day to another. When I wake up in the morning I think, well we haven't been bombed tonight and when I go to bed I always expect it. But it doesn't stop me sleeping. Funny, isn't it?'[33]

Londoners were helped immeasurably by their authorities' determination to do everything after a raid to return conditions to normal, not only the vital logistic services but also other peripheral activities that so characterized the city. The bus and train services were restored as quickly as possible, and during a raid – unlike the First World War – buses continued along their routes with passengers allowed to remain on board. On Friday 23 August 1940, an observer was on a bus travelling towards Hayes when there was a raid. The conductor told his passengers about a shelter nearby if anybody wanted to leave the bus, at which a woman shouted to nobody in particular 'We're British, ain't we?', to which she received no answer[34] – but no one got off either.

These services were a powerful sign of reason and commonsense. Not much more than a month after December's firestorm on the City of London bus services were back to normal, main roads were clear and restaurants, public houses and shops were open with most of the larger stores fairly full. Almost every sign in the devastated areas bore a notice of transfer of a business to a new address. The atmosphere was said to be one of complete normality and pre-occupation with everyday affairs.[35]

In April 1941 another observer went into Holborn on the morning following a serious raid. He found the buses running normally and it seemed the onus was on everyone else to behave in a similar fashion. Wanting to buy seeds from Carter's in Holborn, on his arrival he was invited to walk into the store through a window (the glass of which was absent) because the door was jammed: as he commented, from the sangfroid of the shopkeeper one might have thought it was an everyday occurrence.[36]

The heavy initial raids on East London and the London docks, coming before the emergency services streamlined their operations, might have been expected to have paralyzed such communities. In fact, a report on the Isle of

Dogs stated that food was obtainable and water was only cut off for twelve hours – and the pubs were open.[37]

Stepney took a pasting, but even there all the small tobacconists remained open during the raids and restaurants reported an increase in custom. When the siren went another observer found himself – probably from choice – looking at books outside Joseph's in Charing Cross Road. 'A few booksellers came to their doors but the shops remained open and folk continued to finger books.'[38] In the early days of the Blitz far fewer people tended to go out in the evenings and in Stepney, for instance, with the vital services seriously interrupted 'there was no margin for luxuries like billiards and films and beer'.[39] Some of its cinemas had to close down, and restaurants prepared cold meals only. But even Stepney, reckoned to have been one of the less-impressive authorities, soon recovered (there was no danger of pubs ever being in short supply there, even if some had been destroyed) and the cinema companies did their best to restore their own services.

After the initial shock of the bombing, many people resumed visiting their local cinemas, dance halls and pubs. The Granada chain, for instance, attempted to help by offering nightlong shelter and entertainment for their clients, and those who stayed could look forward to five feature films and community singing. Many brought their blankets for the last house.[40] At Studio One in Oxford Street during the early bombing the manager stopped the film to announce a raid and to tell his patrons where the nearest shelters were, but hardly anybody left and the film continued. The film was stopped again to announce the all clear, when cheers went up and the performance continued.[41]

As revealed in the previous chapter, the tradition of continuing concert attendance was, if anything, stronger still. An observer was in the Queen's Hall, Regent Street, listening to Brahms' *First Symphony*, when suddenly a man in evening dress hurried through the orchestra and Sir Henry Wood stopped conducting. Immediately there came from the audience a sound like mingled laughs and groans with a few claps. The man announced that the siren had gone and asked anyone who wished to leave to do so at once: there came loud applause, then more applause and general conversation. After about two minutes the concert continued. The observer did not himself hear the siren and nobody in any part of the house left as far as he could see.[42]

After the first few weeks of the Blitz, whether resident in central London or in the suburbs, it seemed a matter of honour to continue with traditional leisure activities. Some Londoners, as was their privilege, bought liquor and consumed it, either before going to or when in their shelters; as one witness said, 'I got drunk and I am not ashamed to say so. I had nearly half a bottle of whisky. I felt I needed it.'[43]

In this context Tom Harrisson, in his book *Living Through the Blitz*, instanced the social activities of six 'nippy' girls – waitresses at Joe Lyons near Marble Arch. After the early austere days when they returned home every night to join their families in their shelters,

> in spite of little education and no abnormalities of note [they] have separately and collectively adjusted, managing to resume the main interest of their young lives – a job of sorts, boy-friends, cinemas and pubs, West End outings. They did so in the teeth of Luftwaffe, Lyons, the Landmines, Douhetism, blackout, fear of death, the lot. Whoever managed that in Whitehall in 1938?[44]

During the eight months of the Blitz, Londoners of all ages kept their spirits up by continuing with their normal activities both at work and at leisure. Some few reached unexpected heights of bravery, others (in the minority) were uninterested in putting themselves to further inconvenience. But most adapted to the unique challenge with a determination not to make things any more difficult than they were. The privations of the shelters could be offset by the comradeship they soon discovered there. If they were cinema or theatre buffs no Luftwaffe would keep them away, so they accepted the greater risks involved. The shops might have had less stock and clothing coupons limited spending power, but customers still went. Although extensive trading on the so-called black market was for the very few, most Londoners knew where to obtain a wild rabbit or two for family celebrations. They were bolstered by an ingrained sense of survival and pride in their city that helped them believe that its illimitable resources and their own characteristic talents (with wardens the notable exception) would see them through.

Chapter 10

London and the Doodlebugs

The doodlebugs were so much more terrifying than anything that had come along up till that time because they were supernatural. You accepted a plane with a man in it. You couldn't accept something that was automatic.

Odette Lesley, who as a schoolgirl lived with her mother and sister in Croydon[1]

Although London remained the Luftwaffe's principal target, the second half of 1941 and the early part of 1942 brought a break from the bombing and the city's defenders could have been forgiven for believing that, after sending 2,000 first-line aircraft to other theatres of war,[2] the Luftwaffe had more than enough commitments in both Russia and the Western Desert to prevent it resuming its attacks on them.

That the raids recommenced when they did owed much to the appointment in February 1942 of Sir Arthur 'Bomber' Harris as chief of Bomber Command, with his unwavering determination – supported by both Churchill and the War Cabinet – to promote the strategic bombing of Germany. 'Victory, speedy and complete, awaits the side which first employs air power as it should be employed'[3] he declared and furthermore it would be totally wrong to use it as a subsidiary to land and sea campaigns. Whatever form this strategic bombing would ultimately take, Harris began by 'blooding his air crews' through what he called commercial travellers' samples, by attacking relatively easy targets. In the first instance, this was the undefended Renault factory near Paris and then, on 28 March 1942, he sent 234 bombers to attack the medieval town of Lubeck, the narrow streets and half-timbered houses of which were, he thought, 'built more like a fire-lighter than a human habitation'. Harris's aim was to test the effects on Germany of heavy incendiary attacks as earlier carried out by the Luftwaffe on Britain, and so successful was the raid on Lubeck that 200 acres of the city centre were burned out. His third target was the medium-sized port of Rostock where similar results were obtained. In fact, Harris also used powerful high-explosive bombs as well. 'What we want to do in addition to the horrors of fire is to bring the masonry crashing down on top of the Boche, to kill Boche and to terrify the Boche, hence the proposition of HE.'[4]

Hitler had boasted that any bombing of German cities would be repaid with interest and therefore after the destruction of the historic city of Lubeck, followed by Rostock, his response was inevitable. In fact, after the attack on the Renault factory Hitler had ordered a concentration of his available planes for a heavy attack on London, only for it to be cancelled when the weather deteriorated. After Lubeck, Hitler changed his policy. He reasoned that rather than use his bombing forces in the West against a large well-defended target, he could (like Harris) move against historic cities 'where attacks are likely to have the greatest possible effect on civilian life ... against towns other than London'.[5]

This was the first open threat of bringing terror through bombing. 'Bomber' Harris might still conceivably justify his attack on Lubeck as a Hanseatic port and on Rostock for its Heinkel factory, while the Luftwaffe fire-raising raids against London had also included vital installations. But from now on, the Luftwaffe's raids on Britain would primarily be for the purpose of inflicting terror and loss, a purpose made even more explicit with the German randomly targeted V weapons.

Hitler's Baedeker raids – so called because they were aimed at historic cities worthy of a three-star grading in the German Tourist Guide of Britain – were directed at targets within 50 miles of the coast that possessed few or no defenders. A maximum of seventy-three planes, including some from the Luftwaffe's reserve Training Units, guided by a Pathfinder squadron and the ultrasonic frequencies of the X-GERAT beams, attacked Exeter, Bath, Norwich, York, Canterbury and Ipswich between the months of April and July 1942. Writing about them after the war the official historian on Britain's civil defences rightly concluded that, as with the later RAF raid on Dresden, although their destruction and damage to vital war industries was small, 'from the wider standpoint of the destruction of human life, of the services upon which these various communities depended and of buildings of national significance the enemy's achievements should not be underestimated'.[6] Compared with the earlier raids on London and the later combined attacks by the RAF and USAF on Germany, they were undoubtedly small and, unlike those on London, they were not striking at the British government, nor at its main industrial base.

Less than 900 people died in such raids and the sites where the bombs fell have since been built over (if in many cases by structures of more questionable architectural or visual merit), but if Hitler had ever hoped that such reprisal raids might lead to support being withdrawn from RAF raids on Germany, he was bound to be disappointed.

During the next eighteen months the Luftwaffe's aerial attacks on London and other British cities were reduced to what have been described as 'hit and run' raids. These were usually made by fast, low-flying fighter-bombers, which still succeeded in keeping the country's Ack-Ack and civil defenders on edge. They had good reason to keep alert, for despite its other commitments the Luftwaffe retained 500 aircraft in Europe capable of mounting a heavy onslaught, or series of onslaughts, on Britain. With the growing weight of the RAF's night bombing of Germany it was still possible that planes could be withdrawn – even temporarily – from other theatres for retaliatory raids on Britain. During the early part of 1943 these 'tip and run' raids could be on a fairly large scale. On 17/18 January 100 long-range bombers attacked South London, followed two days later by fighter-bombers who inflicted considerable damage on the Surrey Commercial Dock,[7] but during the year the number of raids decreased sharply.

Meanwhile, the allies increased their raids on Germany. Following a disastrous daylight sortie by the USAF on the German ball-bearings works at Schweinfort on 14 October 1943, they soon received powerful bomber reinforcements and, above all, with the introduction of a potent long-range fighter – the Mustang – the means to protect them. Meanwhile, the RAF's growing capability, and use of Pathfinder planes to improve its target acquisition, would help enable both air forces from early 1944 onwards to mount massive attacks on the German homeland, including its Luftwaffe facilities.

In such circumstances it was virtually inevitable that German planes should be redeployed from other theatres (including all the long-range bombers from Italy) for retaliatory attacks on Britain, and that these should be joined as soon as possible by a specific family of Vergeltungswaffen vengeance weapons, about which there were growing rumours.

Between the third week of January and the end of March 1944 more bombs were dropped on Britain than in the previous year, with thirteen of the fifteen attacks on London in what came to be described as the 'Little Blitz'. These were generally of short duration and although people took to their shelters again, unlike the early days of the Blitz those who went down into the Tube stations emerged quickly upon the sounding of the all clear. On 21 January the largest force since July 1942 attacked London, dropping more large HE bombs than ever before. This was followed by six raids in February, when most of the London boroughs were hit, and four more in March, in the course of which many phosphorus bombs were used. Another two major raids occurred in April, but from this point onwards the Luftwaffe was switched to reconnoitring allied preparations for their invasion of Europe.

During May 1944 German manned air attacks remained slight, but at 4.13 am during the night of 12/13 June 1944 the first of Hitler's long-awaited vengeance weapons – a pilotless flying bomb (Vergeltungswaffe 1) directed at London – dived to earth on farmland south of Gravesend, where it exploded. The rapid development and short operational life of the V1 is one of the most remarkable stories of the Second World War. In many respects it seemed to represent the ultimate reprisal weapon: unmanned, indiscriminate, technologically simple, capable of being produced in large numbers and able to carry a potent explosive warhead of 850kg. Although it was patently in the German interest to keep its existence secret until it could be produced in sufficient numbers to pulverize London, it is fair to say that British intelligence proved remarkably slow in identifying it.

The first mention of what could have been the V1 came from Hitler on Tuesday 19 September 1939, less than two weeks after the outbreak of the war. Speaking in Danzig shortly before the fall of Poland, he announced that Germany had no further quarrel with Britain or France, but if they continued the war 'we have a weapon which cannot be used against us'. Although his words made headlines in the London press, there was as yet no indication about the form such a weapon might take and interest soon died down. Winston Churchill was not, however, content to leave matters there and he appointed a brilliant 28-year-old, ex-Oxford physicist, Dr R V Jones, to discover its identity. During a search of British Secret Service files Jones found they contained a number of possibilities: bacterial material, new gases, flame weapons, gliding bombs, aerial torpedoes and pilotless aircraft, long-range guns and rockets, new torpedoes, mines, submarines and death rays. In his subsequent paper, produced on 11 November 1939, he considered pilotless aircraft among the others and concluded that 'it might be thought by the Germans that such weapons would have a serious effect on our morale, if launched indiscriminately against England'.[8]

At this time, R V Jones also received a set of papers, collectively called *The Oslo Report*, from a 'well-wishing German scientist' about German scientific developments. These did not, in fact, mention a pilotless aircraft, although they reported a major research programme involving long-range rockets at a village called Peenemunde on the Baltic island of Usedom.

By this time the concept of a pilotless aircraft was by no means new, since it had been proposed by a Frenchman, René Lorin, in 1918 as a way of bombarding Berlin. Lorin's proposed aircraft would have been propelled by a so-called pulsejet engine operated by pumping an explosive mixture into a combustion chamber, where it was ignited by a spark plug. The thrust was provided by a series of explosions that were subsequently described as being like a Model T Ford going up a hill,[9] and there were plans to stabilize it by gyroscopes and guide it onto its target by radio. In 1918 it was the Americans who built the first pilotless aircraft that flew: powered by an orthodox 40hp engine built by Henry Ford it was capable of carrying a bomb load equal to its own weight of 300lb. Although plans were discussed to launch thousands of them every day against German rear targets, the war ended before it could go into production.

British designers were also active in the field and in 1926 the chief designer of Gloster Aircraft, Mr H P Folland, forwarded plans to the Air Ministry for a pilotless aircraft – but they were 'not impressed and informed Mr Folland that they could see no future for such a revolutionary plane'.[10]

Finally, in the USA during 1939 a flying bomb, based on their earlier design, achieved a range of 200 miles. General Arnold, the commander of the USAF at the time, was impressed, particularly with its price of $800–$1,000 compared with the $400,000 required for a Flying Fortress. It was, however, not proceeded with because of its limited range and its inability, for instance, to get from Britain into the heart of Germany.

With the German Luftwaffe things were different. Since they had no long-range bomber and no time to develop one from scratch, the flying bomb appeared as a cheap and relatively simple way to regain prestige by achieving Hitler's aim of striking back at the British capital. The Luftwaffe's Secretary to the Air Ministry, Erhard Milch, was keenly aware of the opportunity it offered to get ahead of the army, committed as it was to long-range rockets for its own strategic bombardment of Britain. At the end of March 1942, following the RAF raid on Lubeck and Hitler's furious demands for retaliation, the Luftwaffe gave priority to engine designs by the Argus Aircraft Engine Company: a small, pilotless plane 25ft 4in long, made of thin steel plate rather than the normal aluminium, with a wing span of 17ft 6in, was to be propelled by a simple pulse-jet engine which, unlike a normal jet engine powered by the continuous force of its exhaust gases, worked by forcing air through a narrow tube at the rate of 250 explosions a minute. As with earlier prototypes, its direction finding was governed by a gyroscope, which signalled to its rudder and elevator. An air log measured its maximum range, upon which its elevators depressed and it dived into the ground or, alternatively, continued flying until its fuel was exhausted, upon which it also dived to earth.

By 9 June 1942 the project was codenamed Kirshkern or Cherrystone, and a high-priority contract was granted to the Storch company (makers of small monoplanes) to build its airframe. The target date for production was set at the end of 1943 and in August 1942 testing was transferred to the range at Peenemunde West. With its crude engine incapable of producing enough power to take off on its own, it required a forward push by a catapult along a launching ramp or to be released from an aircraft. During June 1943, actual production figures were discussed with Goering, which were set for 2,000 in December, increasing to 4,800 in April 1944 and levelling off at 5,000 from May onwards. Even with a lower figure of 3,500 missiles a month, it was estimated that a missile could be fired at London every 12 minutes (120 a day). Erhard Milch felt sure that Londoners 'will never endure it. It will be the end of real life in the city.'[11] He even believed that four days would be enough to destroy London – the time taken by the RAF in August to reduce Hamburg to ruins. Goering himself was grossly over-optimistic, envisaging a production of 50,000 a month. To facilitate its launching 196 separate sites were to be constructed to foil any RAF counter-bombing, together with 4 impregnable storage bunkers close by.

On 29 July 1943 another Luftwaffe conference took place with particular reference to security problems at Peenemunde, and these proved fully justified when, on 18 August, a massive RAF raid seriously affected work on the rockets, if less significantly for the flying bombs. Even so, a combination of design problems caused by short cuts in testing, along with production difficulties resulting from the RAF's bombing of Peenemunde and other German factories, brought serious delays. In November Colonel Wachtel, commander of the launch sites, forecast an initial production figure of 1,500 missiles a month rather than the expected 3,500 and, at about the same time, when Hitler visited a flying bomb site he was told the missile could not be fully ready until March 1944 – a statement that caused him to stamp away in a rage. But the Fuhrer's concern was fully understandable, for with the projected allied invasion of Europe and the possibility of the area along the hinterland of the French coast being overrun, the opportunities to use his flying bombs were diminishing rapidly. The high priority granted them was seen in the 40,000 workers who, from September 1943 onwards, were set to construct the launch sites, 59 of which were expected to be ready by the end of November, together with 2 of the 4 giant storage bunkers.

That this work only now came to be recognized for what it was – despite massive allied air superiority – owed much to continuing shortcomings in British security. Following *The Oslo Report* on Peenemunde in late 1939, no more information became available until May 1942, when a Spitfire reconnaissance pilot photographed Peenemunde while on another mission. When the resulting photographs were examined by a young WAAF officer and photographic interpreter, Constance Babington Smith, she pointed out some extraordinary circular embankments rather than signs of pilotless aircraft, but no subsequent action was taken. Later in the year a number of sources gave evidence about a long-range rocket being developed at Peenemunde and in March 1943 two captured German Generals, von Thoma and Cruewell, who were placed in a 'bugged room', duly referred in their conversation to the huge rockets at Peenemunde that had reached the testing stage.

As a result Churchill appointed his son-in-law, Duncan Sandys, a Royal Engineer officer who after being invalided from the service had become an MP, to carry out a special investigation into German activity on secret weapons at Peenemunde and beyond, and to consider possible countermeasures. By Easter 1943 he reported that 'the evidence pointed to research and development being in progress on a long-range rocket, probably ... proceeding side by side with the development of jet-propelled aircraft and airborne rocket torpedoes'.[12] Even so, what Dr R V Jones later described as the 'rockets red glare' blinded the British authorities to the presence of a flying bomb, and when a Cabinet Defence Committee met on 28 June most there still believed that the Germans were solely developing long-range rockets – although Lord Cherwell, the chief government scientist, favoured a pilotless, perhaps jet-propelled, aircraft. Nonetheless, at this meeting two important decisions were made. It was decided that the RAF should bomb Peenemunde in the heaviest night attack possible, and that a most rigorous photographic reconnaissance should be made of the area in northern France within a radius of 130 miles from London.

By September opinion was coming round to the existence of two secret weapons. R V Jones, speaking on behalf of the Air Intelligence Board, said, 'It is probable that the German Air Force has been developing a pilotless aircraft for long range bombardment in competition with the rocket and it is very possible that the aircraft will arrive first'.[13]

By the late autumn, with the help of the codebreaking 'Ultra', the results of the firing tests concerning flying bombs were becoming known to London as quickly as Berlin and, in October, Duncan Sandys ordered a new photographic study of north-west France requiring a hundred separate aeroplane sorties. These revealed what looked like skis turned on their sides pointing at London. By 22 November, fifty-five of these had been identified and on 2 December photographic interpreters, Wing Commander Kendall and Constance Babington Smith, reported to the Chiefs of Staff in London that they were in fact launching pads for flying bombs. Such a build up clearly could not be allowed to continue and it was decided that RAF Bomber Command should bomb the sites when the weather ruled out their bombing of Germany. The raids were also to be supplemented by the heavy bombers from US Eighth Air Force.

As early as 5 December British fighter-bombers, reinforced by others from the US Ninth Air Force, actually bombed the ramps and other facilities. Due to disappointing results (and the heavy casualties suffered) when attempting to attack such small, heavily defended targets, it was decided to use medium and heavy bombers and during December 1,700 tons of bombs were delivered by 1,300 aircraft, half of which were Flying Fortresses, on 24 separate sites. These also proved far from conclusive and until mid-January sites were still being completed faster than they could be destroyed. In all 154 aircraft were lost on these operations, although, by the end of May 1944, 82 of the 96 'ski sites' were believed to have been neutralized. The need to prevent London from being subjected to showers of so-called flying bombs was seen in the additional 25,150 bombing sorties made between December 1943 and June 1944, during which 36,200 tons of bombs were dropped, a greater effort than that expended on any single enemy target up to that time in the war.[14] In total, the allies lost an amazing 443 aircraft and 2,924 airmen on the Crossbow counter-offensive operations against the V weapon sites.[15]

The Germans responded by ostentatiously filling in the bomb craters while at the same time secretly constructing much simpler types of ramp, which were carefully camouflaged or built in woods. These modified sites were largely ignored and their threat underestimated, although only 11 of the 104 original sites escaped the allied bombing. Attempts were also made by the Germans to simplify the missiles' supply chain by storing them in vast bombproof depots, in caves and in a disused railway tunnel. Although British intelligence was slow to appreciate the threat of flying bombs, their bombing of Peenemunde, followed by other raids on their launch sites and factories, undoubtedly slowed their production. Bomber Command's bombing of Kassel on 22/23 October 1943 was particularly serious. On 3 November, ten days after the raid, Erhard Milch received a particularly gloomy report: 'Because Kassel has been lost [nearby] Rothwesten is to all intents and purposes lost as well. The men live in Kassel and their homes and transport are wrecked. In consequence, the final trials of the weapons' power unit, control gear, diving mechanism, compass and air log were held up.'[16] There was a serious shortage of labour at such facilities, for it was felt that co-opted workers could not be used for security reasons.

All this led to the initial strike scheduled for 15 December 1943 not taking place. At the same time it was planned to strike at London with conventional bombers and a long-range gun, none of which took place. Although in the circumstances the date of 15 December might have been wildly optimistic, others came and went, including that of Hitler's birthday on 20 April 1944, all of four months later. It was, in fact, not until 20 May that personnel were moved up to the modified launch sites to conduct the firing. By now the chief concern of Colonel Wachtel, who was responsible for the launching arrangements, was whether 'the enemy would by then be across the Channel'.[17] His answer came at 1.36 am on the morning of Tuesday 6 June when the allied forces succeeded in landing at Normandy. For Wachtel it was now or never and the first salvo of flying bombs was scheduled for 11.40 pm on 12 June, to be followed by a second an hour later. Independent fire was then to be maintained by all sites until 4.45 pm.

In the event, this was still not possible, largely due to allied interdiction raids on the French railways, which in some cases prevented the catapults from arriving together with the permanganate of potash needed to produce the explosive mixture for their warheads. The date was rescheduled for the early morning of 13 June, although the supporting arrangements had also been seriously affected: the German artillery set to fire across the Channel could only manage thirty rounds, while the Heinkel 111s due to bomb London at the same time were destroyed by a chance allied raid on their airfield. After a last-minute postponement of an hour, the massive opening salvo was reduced to a desperate instruction for all commanders to open independent harassing fire at 3.30 am. In the event, just 10 doodlebugs were launched, of which 5 crashed almost at once, another landed in the sea, and 4 crossed over to Britain. Of these, the first landed close to Gravesend, the second in a potato field at Northfleet, the third near a farm in Cuckfield, Sussex, and the last exploded on a railway bridge at Bethnal Green, where six people were killed and thirty injured.

The next day a triumphant Lord Cherwell met Dr R V Jones with the words 'The mountain hath groaned and brought forth a mouse'. Jones responded by asking him not to laugh off the flying bomb campaign at this stage. Sure enough, following the inauspicious beginning, operations at the launching sites were suspended until 15 June to iron out the snags, and by noon the next day 244 flying bombs had been launched. 'Of these 45 crashed, wrecking 9 launch sites, ... one hundred and forty four crossed the English coast. Seventy-one fell in south eastern England and seventy-three reached London. Thirty-three flying bombs were shot down by fighters or AA fire.'[18]

Within 8 days the 1,000th flying bomb was launched, but with the allies ashore and their Normandy bridgehead rapidly building up, the German propaganda minister, Joseph Goebels, was anxious not to raise undue hopes about his country's capacity to win the war – although Goering's deputy in the Luftwaffe, Erhard Milch, was much more sure of the weapon's dire influence on Londoners. 'A weapon against which the public sees there is no real defence, has such catastrophic moral effects that by itself regardless of what the weapon is – it must have immense consequences.'[19]

Since December 1943 when he had learned about the existence of 'air mines with wings', Herbert Morrison, Minister of Home Security with responsibility for London's Civil Defence, took the problem very seriously indeed. He concluded that it was better to keep reckoning on relatively large warheads but, whatever the warheads' size, he believed that 100,000 new individual shelters would be needed. In addition to the Andersons (for people with gardens) there should be other shelters (named after him) located inside houses, in the form of crush-proof tables under which two adults and two children could crouch. These would be so strong that if the house roof collapsed those sheltering would not be killed and the survivors could subsequently be 'dug out'. His proposals were agreed and the steel was reassigned after being intended for two new battleships, the *Lion* and *Temeraire*, on which work had already been suspended, but which were now cancelled.[20]

Morrison also felt the need to consider whether schoolchildren and vulnerable people should be evacuated from the city. The decision to go ahead was made more difficult because estimates of the likely weight of the bombardment not only varied widely, but were periodically revised. By March 1944, for instance, the Air Ministry, which had taken over the investigation of jet-propelled or gliding bombs, calculated that the tonnage expected to fall on Greater London during the first fifteen days of flying bomb attacks would be in the order of five attacks in the earlier Blitz, but as the RAF and USAF bombers concentrated on the small number of sites that they believed would be still operational, totals would drop.[21] The reality was that the allied bombers would continue to experience major difficulties in hitting the sites, especially the modified ones, and any such calculations could never be more than 'instructed guesses'.

Amid the forecasters, the government's chief scientist, Lord Cherwell, took a lone position by believing that the bombs' payload would be under a ton and that less than a third of those launched would complete their journey, resulting in death rates averaging just one per bomb. In the event, Cherwell was surprisingly accurate, but the flying bomb bombardment was quite different from the earlier Blitz in that there was no pattern of strikes to follow, and that during such random attacks the many warnings coming from across the face of London brought much increased concern, if not confusion, for the defenders.

Nonetheless, by 17 July 1944 some 170,000 schoolchildren had been evacuated from 'doodlebug alley' in the southern districts of London like Beckenham, and by the middle of August 'approximately 1,450,000 people had left to escape the flying bombs – a much greater number than those who left to escape the Blitz'.[22] With so many families dislocated, productivity in the British capital fell partly due to the absenteeism when workers were taking shelter or others suffering from 'a loss of sleep and anxiety'.

During the second and third weeks the flying bombs were launched at a rate of about 100 a day and fighters were already bringing down about 30 per cent. The greatest number of bombs crossed the coast at Dungeness and planes from fighter bases at Deanland, Ford, Holmsley, Middle Wallop, Brenzett,

West Malling and Newchurch rose to meet them. In the early stages the latter two gained the greatest successes, although the Spitfires at Deanland and the Mosquitos at Ford were to shoot down a combined total of 359 during the course of the campaign. At West Malling, 316 (City of Warsaw) Squadron, whose pilots including the Polish ace Szymanski, flew Mustangs. By the end of July they had destroyed over fifty flying bombs. At Newchurch the two squadrons of very fast Tempest aircraft of I5O Wing, under the inspired leadership of Wing Commander Roland Beaumont, did even better. By mid-July they were approaching their 500th success.

The pilots quickly learned the most effective techniques against their robotic enemies and, although in the first 6 weeks 18 fighters were badly damaged and 6 airmen killed, this was not repeated. This also applied to instances of early disorganization, which resulted in two Tempests being shot down by the anti-aircraft guns.

The static defences at this time accounted for some 8 to 10 per cent and more than half the bombs that crossed the coast were still reaching London:[23] in the first fortnight 1,600 people were killed and 4,500 seriously injured, with 200,000 houses damaged. Because the flying bombs' blasting power was superior compared with the earlier types, London suffered the same damage to property in two months compared with the nine months of the Blitz, but by now the house repair system had much improved and by the middle of July the daily repairs came to exceed the rate of damage.

What no one – Herbert Morrison, Lord Cherwell or the Prime Minister himself – could doubt was that with the war entering what was expected to be its final victorious stage, London deserved to be protected in the most effective way possible, for the 'flying bombs' could soon be joined by massed rockets and attacks from long-range guns. As in the previous war, the vast manpower and equipment involved were not the prime consideration: there were also the very costly aircraft attacks on their bombs' points of delivery, both on the classic 'ski launching sites' and the later modified ramps. The campaign could, of course, only be concluded successfully by occupying the launch areas along the French and Belgian coastline, from Normandy's Cotentin peninsula northwards. Given the traditional tenacity of German defenders this was likely to take time, and meanwhile the citizens of London were reliant on the successive defence lines of the air and ground defenders. Upon the radar's first warning, fighters set off to patrol 20 miles out from the English coast. Once they had spotted the incoming flying bombs, a second group were despatched to destroy them. The surviving doodlebugs then had to pass through a concentration of 400 heavy and 346 light ack-ack guns, accompanied by 216 searchlights, positioned south of London. Finally, they came upon a barrier of 480 barrage balloons positioned on a belt of high ground between Cobham in Kent and Limpsfield in Surrey.

Despite a warning from Winston Churchill about the V1's potency, General Pile, who commanded the ground defences, acknowledged later that in the first instance he did not consider the flying bombs would be a great challenge. They flew at a constant altitude, at a constant speed and on a straight and level course, seemingly presenting dream targets for his gunners. It was to his considerable surprise, therefore, that at the very best they succeeded in bringing down a mere 8 to 10 per cent of the targets they engaged, which was, of course, unsatisfactory, but he also quickly came to understand that, contrary to the earlier Blitzes, Londoners' reactions to the doodlebugs getting through had come to resemble the First World War attitude that 'now that the end of the war was fairly clearly in sight there was a great and increasing disinclination on the part of the civilians to getting killed'.[24] The guns' disappointing kill rates owed much to the fact that, although the V1s' route paths were predictable, they presented very small targets and flew at between 1,500 and 3,000ft, which was too low for the heavier AA guns. Their speed of between 370–400mph was only marginally slower than the latest piston–engined fighters, nor were they restricted by a lack of daylight or bad weather. They also proved less susceptible to damage than manned aircraft.

There were other factors as well. In the opening stages the guns were not best positioned, nor were they all fully up to the task. There was, too, a serious lack of fully automatic radar direction-finding equipment which could handle targets up to 60,000ft. At the end of June, General Pile appealed to Washington for more predictors, especially the American SCR 584 radars, and a shipment was sent directly[25] which were to prove so valuable that Pile believed that without them his guns would not have defeated the flying bomb.[26] Pile also replaced his mobile 3.75s with heavier ordnance, which had to be uprooted from their fixed emplacements all over Britain onto specially adapted platforms made from railway sleepers and rails bolted together, all set in heavy ballast.[27]

This was still not considered enough and on 13 July Sir Roderic Hill, commanding the Air Defences of Great Britain, had Pile move his guns forward into a new belt 5,000yd wide directly along the coast from St Margaret's Bay, Dover, to Cuckmere Haven near Beachy Head.[28] From there they could fire 10,000yd out to sea leaving the inland area for aircraft, except for the barrage balloons which remained close to London. This operation involved relocating 23,000 men, women and equipment, together with their guns, but it was nonetheless achieved in a week by drivers who covered approximately 2,750,000 miles: by 17 July all Pile's heavy guns were in position, followed by his light guns two days later.

Although on 27 June the allies captured Cherbourg at the tip of the Cotentin peninsula, the number of incoming V1s rose during July and August and from 27 June the guns were reputedly in action for 108 hours of the 120 over the next five days with their crews having 'to snatch forty winks whenever they could'.[29] Pile's move and re-equipping brought startling success, for during July and August their kill rate rose from about 9 per cent to 17 per cent, and then to some 50 per cent. The searchlights were instrumental in illuminating the missiles for the night fighters and by 5 September the barrage balloons had also claimed 231 flying bombs close to their London target.

In spite of the spectacular growth in the guns' successes, those of the fighters still exceeded them: of the 5,823 incidents reported between mid-June and early September 1944, the planes accounted for 1,772 missiles with the guns destroying 1,460. As in the earlier Battle of Britain, pilots from almost all the allied countries combined in the attacks on the V1s, including Britons, Canadians, Australians, New Zealanders, South Africans, Dutch, Belgians, Poles, Czechs, Norwegians, Free French, Americans and even one Swede. Of those who took part, two were one-legged pilots – one British, one French.[30] As before, the Polish pilots did exceptionally well, quickly accounting for 150 flying bombs. But most importantly, of all the 9,251 flying bombs plotted only 2,419 reached London.[31]

By 5 September the allied ground forces reached Antwerp, having cleared the French coastline opposite Britain from Calais to the River Seine, and on the 7th Herbert Morrison officially ended the evacuation of London. At a press conference on the same day, Duncan Sandys praised both the people of London for their courage and the Americans for their help through their dangerous sorties against the doodlebug sites, before going on to declare, 'Except, possibly, for a few last shots the battle of London is over'.[32] By any standard it was a rash statement, for the Germans not only adopted new methods of despatching their flying bombs but mounted fresh strikes on London – this time with rockets, a truly revolutionary weapon.

On 8 September Duncan Sandys' statement had scarcely been reported when the first two V2s fell on Chiswick and Epping, while from 16 September a number of V1s reappeared, after He 111 and Ju 88 aircraft had been adapted to carry a flying bomb under one of their wings. At a selected point 25 miles from the English coast its jet motor was ignited, and with its instruments already pre-set it accelerated away from its mother craft. In an attempt to avoid detection the planes' crews operated without radio or radar transmissions, using dead reckoning to determine their positions. On the morning of 16 September the 15 aircraft of Kamfgeschwader 53 succeeded in launching only 9 flying bombs between them, of which the navy shot down 2 into the sea, the fighters destroyed another 3, 2 dived prematurely into open countryside in Essex and just 2 landed on Woolwich and Barking.[33] Such launches continued until 14 January 1945 but they proved remarkably inaccurate, for the mother bombers, although only on the coastal radar screens for an average of seven minutes, tended to rush their release.

On 21 September General Pile decided to counter this new challenge from the east by making the gun belt in Kent and Sussex non-operational and extending his gun positions up to Harwich. This took an unexpectedly long time because of transport shortages caused by the priority demands given to 21st Army Group, and it was not until mid-October that the benefits began to be felt, with success rates rising from 60 to 80 per cent. On 24 December, in a sudden change of direction, thirty bombs were launched against Manchester and other northern towns, although by far the majority continued to be directed at London. By mid-January 1945 the air-launched attacks also ceased and, compared with the earlier V1 attacks, London came off very lightly. Out of a total of 495 doodlebugs that crossed the east coast and came within gun range, 320 were shot down, aided by Pile's searchlights that illuminated 14 of the 42 intercepted by night fighters. The extent of the defenders' success can be seen in the fact that only thirteen reached London.

The doodlebugs final throw came between 4 and 29 March 1945 when, after the Germans succeeded in extending their range, they were launched from Holland, but by now the balance of success lay firmly with the defenders. Of the 125 flying bombs approaching the English coast, 87 were shot down by ack-ack guns and 4 by fighters, leaving just 15 to reach London.[34]

Although the allies undoubtedly won their contest against the pilotless planes, their adoption was a brilliant move on the part of the Germans. With no strategic bombers and a crippling shortage of experienced pilots, during the final stages of the war the Luftwaffe gained a fresh opportunity to bomb London and south-east England at remarkably little cost in either manpower or resources. In fact, the cost of mass-producing each missile was put at an amazing £125.[35] This was, of course, quite apart from the weapon's relatively modest technical development, its launching sites and storage facilities, and the regiment devoted to its launching. The respective costs on both sides for the flying bomb offensive have been estimated in the order of £70 million for Britain and £14 million for Germany.[36]

For the allies, London as the exemplar of the free world had to be protected, almost regardless of cost. A total of 177,050 men and 77,000 women were committed to its ground defences against the V1s, as well as the RAF squadrons engaged on both day and night operations. Extensive use was also made of the Allied Expeditionary Air Force and the US Eighth Air Force to attack the flying bomb sites, during which they suffered high losses in both men and machines. In such a situation direct comparisons are near impossible but the casualties suffered by Colonel Wachtel's launching regiment were put at just 185, compared with over 6,000 civilians and 2,000 servicemen killed and 8,000 civilians and 1,500 servicemen seriously injured by the flying bombs in London and elsewhere.[37]

Following the V1s' defeat there has been an understandable tendency to forget the extent of their threat. Roy Irons, for instance, in his book on Hitler's terror weapons[38] points out that, although the allies had considered them as an adjunct to air power, they rejected them because they were committed to the use of large manned bombers for strategic purposes. The Luftwaffe was not so equipped and hence the V1s gave them a genuine option for attacking London: if it had not been for the damage to their production facilities and launch sites the capital could have been bombarded at a rate of at least 60,000 missiles a year.[39] This would have meant more than 160 bombs a day, and even with the anticipated successes gained by London's defenders swathes of the capital would soon have been reduced to rubble.

From the end of November 1944 to March 1945 they were also used against Antwerp and Liège when despite the allies' massive air superiority, they succeeded in much restricting the volume of supplies, particularly ammunition, passing through Antwerp for delivery to the invading armies. General Eisenhower had such regard for them he considered that had they come into operation sooner and made the Portsmouth/Southampton area one of their principal targets, Overlord might well have been written off.[40] He reached such conclusions while the V1 still had serious shortcomings in both reliability and accuracy: had their accuracy been greater the threat to Antwerp or Portsmouth/Southampton could have been far more serious, although in the case of London the weapon's inaccuracy was less of a disadvantage, for the random and spread nature of the attacks increased their terror and tested the defences to the limit.

Coming into service during the last year of the war, the V1s are commonly seen as a last-ditch weapon, but the Americans twice considered them for their offensive use first against Germany during 1918, and then in their thousands against Japan as a viable alternative to the conventional or atomic bombing of that country. Although by the closing stages of the Second World War the weight and potency of their attacks was enfeebled by bombing and a lavish defence system, they were, however, not finally defeated until the occupation of the launch sites along the French, Belgian and finally the Dutch coasts.

Their destructive powers may have been reduced but, most significantly, they were also launched against a great city, however war torn, whose people, although undoubtedly tired and angry at having to face a fresh bombardment, were still far from willing to give way to terror or despair. Yet had they only been developed six months earlier and given genuine guidance systems, swarms of Hitler's cut-price but potent missiles could conceivably have swamped London's defences prior to the arrival of the even more terrifying weapon – Hitler's V2 rockets.

Chapter 11

London and the V2s

It is a strange way of living, when quite feasibly one may be dead next minute, next hour, or to-morrow with no warning and no escape ... a slaying that is purely a matter of luck.

C Jory, Fleet Street journalist[1]

At the end of the First World War *The Times* rightly concluded that the bomb loads carried by both Zeppelins and aeroplanes had been insufficient to do London great harm and that in fact 'it was let off very lightly indeed'.[2]

It might have been different had there been other means of delivery, and while science-fiction writers Jules Verne and H G Wells had certainly considered the possibility of rockets travelling long distances, even crossing to other planets, no serious rocket development had occurred during the First World War. In fact, relatively small rockets had already been utilized as a weapon of war in the nineteenth century when the British rocket inventor Sir William Congreve demonstrated their advantages over conventional artillery due to their recoilessness, lightness, portability and economy.[3] During the Napoleonic War they were used in a British attack on Copenhagen in 1807, when the greater part of the city 'was burned to the ground, set aflame by a mass expenditure of 25,000 rockets'.[4] However, during the First World War in terms of warhead weight, accuracy, range and control, artillery had developed beyond the capability of any known rocket and interest in rocketry therefore lapsed.

It remained low, in spite of inter-war pioneers like the Russian schoolmaster/ cosmologist Konstantine Tsiolkovsky (whose genius was belatedly recognized in the 1930s) and the American physicist Robert Hutchings Goddard, who in 1926 was the first to launch a rocket propelled by a liquid fuel (using a mixture of liquid oxygen and gasoline). Both fought a losing battle against sceptical War Departments and less-inspired colleagues, and events might have continued in this way if Germany had not possessed an especial reason to favour them. The 1919 Treaty of Versailles imposed on Germany not only limited its army to 100,000 men, but also banned heavy artillery, chemical weapons, tanks and aircraft; there were, however, no restrictions on rockets. The writings of Germany's own astronautic pioneer, Professor Hermann Oberth, a mathematics and physics teacher from Transylvania, with his 1923 treatise *Die Rakete zu den Planeten Raum* (*The Rocket in Inter-planetary Space*), had led to the founding of a German rocket society (the *Verein fur Raumschiffahrt* or Association for Space Travel), commonly known as the VIR, whose scientists included the young Wernher von Braun.

During the Depression years this met with both major developmental problems and a falling membership, which led in turn to the German Army Ordnance Board adopting a rocket programme of its own. On 17 December 1933 their Army Weapons Department appointed a 35-year-old captain and enthusiast in rocket technology, Walter Dornberger, to head a research unit into rockets for military use rather than for inter-planetary travel. He was to develop a liquid-fuel rocket with a greater range than any conventional artillery piece which, by using a multi-axis gyroscope control system invented in 1929, would have a greater likelihood of reaching its proposed target than more vulnerable aircraft. This work was to be carried out in secret on the Kummers-dorf artillery range some 17 miles from Berlin where Dornberger's laboratory was given the neutral title 'Experimental Station West'.

Dornberger was quick to recruit two outstanding helpers, the 28-year-old Wernher von Braun from VIR and Walter Riedel, an engineer who had already worked on rocket-powered cars. The tall, fair-haired von Braun was both shrewd and personable and apparently possessed astounding theoretical knowledge.[5] Once he grasped a problem he was always intent on laying bare the difficulties and he not only became the outstanding member of Dornberger's team but, following the Second World War, the Director of the American NASA's first Space Flight Centre. The versatile Riedel was the project's designer and test engineer who apparently acted as the steadying hand to von Braun's 'bubbling stream of ideas'.[6]

As technical manager, von Braun's first assignment was to build a 650lb thrust rocket motor (burning liquid oxygen, ethyl alcohol and water). Despite major teething troubles, by 1935 he succeeded in propelling rockets to a height of 15 miles,[7] but by now it was no longer acceptable to launch such unreliable devices from Kummersdorf, where there was a real risk of them falling on other European countries. Von Braun believed he had found the solution when, during a visit to his home, his mother reminded him of his father's duck shooting on the remote island of Usedom off the Baltic coast with its fishing village of Peenemunde consisting of 96 houses and 447 inhabitants. From here, rocket flights could be aimed out to sea. Dornberger proved enthusiastic and the island was purchased by the German Air Ministry as a joint research centre with the army. Substantial funds were then allocated for establishing a rocket-building facility which was destined to become not only the most advanced but largest of its type in the world, with some 10,000 employees.[8]

By May 1937 Dornberger's 100-strong scientific team had moved to Peenemunde and, under von Braun's impulsion, by the autumn of that year they had launched experimental A5 rockets which succeeded in rising to a height of 5 miles and reaching the speed of sound. By the following year, with Hitler's incorporation of Austria into the Reich, his humbling of Britain and France at Munich and seizure of Czechoslovakia, it was clear that war could not be long avoided. However much the Peenemunde scientists might be absorbed in their particular technological problems, their progress was such that their rockets already represented a potential weapon against European targets, including London. Despite the cost of over ½ million Reichmarks the facility continued to enjoy the valuable support of von Brauchitsch, the Army Commander in Chief, and there was even talk of December 1941 as a possible date for the large-scale manufacture of a rocket that could conceivably hit London and reduce it to rubble by constant bombardment.

Despite successful experimental launches, the programme's future depended on its A4 rocket which, following unsuccessful attempts to take off at an angle, was to be launched vertically 'after which it would gradually tilt at an angle of 49 degrees as it climbed upwards'.[9] At a given point its fuel was scheduled to be cut off following which it was hoped it would descend onto its intended target area. After a disastrous test on 18 March 1942, which compelled all its components to be retested, a fifth launch was scheduled for 3 October. Walter Dornberger described his feelings and those of his senior operatives watching events on a state of the art television screen, 'We knew only one thing, that we must not fail that day ... If today's test failed I should have to propose the transfer of all our armament potential to aircraft or tank construction'.[10] In the event the launch proved faultless and the 5½-ton missile, which was capable of carrying a 1-ton warhead, travelled 120 miles before it came down just 2½ miles wide of its aiming point. Afterwards Dornberger held a modest celebration party at which he told his gathered scientists, 'We have invaded space with our rocket and for the first time – mark this well – have used space as a bridge between two points on the earth; we have proved rocket propulsion for space travel'. He then reminded them of their essential responsibility: 'So long as war lasts, our most urgent task can only be the rapid perfection of the rocket as a weapon.'[11]

The work of Dornberger, von Braun, Dr Theil and others offered Hitler a new attacking option against which, in contrast to the First World War or during the earlier blitz of London by his aircraft, the capital would have no defence. What had yet to be decided was the degree of priority for such a sophisticated (and expensive) weapon of random destruction, with its 20,000 individual components, when the land war was already turning against Germany both on the Eastern Front and in North Africa and when the allied strategic bombing of Germany's own heartland was about to gather pace.

Concentrated rocket attacks on Britain seemed attainable when on 22 December 1942 Hitler signed the order for mass-production in the region of 5,000, although he still failed to give it his special priority. Even so, Albert Speer, the Munitions Minister, sent one of his most energetic officials, Gerhard Degenkolb (the German Beaverbrook) to work with Dornberger on mass-producing them. The cosy, if hardworking, days at Peenemunde were about to end; Dornberger complained of Degenkolb being relatively unaware of the technical problems and 'acting like a burly, unendingly foul-mouthed and dreaded slave driver'.[12]

Degenkolb aimed to produce 300 A4s monthly by December 1943 at three factories, Peenemunde, Friedrichshafen and Wiener Neustadt, while Dornberger's lesser target was for a total of 5,150 rockets by September 1944, when the war might already be over. Whatever their differences, both men were seriously handicapped by Hitler not granting the A4 his special priority. He gave his reasons to von Speer, apparently telling him 'I have dreamed that the rocket will never be operational against England. I can rely on my inspirations. It is therefore pointless to give more support to the project'.[13] The outrage of a scientist like Dornberger at Hitler's reliance on a mixture of intuition and superstition was justifiably predictable.

The other main cause of Dornberger's problems was the rival development by the Luftwaffe of an unmanned air torpedo designed to carry a similar warhead. Far less challenging technologically, it was, of course, notably cheaper. Even when the amazingly low estimate of £125 for each missile was increased tenfold by including its launching costs, the £1,250 still compared most favourably with the estimated cost of some £12,000 for each rocket. There were, of course, considerations beyond purely financial ones, including the inability of the British defences to stop the rocket attacks and the power to fire them from mobile launching bases instead of the V1s' highly visible 'ski sites', or from their smaller catapult installations.

An attempt was made to compare the systems on 26 May 1943 when a joint demonstration was arranged before von Speer and senior military figures. In the course of two launchings, the rockets took off perfectly (although the second only travelled 17 miles because of an engine cut out), whereas both flying bombs crashed very shortly after take off. Nonetheless, it was recommended that both types should be given top priority and put forward for mass-production, for by using them in tandem it was thought that London's defences could be brought to breaking point. However encouraging this might have been for the rocket designers, Hitler had yet to give his full approval, which came on 7 July following a colour film presentation accompanied by a brilliant commentary by von Braun on the rockets' historic ascent.

Hitler was much impressed and informed the rocket designers that he regretted he had not believed in their success earlier, even telling Dornberger that if Germany had possessed such rockets in 1939 'we should never have had this war'. He finally gave the A4s his top priority by putting them on an equal rating with tank production. He believed rocket attacks on London could bring about a turning point in the war. So much depended, of course, on how quickly they could be manufactured and launched and in what quantity. Whatever the difficulties, the British capital and the south-east of the country seemed likely to face unparalleled assaults.

It was inconceivable that the British would not make a counter-response, and a decision about their first measures was taken during a meeting of the Cabinet's Defence Committee on 29 June 1943, with Winston Churchill as chairman. It was made in the teeth of opposition from Lord Cherwell, the government's chief scientist, who, completely unaware of the advances in liquid-fuel technology, believed that 40 miles was the maximum range for a single-stage rocket and that a new type of fuel to propel it further was scientifically out of the question. Notwithstanding this, the committee decided that on balance a rocket threat had to be acknowledged and, as Peenemunde was the only location suspected of rocket activity, this should be bombed by the heaviest possible night attack.

The RAF decided to bide their time and wait for the longer nights when their bombers (Lancasters and Halifaxes) could not only reach Peenemunde but return under cover of darkness, and so it was more than six weeks later when the raid was finally mounted on 19 August 1943. The mission, codenamed Hydra, which included a diversionary raid on Berlin to occupy the German fighters, was made by no less than 596 4-engined aircraft split into 3 waves that dropped 1,600 tons of high explosive and 250 tons of incendiary bombs. Despite the diversion the cost was high – forty-four aircraft were lost, against thirty-nine defending fighters – but by the time the last group departed the crews were convinced they had destroyed the installation,[14] and an offer made by the US Eighth Air Force to finish the base off in daylight was refused. In fact, despite the destruction and fire, the damage to the main installations, including the wind tunnel and the Great Hall where the rockets were assembled, was not that serious. The greatest loss was the 550 people working on the campus who were killed, most of whom were foreign prisoners.

The Germans accentuated the damage by placing charred beams over buildings that remained intact. Dornberger estimated that the raid delayed the research and production work at Peenemunde by 4 to 6 weeks, although British scientist R V Jones, writing after the war, was sure that it was at least 2 months – a very significant setback to attacks on London or even the seaports from where the allied invasion of Europe were due to assemble.

The raid had other important, if unexpected, effects. In particular it gave Heinrich Himmler the opportunity to become involved with the A4 rocket project, and he proposed safeguarding the programme by moving production work from Peenemunde to an underground site which would be invulnerable to future raids. They could use labour taken from his concentration camps to help further maintain its security. It was also agreed that the main testing range for the rockets should be transferred from Usedom to the one-time SS training ground at Blizag, about 100 miles south of Warsaw, from where missiles could be directed towards the Pripet Marshes near the River Bug some 20 miles away. Following the bombing of Peenemunde, the RAF also badly damaged a factory at Friedrichshafen on Lake Constance, which was preparing to produce 300 A4s a month, while an attack by US Ninth Air Force on a factory at Wiener Neustadt, producing rocket parts, also inflicted massive damage.

These attacks led to the work on rockets being transferred to less-vulnerable installations in north Germany. Nordhausen, in the Harz mountains, was chosen by Degenkolb as the site for the main underground factory, since there were tunnels and galleries previously used for the storage of oil. Here the works were built from scratch under the supervision of Himmler's representative SS Grupenfuhrer Hans Kammler. Work proceeded rapidly and by November 1943 the number of rockets being assembled exceeded those at Peenemunde. For the slave labour involved, the costs were high and conditions in the dank tunnels were extremely adverse, particularly in the initial stages when facilities were rudimentary. Under the brutal driving of their SS overseers many operatives, after coming from concentration camps in an exhausted state, were worked to death. 'After twelve hours of hard labour a further six and a half hours had to be spent on roll calls, getting to work, and standing in queues for food as well as finding a place to sleep, barely 5½ hours were left for rest.'[15] There were piles of prisoners' corpses next to the sick room every day.

After a visit from von Speer, who concluded that the extremely high death rates slowed production, conditions improved. Better food and sanitary conditions were introduced together with brick buildings for the hospital, kitchens and laundry facilities – there was even a cinema, canteen and sports hall.[16] The supervision continued to be extremely harsh, however, and, despite the earlier use of slave labour at Peenemunde, there would never be the same general air of scientific adventurism there. When, on 25 January 1944, von Braun visited the factory following many of Speer's improvements, he still noted the silent Polish workers forbidden to look him in the face and, after walking round all the corridors, he left despondent. By February 1945 the numbers working there totalled 42,074.[17]

The relationships between the scientists and those responsible for the production and pre-launch arrangements were also far from good. Apart from the clashes between Degenkolb and Dornberger, Kammler described von Braun as 'too young, too childish, too supercilious and too arrogant' for his job.[18] Even so, they had to work together.

Whatever the human costs, the streamlined production facilities built at Nordhausen were capable of producing 1,800 missiles a month, although in practice the limited amount of liquid oxygen that German industry could supply reduced the actual production quota to 900 a month (the same as that set by Degenkolb at Peenemunde). At this rate London was still about to receive thirty rockets each day, more than the British authorities thought the population could withstand.

In reality, before the missiles could be released, launching batteries had to be established and their personnel trained, and appropriate storage facilities constructed for rockets that, for the most part, had to travel by land from Nordhausen across Germany and France to the Channel coast, all under conditions of allied air superiority. This brought further understandable delays. However, two rocket batteries were formed in October and November 1943 and moved for preliminary training to the firing ranges at Blizna, although the launch sites in northern France were not expected to be ready until the end of June or early July 1944. There were further delays when, following attacks by allied bombers on bunkers at St Omer near Calais and Wizernes near Bologne, an alternative storage facility had to be readied in caves near Mery-sur-Oise.

These difficulties were paralleled by serious problems with the rockets themselves during launch tests without live warheads, which did not manifest themselves until the battery training at Blizna[19] since Hitler had refused to sanction a pilot production facility. Of the 57 rockets launched, only 26 left the ground and only 4 of these landed within the target area. The engines of some stopped less than 100ft above the launch pad, others exploded when they reached altitudes of 3,000–6,000ft and some that travelled the full range exploded a few thousand feet above the target. At first sabotage was suspected but this was discounted. Dornberger and von Braun, crouching in slit trenches first on the range at Blizna and then, after the Russian advances, on others further west at Heidelager and Heidekraut, charted the rockets' erratic behaviour while flying over their heads. It was not until the summer of 1944 that the problems were finally solved. Tests then followed on the warheads whose load was decided at 1,650lb of amatol explosive scheduled to explode either at 10ft above the ground or on contact with it. All this meant that the earliest possible date for a sustained bombardment of London could not be before early September 1944. As a result, the Luftwaffe, with its flying bombs, succeeded in launching first, upon which Hitler decided to increase flying bomb production at the expense of the rockets and to transfer work at a second underground factory scheduled for rocket production to producing tanks.

Continuing work by Dornberger and his team on perfecting the A4 rocket, which had involved no less than 65,000 engineering modifications since 1942, was forcibly interrupted when on 15 March 1944 he was called to Berchtesgaden to discover von Braun, Klaus Reidel and Helmut Grottrup had been arrested by Himmler on charges of sabotage. They had been overheard talking at a party about the future use of rockets in space and were accused of not giving their full attention to their use as weapons. Dornberger was taken to task for his own lack of loyalty but he succeeded in persuading Speer to remind Hitler that his scientists were irreplaceable and that without their skills the rocket programme would certainly collapse. The crisis might well have arisen because of an earlier incident when Himmler offered his personal support for the rocket programme only to be told by von Braun that his offer was 'akin to watering a delicate flower with a fire hose of manure'.[20]

Although the scientists were released to continue their work, other problems that would affect them and the rockets' launch timings were, in fact, multiplying. The allied invasion of Normandy on 6 June 1944 stopped all work on the missiles' storage and launching sites in France, and a fortnight later an attempt to assassinate Hitler by a group of disaffected high-ranking officers brought other significant results. With Himmler remaining faithful and rounding up the conspirators, he at last succeeded in gaining control of the A4 rocket programme and, as a result, appointed Hans Kammler as its Commissioner General. Dornberger found himself reduced to being a senior (and heartily despised) member of Kammler's staff. On 29 August Kammler received orders from Hitler to commence the bombardment of London as soon as possible. After establishing his headquarters at Brussels he ordered the firing batteries (made up of 5,306 soldiers and 1,592 vehicles) to take up their positions in Belgium and be ready to commence firing on 5 September.

Meanwhile on the allied side, following the RAF raid on Peenemunde, further initiatives had been undertaken to counter the V weapons. On 8 November 1943 an inquiry was held in the British Cabinet Office into gaining further evidence about their existence and development, during which Wing Commander Kendall of the Air Intelligence Photographic Branch reported on the existence of concrete ramps in the Pas de Calais area pointing towards London, which it was thought were for launching flying bombs rather than rockets. This more pressing menace caused the rocket threat codename 'Bodyline', which had rockets chiefly in mind, to be downgraded and replaced by 'Crossbow', to be used principally in connection with the flying bombs. A growing belief that the first attack on London would come from flying bombs was apparently confirmed when on 2 December 1943 an aerial photograph of Peenemunde showed a pilotless aircraft standing on a ramp identical to those at the Pas de Calais. The priority accorded to flying bombs was confirmed at a meeting of the Civil Defence Committee on 31 December 1943, although its report acknowledged that 'the possibility of long distance rockets being utilised, probably at a rather late stage, should certainly not be ignored'.[21] With greater knowledge becoming available about the different V weapons, their codenames were changed to 'Diver' for the pilotless aircraft and 'Big Ben' for the rocket.

Understandably, by far the greatest attention at this time was directed towards the allied invasion of Europe, although the forecasts relating to the V weapons proved correct when a week after the Normandy landings the flying bombs commenced their attacks on London. Despite this, Londoner Herbert Morrison, then Minister for Home Security, continued to show a deep concern about the second V weapon, which he believed, among other things, 'could put the tubes out of action for months'. On 27 June he spelt out what he saw as the much-increased menace to his beloved city and its people if the flying bomb attacks were joined by rockets as well: 'I am apprehensive of what might happen if the strain continues, and, in addition to flying bombs, long range missiles are used against the metropolis. I have a high degree of faith in the Londoner and will do everything to hold up their courage and spirit, but there is a limit and the limit will come.'[22]

The difficulty still facing Herbert Morrison and others concerning the rockets was the lack of information regarding their size and performance – some estimates pictured them as 60-ton monsters with 10-ton warheads. Although the Polish resistance sent reports about rockets at Blizna that appeared to be radar controlled and used concentrated hydrogen peroxide, more accurate information did not become available until a test rocket fell on Swedish soil and information about it was relayed to London. This enabled Dr R V Jones to give an interim report on 18 July 1944 to a Crossbow Committee chaired by Winston Churchill. Concerning numbers, Jones said he believed that 150 experimental rockets had been manufactured, together with some 1,000 production models. At this Churchill reacted violently: he considered the use of poison gas on Germany and proposed the bombing of nine major hydrogen peroxide plants, as well as developing means of jamming what was believed to be their radio control system. Neither initiative could ensure the expected attacks would be checked, and on 31 July the Joint Intelligence Sub Committee dealing with rockets pointed out that the rocket launching sites were very small and of simple design, thereby offering virtually no chance of being bombed. Such evidence led the authorities to question why the rockets had not yet been fired. The favoured opinion was that the Germans were waiting until they could launch them at a greater intensity, with August felt to be the most likely month for an assault that was by now confidently expected. By 26 August Dr Jones had finally come close to an accurate estimate of the size and scale of the A4 rocket, which he put at 10 to 12 tons with a warhead of 1 to 2 tons. He believed that about 2,000 were probably in stock, with a monthly production of some 500 and the intended monthly rate of launch likely to be about 800.

While the rejection of the imagined 60-ton monsters brought relief, such a relatively modest bombardment delivering some 800 tons of high explosive a month – less than during the early Blitz or from the flying bombs – raised questions from Lord Cherwell and others about why the Germans would go to so much expense and trouble to produce such a relatively modest return. The highly gifted and imaginative scientist R V Jones concluded that developing the rockets went beyond economic considerations 'with such a thing as this rocket we are forced to enter a fantasy where romance has replaced economy – a missile which traces out a flaming ascent to heights hitherto beyond the reach of man and hurls itself 200 miles across the stratosphere at unparalleled speed to descend – with luck – on a defenceless target'.[23]

Hitler's support for them came, of course, from his belief in their qualities of terror and the ability to swamp London with large numbers of them. Whatever their differences concerning the rocket, the British authorities were united in knowing that once launched there seemed no way of stopping it. Although the site of the rocket factory at Nordhausen had been discovered on 31 August 1944 it was considered virtually impregnable, and since the rockets needed small launching sites only, their storage complexes (which could equally be used for V1s) remained genuine targets for bombing. No one could accuse the Allied Air Forces of not trying, for during the 12½ months after the first bombing of Peenemunde no less than 118,000 tons of bombs were dropped on the V weapon sites.

After such intensive bombing and the Normandy breakout that enabled the allied ground forces to race across France and Belgium towards the German border, it was hard to believe that a fresh bombardment of London by rockets would actually begin. On 5 September 1944 Herbert Morrison's Rocket Consequences Committee, a body that previously had been notably alarmist, wrote that, 'The enemy is unlikely to be able to launch rockets or flying bombs across London on any appreciable scale after the allied armies have crossed the Franco-Belgian frontier'.[24] The next day the Vice Chiefs of Staff went further in their stated belief 'that the rocket attacks on London need no longer be expected'. It was left to Air Marshal Sir Roderic Hill to point out to them that western Holland was well within rocket range of Britain and still in Nazi hands. Even so, the euphoric mood was not to be denied: all the daily papers believed that a V2 offensive was now remote and on 7 September Duncan Sandys held a massive press conference when he asserted that the Battle of London was materially over.

* * *

Following the bewildering twists already seen in the course of the war, together with the undoubted staunchness of German resolve, such an opinion was rash. With SS General Hans Kammler responsible for launching the rocket offensive there was every likelihood it would still take place. Although the time lost in development meant that launching sites in France and Belgium were already in allied hands, as Sir Roderic Hill had observed, Holland and Walcheren Island were not – in any case, Dornberger had always believed that launching would be best accomplished by mobile regiments operating from constantly changing sites. Such units consisted of a small convoy of vehicles, made up of staff cars, tankers carrying fuel and three ingenious 'Meillerwagen', which acted as both rocket transporters and firing frames with each including a gantry and servicing structure. Upon reaching the selected launching site each Meillerwagen (with a rocket in its firing frame) was then tilted to the vertical to form a structure over 40ft high upon which the launch crew set the rocket's gyroscope (near its nose), filled its fuel tanks and checked the electrical current to it before declaring it ready for ignition and take-off. This process lasted approximately an hour. Following the launch, the Meillerwagen could be returned to the horizontal and loaded with another rocket for further use.

On the day of Duncan Sandys' press conference Kammler had 12 launching units at his disposal and on that very day 3 rockets were fired at Paris, 2 of which malfunctioned. At 6.38 am on the next morning, Friday 8 September 1944, the order was given to ignite two rockets aimed at London, which were scheduled, after a flight lasting five minutes and twenty seconds, to land at a point 1,000yd east of Waterloo Bridge. The first fell on Chiswick, on a road through a housing estate, creating a hole 20ft deep and killing 3 people, injuring 10 and slightly wounding a further 10. Just sixteen seconds later the second fell on some wooden huts at Epping, 20 miles away, causing no injuries.

Thus commenced a new and unexpected bombardment of London, although coming so late in the war when France and Belgium were already in allied hands, only Hitler believed it could genuinely tilt things back in Germany's favour. For Londoners under attack a new noise was added to the V1's rough, uneven pulses, followed by a terrifying silence as it plunged down, namely a distinctive double bang, caused by the sound of impact when the rocket hit the ground, followed by its sonic boom when re-entering the atmosphere.

With the relatively few early strikes (only six rockets were despatched between 16 and 19 September) the British authorities' first reaction was to deny them, and to instruct newspaper editors that to prevent the Germans from gaining any knowledge of their strikes they also should ignore them. At the same time a signal was sent to Field Marshal Montgomery at 21 Army Group asking him how quickly he could occupy the coastal area containing Antwerp-Utrecht-Rotterdam and thus end the threat. With the possibility that he could move rapidly, the Cabinet decided to maintain their silence on the rockets until the 24 September. As a consequence, Montgomery mounted his Operation 'Market Garden' at the shortest notice, using airborne forces with which he hoped to establish a bridgehead over the Rhine at Arnhem and, after over-running the area from where the rockets were being launched, move into Germany itself. 'Market Garden' was launched on 17 September but by the 25th it was clear that Montgomery's gamble had failed, and the Chiefs of Staff formally reported to the Cabinet upon the rocket attacks.

Later that day the Cabinet decided to continue its policy of silence and asked the American Chiefs of Staff to do their best to prevent references to the explosions appearing in the American press. This led to a remarkable period in which a few Londoners actually knew about the rockets, others guessed at the truth, while the majority were not aware that the rockets had arrived. All kinds of rumours circulated: the explosions were attributed to crashing German bombers, exploding gas mains and demolitions of buildings damaged in previous raids. It proved a dangerous policy, for with people fearful of other unknown German weapons, such as novel forms of poison gas, morale tended to plummet and the official line invited derision from those on the staff of hospitals, for instance, with casualties arriving as a result of something that was not officially happening. Among London's citizens there was no shortage of in-jokes, such as the one about flying gas mains.

On 11 November Churchill formally announced the attacks by V2 rockets, while on the previous day the London newspapers had featured stories about the new weapon. For the Germans, the relatively light attacks so far reflected the major difficulties being experienced by Kammler and Dornberger in getting the rockets to their launcher vehicles and despatching them, and although Speer received a directive from Hitler on 23 September that the monthly production of A4s should rise to 900, this was by now quite impossible. The central works were able to meet this total, but shortages of alcohol and liquid oxygen following the overrunning of underground generating plants at Liège and Willengen severely restricted the number capable of being launched.

On 21 September Kammler, mirroring the V1 tactics, opened a secondary offensive against Antwerp and other European cities but this was seriously impaired by the large percentage of failed missiles, brought about by the allied bombing of the storage centres which forced rockets into temporary depots where their sensitive components were subject to the wind and weather. Dornberger solved this by ensuring that rockets were delivered from the production line to the firing units within three days, and while this largely cured the component breakdowns the shortages of alcohol and liquid oxygen could not be sorted out so easily. After largely abortive attacks against Norfolk and Ipswich, Kammler returned a battery to The Hague, thus bringing London back into range, and on 12 October Hitler ordered London to be the sole British target (although Antwerp should continue to be bombarded). Despite anti-rocket sorties by fighters based in Britain and the bombing of The Hague's southern outskirts, neither of which had great effect, London faced renewed and heavier rocket attacks. These were likely to continue until the resumption of the land offensive and the Rhine crossing, which did not occur until 23 March 1945, following which the allied forces were able to fan out along the Dutch sea coast.

During the week ending 1 November 1944 Kammler succeeded in launching twenty-six rockets on London against the eight which dropped elsewhere. Even at the eleventh hour, with the British and Canadians occupying Holland and the Americans and Russians converging on Nordhausen, he continued to despatch them. In the week ending 7 March 1945, 58 V2s were launched, 36 of which reached London; the next week there were 62 and still 46 during the week ending 29 March. Somehow Kammler kept the rocket transporters moving through the night, using infra-red devices to pave the way, despite the Dutch resistance blowing up the only railway line to The Hague. The Nordhausen factory churned out rockets until the very end – 690 during January, 617 in February and 362 in March.

The campaign finally ended when, on 27 March, Kammler was ordered to disband his rocket troops and form them into an infantry battalion to defend the Nordhausen area. While attempting to make a final defence of Czechoslovakia against the Russians this fanatical Nazi died, most probably as a result of his own orders to his Adjutant who shot him to prevent his capture. On 26 April the American and Russian forces met on the Elbe and a few days later the American armies occupied Nordhausen, released its workers and took its arsenal of approximately 250 incomplete rockets (filling 300 railway wagons) for shipment to the USA. In July of the previous year, after the Russians had occupied the Blizna Artillery Target Field, they had flown the mangled rocket parts from there to Moscow to reconstruct Hitler's 'miracle' weapon for themselves.[25]

Dornberger and von Braun surrendered to the Americans. Had they stayed in Europe they would have been tried for their activities, but they and their families, together with other selected rocket experts, were transported to the USA where, by September 1945, they had entered into a contract with the American government to launch V2s from the USA's White Sands testing range in New Mexico. The first launching occurred on 16 April 1946, thus providing the USA with the opportunity of launching payloads into space. Other scientists from Peenemunde signed long-term contracts for collaboration with the Soviet authorities, leading to the completion of that country's first rocket launch in September 1947.

In London reactions were different. Unlike the Americans' seizure of the rockets and conveyance of the scientists back to the USA, together with the Russian recruitment of others, the main feeling was cautious relief over the cessation of the attacks, with no positive intention of using German rocket expertise to inspire and excite their own rocket programme. After Duncan Sandys' premature declaration on 7 September 1944 that the Battle of London was over, two months elapsed between the first V2 strike and the news being made public and it was not until 26 April 1945, a month after the last strike, that, in answer to a question in the House of Commons, Winston Churchill declared 'They have ceased'.

Such a curt comment typified the official attitude to the V2 rockets. Churchill mentions them only briefly in his War Memoirs and the Official Report on the V weapons by Air Chief Marshal Roderic Hill was similarly sparing, compared with his references to the V1s. Could this be because, with British scientists found to be so unequal to their German counterparts and unable to protect Londoners from such attacks, it was too awkward a subject to face? It is also just possible that, coming so late in the hostilities and being launched in such relatively small numbers, their 2,000lb warheads could never have been considered capable of changing the course of the war. Yet in so many respects they were a far more formidable weapon of war than the V1s.

As for the statistics, over a seven-month campaign the actual number of rockets reported to have struck Britain was 1,115, of which 518 reached London, killing 2,511 people and seriously injuring 5,869. (Elsewhere in Britain 213 were killed and 598 seriously injured.)[26] Yet whereas the V1 caused 2.2 deaths per bomb, the V2 average was 5.3 for a similar sized warhead. This greater lethal effect was due to two main reasons: they gave no warning for people to take shelter, and their massive impact (which has been likened to fifty 100-ton steam locomotives hitting the ground simultaneously)[27] caused craters 30ft deep and 75ft in diameter. This earthquake effect brought a greater pulverization of the rubble, causing more people to be burned and suffocated, and thus resulted in such higher mortality.

The V2 also had a much greater effect on morale than V1s during that last winter of the war. General Pile tried to counter them by investigating the use of radar to predict the fall of the rockets and fire shells in their path, but for any chance of success the guns had to be fired within a two-second window when the rockets were more than 30 miles from London. Although he was by nature optimistic, by April 1945 Pile's research here still had far to go.[28]

No one could claim that London's own defences had any measurable success against V2 rockets, which if used soon enough and in sufficient numbers could have given Germany – despite its lack of a strategic air force – the opportunity to strike devastatingly against its opponent's capital city. They failed to do so for several reasons, notably because of Hitler's early scepticism towards them which affected the hard choices that were necessary between competing weapon systems, and also because their advanced technology necessitating countless modifications was not fully appreciated by the programme's Gestapo directors. It was also delayed by the allied bombing of Peenemunde – even if this was not as devastating as it might have been – and by British fighters raiding the launch areas,[29] before being neutralized by the allies overrunning their potential launch sites in France and Belgium and finally in Holland. It was most fortunate that they did for, unlike the other attacks upon London, once launched the V2s were impossible to counter.

PART 4

Terrorist Attacks

Chapter 12

The IRA

The fact that the bombs were going off in England was bringing home to the British people what was happening in the North (of Ireland).

Paul Holmes, London IRA bomber[1]

The vast crowd of Londoners who on 8 May 1945 – Victory in Europe Day – gathered in front of the Ministry of Health building in Whitehall to applaud Winston Churchill and his colleagues standing on its balcony were for the most part looking forward to getting back to normal. Japan still held out but, with the German surrender, London was finally free from airborne attacks.

The next day large numbers congregated before the same balcony to hear Winston Churchill pay tribute to London's contribution towards Germany's defeat. To sporadic cheers he likened the capital to a large animal with a thick hide – he was not sure which animal represented it best – 'London like a great rhinoceros ... a great hippopotamus', then looking down on the smiling faces he praised them for never failing 'in the long, monstrous days and in the long nights black as hell'.[2] A few days later, while some were still celebrating the victory, the erstwhile cherubic figure on the balcony had despatched a telegram to the American President, Harry Truman, with a far more sombre message: 'An Iron curtain is drawn down upon (the Russian) front. We do not know what is going on behind it.'[3]

During a speech made at Fulton, Missouri on 5 March of the following year, Churchill expanded on this by outlining militant communism and the need for the Western democracies – especially Britain and the USA – to stand together against it. In the case of Britain, with conscription still in force and two great opposing alliances of NATO and the Warsaw Pact confronting each other in Berlin, many in London and the other great cities of Europe justly felt themselves in renewed danger. Yet because of the unparalleled destructive power of the atomic bombs dropped on Japan, in reality things had changed forever.

This was recognized by Clement Atlee, Churchill's successor as Prime Minister, when he told his Cabinet that another war could bring the world's statesmen into making decisions affecting 'the very survival of civilisation'.[4]

Atlee still thought in terms of <u>using</u> such weapons, however serious the results, and he told the British advisory committee on nuclear energy meeting on 29 August 1945 that 'the answer to an atomic bomb on London is an atomic bomb on another city'.[5] Such a statement was soon invalidated by the development of thermo-nuclear devices many times more powerful than atomic ones, initially by the USA in 1952, followed by the Soviet Union in 1953 and Britain in 1957, making any such exchange unthinkable.

Britain's determination to have its own nuclear weapons led to the development of the country's V bombers and nuclear submarines and after Prime Minister Harold Macmillan's negotiations with the Americans at Nassau in 1962 it was agreed that British submarines would be equipped with multi-headed missiles, before subsequently being updated with missiles equipped with independently targeted warheads. London and the home island were now protected from attack by Britain's capacity to respond with overwhelming force; such destructive capability finally realized the expectations for deterrence voiced earlier by Hugh Trenchard, with London and the British state seeking security through the so-called 'sturdy child of terror'.

Yet while the possession of such weapons made nuclear war virtually unthinkable, the second half of the twentieth century and the early part of the twenty-first century saw continued hostilities beneath the nuclear umbrella. Britain became involved in a number of campaigns against nationalist forces, especially during the decades 1948–68, as governments of its member countries sought independence and by the 1970s London would again come under attack, this time from Irish Republicans determined to complete their own unfinished colonial business following the 1921 partition of Ireland. London had experienced attacks from Irish Fenians during the 1880s and from the Irish Republican Army (IRA) during 1939–40 but, from 1970 onwards these would be more formidable and far better directed.

Although the IRA had long prided itself on being one of the world's oldest guerrilla groups[6] the attacks on London during the last third of the twentieth century were, in the main, mounted by an aggressive Northern Irish faction calling itself the Provisional IRA (a title taken from the proclamation in 1921 which referred to the provisional government for the new Irish Republic). This subsequently took over the IRA and its political wing, Sinn Fein. The extent of the Provisional's ambitions became evident on 10 December 1969 when its Executive declared its intention to use violent means to bring down Ulster and to induce the Dublin leadership into creating a national democracy through a united, independent and free Ireland.[7] Among its leading figures at this time were Joe Cahill, Seamus Twomy, Gerry Adams and Jimmy Drumm. In their Green Book, the Provisionals justified such pretensions through historical allusions. Their tone was uncompromising.

> For the past 800 years the British ruling class have attempted to smash down the resistance of the Irish people. Campaign after campaign, decade after decade, century after century, armies of resistance have fought and despite temporary setbacks, slavery and famine, penal laws and murder, the will of the Irish people in their desire to cast off the chains of foreign occupation continue(s), an unremitting and relentless war against enemy occupation.[8]

Whatever its historic pretensions, in practice the Provisional IRA took its inspiration from the seminal Easter Rising of 1916 (by a relatively small number of Republican idealists) which brought about the treaty of 1921 when Ireland was partitioned between an Irish Free State, containing twenty-six of Ireland's thirty-two counties, with a predominantly Catholic population, and a separate Northern Ireland with its two-thirds Protestants who had emigrated there from Scotland and England and who were favourably disposed to Britain. The Provisionals considered the terms of the Treaty in Northern Ireland were unjustly set against the Catholic third who thought of themselves as Irish, and they viewed the new state as unsatisfactory, if not illegitimate: because Ireland had been denied its rightful self-determination by an Imperialist Britain, justice could only be gained through violence. Just as the British colonies had been freed by force, the Irish colony (of Northern Ireland) had similarly to be freed by force.[9] The best place to apply such violence was, of course, London, the capital of the British state, although the Provisionals' natural battlefield was Northern Ireland and any military campaign against London was likely to develop from there.

In Northern Ireland the Provisionals' cause was undoubtedly helped by the fact that the prevailing conditions were hardly equitable for the Catholics. Not only did the Unionists have a regular and overwhelming majority in the Northern Irish government and de facto control over the judiciary, police and large industrial organizations, but the Orange Order (founded in 1795) dominated Ulster society.

During the early post-war years there seemed little chance of achieving greater equity for the Northern Irish Catholics through political means. As for those committed to achieving it through violence, the Traditional IRA prior to 1969 was far from robust, wedded as it was to Marxist ideas rather than mainstream Republicanism. Changes finally came in 1963, not as a result of terrorist actions but with the election of a new Unionist Prime Minister, Captain Terence O'Neill, who embarked on a programme of reform and modernization which he naively believed would not endanger 'the Union with Britain nor his own party's unbroken run in government'.[10]

In reality, it led to developments he was unable to control. The arrival of a rabble-rousing Ian Paisley helped stir rising tensions, while on the Nationalist side he was opposed by John Hume, a 27-year-old schoolmaster who argued for Catholics to be given greater participation in the Ulster state, while Gerry Fitt, now MP for West Belfast, had gained support at Westminster for his Republican Labour Party. The touchstone for much increased Catholic agitation was the Northern Ireland Civil Rights Association, inspired by images of Martin Luther King in the USA that attempted to redraw the electoral boundaries.

Major unrest after a public rally organized for the civil rights movement was followed by a protest march in Londonderry. The violence with which the RUC treated this march and the television pictures of well-known personalities such as Gerry Fitt being beaten by batons and heavy blackthorn sticks aroused widespread anger among the Catholic community. It also gave those who during the next year officially established the Provisional IRA a golden opportunity to pursue a campaign of violence in pursuit of Irish independence.

O'Neill was succeeded in May 1969 by his cousin, James Chichester-Clark, a gentleman farmer from Londonderry who, like O'Neill, had previously served as an officer in the Irish Guards. Chichester-Clark also failed to rally support and, with increasing violence, the situation deteriorated further. In 1969 the RUC lost control during major rioting that followed a march by the Apprentice Boys of Derry. This opened the way for even more violent clashes within Protestant and Catholic areas of Belfast, where on both sides people were driven out of their homes, following which the historic request was made for British troops to be brought in to restore order. With British troops in Ireland it could only be a matter of time before the IRA mounted active operations against the British mainland, with London its traditional target.

Following Chichester-Clark's resignation in 1971, businessman Brian Faulkner became Stormont's Prime Minister and under him violence escalated. His decision for the army to carry out a mass round up of the IRA on 9 August 1971, and then intern them, proved disastrous and major shooting exchanges occurred between the Provisional IRA and the army as well as the Protestant paramilitaries, and Republican recruits flocked in large numbers to the IRA. In fact, 1972 saw the highest level of casualties ever.

On 30 January 1972 came Bloody Sunday, with the killing of thirteen people and the wounding of thirteen more at the hands of the Parachute Regiment following an illegal civil rights march. With the Catholics boycotting Stormont, the British Prime Minister, Edward Heath, adjourned it on 28 March 1972 and imposed direct rule from London through the Northern Ireland Office headed by Willie Whitelaw. During 1972 a state of war existed in Northern Ireland, where 500 people were killed and almost 5,000 injured, with over 10,000 shooting incidents and 2,000 armed robberies that netted £800,000. In July alone almost 100 people died as Republican and Loyalist forces battled in the streets, and before the end of the year the British garrison of 17,000 soldiers had to be increased to 29,000.[11]

With 'politicians, churchmen, paramilitaries, governments and the British Army failing to resolve things'[12] it promised to be a long war and the Provisional leaders decided to apply pressure on the British state where it most hurt, by raiding London and elsewhere on the British mainland. Their favourite weapon here would be the car bomb, indiscriminate but capable of inflicting many casualties and causing enormous damage.

On 3 January 1972 the Parachute Brigade lines at Aldershot had been bombed by the Official IRA in direct revenge for Bloody Sunday, an attack, however, that failed to bring about the damage and loss of life anticipated, with the deaths limited to a gardener, a Roman Catholic padre and five women on the staff of the Brigade's Officers' Mess. For the Provisionals London, rather than Aldershot, would always be their prime objective, where the priority targets were the Old Bailey, the heart of the English judicial system, and the Metropolitan Police Headquarters at New Scotland Yard. To this end, four cars with false number plates were sent over from Dublin: one was parked outside Scotland Yard, another outside the Army Central Recruiting Depot in Whitehall, a third close to the British Forces Broadcasting network on Dean Stanley Street, Westminster, and the fourth at the Old Bailey. The terrorist leaders were two trainee women teachers, Dolours and Marion Price, and Hugh Feeney, a male volunteer, all three of whom subsequently became hunger strikers. On 8 March 1973 the car bomb outside New Scotland Yard, containing 170lb of explosives, was discovered by two alert police constables and successfully defused, while the gang's ringleaders and others were detained at Heathrow on their way back to Dublin. After a massive police search, the bomb at the British Forces Broadcasting Network was also defused, but the other two exploded shortly after 3.00 pm causing injuries – some of which were serious – to scores of people.

Following the capture of their gang members, the Provisionals decided to limit the size of their attack squads. The attacks resumed on 10 September 1973 when an incendiary device was placed in Harrods department store and there were also explosions at two London railway stations. On the 20th a bomb exploded at Chelsea Barracks, followed by further explosions before Christmas in the same year.

Meanwhile, the Irish Secretary, Willie Whitelaw, was exploring new power-sharing arrangements designed to meet the wishes of Northern Ireland and Great Britain which would 'as far as possible [be] acceptable to [and accepted by] the Republic of Ireland'.[13] In late 1973 Northern Irish politicians, together with representatives from London and Dublin, met at the Civil Service Training Centre at Sunningdale, and on 1 January 1974 a so-called power-sharing executive took office at Stormont. This soon encountered opposition from opposite poles – Unionists on one side and the Provisional IRA on the other – and a general strike by the Ulster Workers Council brought about its resignation.

With the end of power-sharing the IRA returned to London in June 1974 with an attack on the Tower of London, the City's historic stronghold, where a woman was killed and 41 other people injured, and in November an explosion in a public house opposite Woolwich Barracks saw another 2 people killed and 28 injured. (During October and November indiscriminate attacks were made outside London, with 5 killed and 54 injured at a public house in Guildford, Surrey and a further 29 people killed and 182 injured in Birmingham bars.) In December explosions occurred in London's Chelsea, Soho and Tottenham Court Road districts and in Selfridges and Harrods department stores. During the following year, while another Irish Secretary, Merlyn Rees, attempted to bring the Ulster politicians together, IRA bombs continued to explode in London, this time in its hotels, including the Hilton, and at Green Park Underground station.

For much of 1974 and 1975 Merlyn Rees succeeded in negotiating cease fires with the Official IRA after declaring the end of internment, but the Provisionals viewed such initiatives as a British device to create divisions between themselves and the Officials, for they had no intention of ending their attacks on London. Although the year 1975/6 saw continued violence in Northern Ireland where another 600 people were killed (most of them by the Provisional IRA), the British army inflicted and suffered far fewer casualties than before. At the same time the Provisionals kept up their pressure on the mainland when, in March 1976, fifty people were injured in an attack on London's Ideal Home Exhibition, and a London Underground train driver was killed while pursuing a bomber.

By the autumn of 1976, following Roy Mason becoming Northern Irish Secretary, there were changes on both sides: the British government's emphasis shifted from large political initiatives to a concentration on security and economic measures within Northern Ireland, while by the spring of 1977 Gerry Adams and Martin McGuinness succeeded in assuming control of the IRA as a whole and Adams again acknowledged that it was likely to be a long war of attrition, where 'political stalemate, continued violence, occasional attacks on Britain, international pressure, the enormous cost and the apparent insolubility of the problem would ultimately sap Britain's will to stay in Northern Ireland'.[14]

In such a context further attacks – and threats of attacks – against London were obligatory, despite an eighteen-month lull brought about by further feuding within the IRA itself. In December 1978 the targets were pre-Christmas shoppers and during the spring of the following year (March 1979) came the assassination of Margaret Thatcher's close aide, Airey Neave, by a booby trap bomb exploding under his car as he left the House of Commons; although the Irish Liberation Army (INLA) claimed responsibility for the attack, it was all the same for Londoners. In Ireland during August the IRA demonstrated its own deadly skills when Lord Mountbatten was killed in a boat off the Sligo coast, and nineteen soldiers, mainly paratroopers, and a civilian died in an ambush near Warren Point in County Down.

Terrorist initiatives over the next two years were dominated by hunger strikes at Belfast's Long Kesh prison with Republicans determined to regain their prisoner-of-war status. Although initially opposed, Gerry Adams seized the chance of putting hunger striker Bobby Sands forward as Sinn Fein's candidate for Fermanagh/South Tyrone, a seat that he won by a narrow margin. The hunger strikes not only boosted the IRA's political initiatives but brought a great propaganda coup, which earned international sympathy and caused a flood of new recruits that not even the bombing of London could effect. Bobby Sands died on 5 May 1981 on the sixty-sixth day of his strike and his funeral was attended by tens of thousands of mourners: the deaths of nine other prisoners followed. Upon this, Margaret Thatcher's Northern Ireland Secretary, James Prior, granted limited concessions to the prisoners' demands.

The hunger strikes led to Margaret Thatcher being placed at the head of the IRA's assassination list, but in 1982 under her premiership James Prior again proposed elections to a Northern Ireland assembly, which in this case could gradually assume power as it was devolved by stages. Following such concessions the IRA exploded more bombs in London, this time predominantly against servicemen: on 20 July two carefully planned attacks were made on a single day in London's parks that killed eleven soldiers. Two troopers were killed and seventeen civilians injured during the first, which was detonated as the mounted Household Cavalry rode in ceremonial uniform through Hyde Park. Just two hours later a second bomb exploded under the bandstand in Regent's Park, killing six soldier bandsmen and injuring twenty-four civilians.[15]

In the British General Election the following year the IRA's decision to support Sinn Fein as its political wing was rewarded when they polled 100,000 votes and their leader, Gerry Adams, succeeded in becoming

Westminster's MP for West Belfast. However, the Unionists still won fifteen of the seventeen Northern Ireland seats.

In December 1983 the London bombings continued with a device placed outside Harrods while more than 10,000 shoppers thronged the store, resulting in 6 civilians being killed and 91 injured. Although undoubtedly a terrifying demonstration of IRA capability, the number of people injured caused the leadership to consider it counterproductive. Notwithstanding this, the incidence of attacks continued and that on Harrods marked the start of what would turn out to be a decade of operations by the IRA's shadowy 'England Department'.

Such attacks on London did not stop the IRA mounting an assassination attempt on the British government at the Grand Hotel, Brighton in October of the following year where the 1984 Conservative annual conference was being held. A pre-placed Semtex bomb killed five and injured thirty Conservative MPs and their dependents. Although Margaret Thatcher – their main target – escaped, the IRA issued a personal statement reminding her that 'Today we were unlucky but remember we only have to be lucky once'.

Alarm in both London and Dublin at the IRA's new electoral initiatives helped to bring about the Anglo-Irish Accord of 1985, signed at Hillsborough, County Down, which marked a new convergence of both governments and their recognition of Northern Ireland as a common problem. At the same time the IRA's continuing commitment to violence and its determination to have more potent arms than the Protestant paramilitaries led to it undertaking a major re-armament programme helped by the Libyan leader, Colonel Gaddafi. Four shipments from Libya during the mid-1980s brought the IRA 1,000 rifles, Semtex plastic explosive, heavy machine guns, flamethrowers, SAM-7 missiles and anti-aircraft guns.[16] With such supplies the IRA could step up its violence in England and change earlier hit and run tactics into a more sustained offensive; it also now possessed a capability for a number of 'spectaculars', both in London and elsewhere.

One was seen in 1987 with the bombing at Enniskillen on Remembrance Day causing eleven deaths and sixty injuries, although this desecration of a ceremony to remember the dead rebounded against the IRA. During 1988 a damaging attack was made on an army barracks at Mill Hill, London and in 1990 came the killing and maiming of army careers' personnel, the bombings at London's Honourable Artillery Company's headquarters and at the Carlton Club, favoured by the Conservative Party. During September 1989 a bomb containing Semtex had exploded at the Royal Marines' Regimental School of Music at Deal, killing eleven bandsmen, while in East Sussex during July 1990 Margaret Thatcher's friend and strong Unionist supporter Ian Gow was killed by a bomb placed under his car.

Back in London, during February 1991 another IRA 'spectacular' only narrowly failed when an audacious mortar attack (originally intended against Margaret Thatcher) rained bombs on the garden of No. 10 Downing Street, shattering the windows of the nearby Cabinet Office where the Cabinet was in session. A plastic covering over the windows saved those within from suffering injury, but an attack on Downing Street itself was a chilling demonstration of the IRA's continuing resourcefulness. In the same month Victoria and Paddington stations were also attacked.

In 1992 the IRA changed its policy of using bombs to scare ordinary citizens into awareness of the troubles, to causing serious economic damage in the City of London. During April 1992, following an attack on London Bridge railway station, a truly extraordinary operation was mounted which involved placing an explosive device weighing 1,000lb (using Semtex as its trigger) outside the Baltic Exchange in the City of London. This, the largest bomb to be exploded on mainland Britain since the Second World War, was expected to have a devastating effect on the City's tall buildings so closely packed together. The damage to the Baltic Exchange alone was estimated at £700 million – more than the cost of all the previous explosions in Northern Ireland so far, which stood at £600 million. Damage on this scale represented a measurable blow to the British economy as a whole and, although three people were killed and ninety-one injured, the aim was to cause the maximum material damage. There followed another attack, this time on a DIY store at Staples Corner.

The campaign could have had even more serious consequences if two similar devices, a 1-ton van bomb outside Canary Wharf and a 1,000lb bomb on London's Tottenham Court Road, had not been defused. Meanwhile, a number of lesser bombs were detonated at the Royal Festival Hall, the Hyde Park Hilton, in Covent Garden, outside railway and Underground stations and in the West End.

During February 1993 an explosion near Camden Market in north London led to eighteen people being injured, and in April a bomb was placed outside a central London Conservative club. During the same month there was another IRA 'spectacular', when a homemade bomb containing almost a ton of explosive was carried in a tipper truck to devastate the Bishopsgate area of the City. Initial estimates of the cost were set at £1 billion, although this was subsequently reduced by somewhat over half. In Northern Ireland the IRA's foot soldiers continued with their violence, but the largest operations were directed at the City of London and as a result a security cordon – 'a ring of steel' – was constructed to prevent future large-scale attacks. This involved checking 7,000 vehicles a day and imposing limitations on freedom of movement in and out of the City.

In August 1993 the IRA reminded the authorities of its continuing capability by planting a bomb in the City, although such 'active operations' were now being scaled back in line with Sinn Fein's aim of being seen to support the peace process. This, in December, saw the Downing Street Declaration between John Major and the Irish Taoiseach, Albert Reynolds, which 'included a commitment that the people of Northern Ireland would [be able to] decide its future, along with a demand that the IRA permanently renounce violence'.[17]

Even so, the IRA showed it could still mount new operations when on 9, 11 and 13 March it placed mortar bombs on the runways at Heathrow – although none ignited because the Semtex used had been (deliberately) doctored not to explode.[18] Finally, on 31 August 1994, following a series of high-level meetings between the IRA and the British government, the decision came to call a halt to the twenty-five years of conflict that had kept London under siege. Its leadership duly issued the following statement: 'Recognising the potential of the current situation and in order to enhance the democratic peace process and underline our definitive commitment to its success the leadership of Oglaigh nah Eireann have decided that as of midnight Wednesday 31 August there will be a complete cessation of military operations. All our units have been instructed accordingly.'[19]

In October 1994 the Combined Loyalist Military Command followed with a ceasefire of their own. However, after eighteen months of negotiations, chaired in the later stages by the American Senator George Mitchell, when there came a sticking point over the decommissioning of terrorist weapons, the IRA ended its cessation – with declared reluctance – and demonstrated its continuing ability to mount military operations on the British mainland. This resulted in a huge bomb explosion at London's Canary Wharf, killing two people, injuring many more and causing enormous damage. As intended, the prospect of another generation being exposed to such violence galvanized political activity and the peace talks re-opened with renewed purpose.

After the election of Tony Blair to Downing Street with a landslide majority, another IRA cessation in July 1997 was followed on 10 April 1998 with the Good Friday Agreement, which granted devolved government in Northern Ireland. Referenda in support were then held on both sides of the Irish border, bringing massive approval, and in the year 2000 came the agreement for the inspection of a number of IRA arms dumps by international monitors.

Following the prolonged IRA cessation, the subsequent monitoring of its arms and the partial realization of its political aims with devolved government in Northern Ireland, London could finally hope to be spared from violence. While in the first instance the attacks had been somewhat haphazard, by the early 1980s, under the more sophisticated leadership of Gerry Adams, the violence was not only more carefully controlled but carried out with extreme professionalism. The small cells used by the organization's 'England Department' proved virtually impossible to penetrate and the bombing was always designed to force the Westminster government towards a political settlement in the IRA's favour and to loosen the ties of the capital's senior politicians with the Unionists.

With this end in view, the attacks progressed through ones against military targets, the city's communication system and normal places of recreation to assassination attempts on senior political figures and, finally, to massive bombs aimed at bringing heavy damage to the city's infrastructure. The intention had never been to bring about extensive loss of life – and early warnings were often given, although these varied in their effectiveness – for the IRA leadership well understood that the resulting anger and revulsion to attacks on ordinary Londoners, who a few years before had endured prolonged and heavy assaults during the war, would more than likely prove counterproductive.

For the terrorists meticulous planning was essential to avoid bungled attacks – for every successful one demonstrated the seeming inability of the security forces to prevent it. In fact, the IRA's twenty main attacks from 1983–93 proved highly successful: apart from bringing major dislocation to the city, 35 people were killed, 544 injured and billions of pounds worth of damage caused for the conviction of just 3 raiders.[20]

Considering the bombers' expertise, particularly in the later stages, it was no wonder they succeeded so frequently, despite the intelligence services ranged against them. Terrorists were heavily favoured by the enormous size of the capital, while the security forces had to second-guess their possible targets from the vast number of national treasures, including monuments, banks, railway stations, department stores, museums and famous restaurants. Unsurprisingly, precautions were often implemented only after an attack had occurred.

Even so, the cellular structure adopted by the terrorist teams – with no liaison (and often no knowledge) of each other – coupled with their ability to move, if necessary, to other cities or to return to Ireland was very effective. With London so close to Ireland and with the normal extent of travel between the two countries, experts could be despatched to support individual cells, only to be removed prior to an operation being carried out. Another unquestioned advantage of using small cells was that, if some individuals were apprehended, they could quickly be brought back to strength. They were also not particularly expensive due to their use of highjacked vehicles and homemade explosives to augment their quantities of Semtex.

They could, however, never relax in their precautions for, despite London's size, the many thousands of innocent Irish nationals working there and the ability of agents to blend in with the community at large, alert citizens could still make it an inimical place. There was, for instance, the case of the English 'helper' Vincent Wood, a sales executive with no criminal record, who had become an IRA quartermaster and placed a sealed tea chest containing Semtex and timing devices in a friend's shop. He was discovered when the shop's staff became curious and, after opening the chest, informed the police of its contents.[21]

One undoubted result of the deadly interplay between the terrorists and the security forces has been the growth of restrictions on individuals, where at times the level of security arrangements in London has equalled those in Belfast or Derry. Following the Billingsgate bombing, for instance, certain routes within the City of London were permanently closed to vehicles, while those entering the city are currently subject to CCTV cameras which read vehicle's registration plates and monitor the drivers and their passengers. Anyone entering a public building or an airport for any reason faces vigorous search procedures and heavy restrictions on personal baggage. Londoners are also subject to very high levels of surveillance and storage of information from security cameras and other electronic measures.

The plurality of security organizations include MI5 (in overall control), Scotland Yard's Anti-Terrorist Squad, MI6, military resources and even teams from regional police forces. Under the Prevention of Terrorism Act the police enjoy extended rights of search and arrest and also the right to hold suspects for twenty-eight days without the need to charge them (the authorities would have preferred it to be longer). While many raids might have been foiled by such measures during the troubled years, many Londoners, particularly ordinary Irish families, have reason to wonder how far their traditional freedoms might have been lost forever. Police in various forms of combat dress, engaged in covert searches of buildings during the night hours, have also forfeited some of the former trust and affection of London's citizens for their 'bobbies on the beat'.

In short, IRA violence over the last twenty-five years in London not only brought it political success but changed London's security landscape even more than the two world wars. Although the violence during wartime was undoubtedly higher, the enemy was more easily identifiable and with peace violence was expected to end; with terrorism there is always a possibility of future outrages. In this regard, although the IRA has denounced violence and its leadership at Westminster is committed to political rather than military solutions, Northern Ireland remains a divided community: Unionists are far from embracing a common Ireland or willing to cede real authority in Northern Ireland, while Nationalists are unwilling to place limits on their own objectives.[22]

As a result in February 2010 another generation of British and Irish prime ministers became engaged in lengthy, and for a time seemingly insoluble, problems concerned with the latest plans for power-sharing. Furthermore, inseparable from Irish politics is the possibility of an assault by Republican (or Unionist) gunmen wedded to continuing violence against the present IRA leadership.

Apart from such real and continuing concerns about Irish terrorism, London presently faces new threats from a truly international terrorist organization under the mantle of al-Qaeda.

Chapter 13

Al-Qaeda

I didn't dream. I slept fine. I knew I was going to paradise so I was very calm.

Didar, suicide bomber, aged 17[1]

With the IRA eschewing violence there appeared to be genuine hopes that London might now be free from its attacks – unless, of course, some putsch or similar bloodletting were to bring about a massive change of leadership.[2]

Not so with al-Qaeda, a much more loosely structured fundamentalist movement whose political aims – unlike the IRA's predominantly concerned with Britain and Ireland – are to mobilize and radicalize the whole Islamic world against what is seen as the current flawed beliefs and practices of the West. In such circumstances, as a foremost symbol of Western civilization London must expect to be in the firing line, whether such attacks are co-ordinated by Osama Bin Laden or any other of the al-Qaeda leaders. With their less-focused but far more sweeping objectives, such threats are fiendishly difficult to counter, particularly in the case of suicide bombers determined to cause the maximum loss of life.

In spite of this, the West's intelligence services and counterterrorist organizations might have felt reasonably confident against such opponents until the success of the first attack in February 1993 upon New York's World Trade Centre, when 6 people were killed and 1,000 injured, and when 2 years later, on 26 January 1995, a bomb was placed on a Paris commuter train killing 4 people and wounding 60 others. The suspects were part of a fundamentalist Islamic group committed to stopping France shipping arms to Iraq; the year after another explosion on a Paris commuter train killed a further two people.

Then came the pivotal attack of 11 September 2001 when 19 suicide bombers, working in unison, hijacked aeroplanes and launched them against New York's World Trade Centre's twin towers (and also the Pentagon in Washington), bringing about the deaths of 2,975 people and causing $2 trillion's worth of damage in New York. Apart from changing the level of immediate threat it was inevitable that the 9/11 attack should lead to increased fears of similar attacks on

London and other European capitals, a likelihood further increased by improved American countermeasures following 9/11 that made repeat attacks on the USA far more difficult.

The first European city to be attacked in the twenty-first century was Madrid where, on 11 March 2004 (in similar style to Paris), the terrorists targeted the Metro system, leaving 191 people dead. There could be no doubt about the political intent since the attack was timed to coincide with Spain's elections and, in fact, it succeeded in bringing about the withdrawal of Spanish troops from Iraq. The Spanish security services expressly warned Scotland Yard that London might be likely to suffer a similar attack because of the links they had discovered between al-Qaeda operatives in Madrid and radicals in North London.[3]

Remarkably, in spite of such warnings and the thwarting of al-Qaeda's plans during 2003 to hijack a plane from Eastern Europe, crash it into the airport at Heathrow and follow up with an attack by remotely controlled mortars, when the awaited attack on London came on 7 July 2005 it was unexpected. Only a month earlier the British Joint Terrorism Assessment Centre, co-ordinated by MI5, decided that 'at present there is not a group with both the current intent and capability to make an attack on the UK'[4] – this despite the relatively recent involvement of British nationals such as Richard Reid, the so-called shoe bomber, in suicide attacks elsewhere. During December 2001 Reid attempted to blow up an American Airlines flight from Paris to Miami with explosives concealed in his footwear, and during the same month there was an identical attempt by another Briton, Sajid Badat, which came to nothing.

Before the 7/7 attack, which was described as coming out of the blue, the level of terrorist threat (indicated by seven stages of ascending risk) had been downgraded from severe general to substantial, the lowest since the 9/11 attacks on the USA.[5] Whether seven different stages actually gave the security forces greater control than those of a shorter series, London's Metropolitan Police were plainly confident about their capacity to react in the event of an attack. Their Commissioner, Sir Ian Blair, speaking on the BBC's *Today* programme twenty-four hours earlier, declared that, 'We have been described by Her Majesty's Inspectorate of Constabulary as the envy of the policing world in relation to counter-terrorism and I am absolutely positive that our ability is too'.[6] For good measure he added that 'We've upped the game'.

Such complacency might have been partly due to the fact that ten days before officers from Scotland Yard had arrested a computer expert who apparently provided them with vital information about the terrorists' internal communications, including the code that al-Qaeda was reputedly using – a breakthrough over optimistically described by one insider as similar to breaking the German

Enigma code during the Second World War. Whatever the degree of over confidence, the attack would demonstrate, in spite of accomplished security services, the difficulty of anticipating such a move from unremarkable home-grown terrorists with no obvious criminal record,[7] whether they were in communication with al-Qaeda's representatives or not. As in Madrid earlier, the shrewd timing of the London attack undoubtedly pointed to external direction. The capital had just received news of its success in being made the Olympic capital for 2012, while at Scotland's Gleneagles Hotel a G8 Summit of the world's leading nations was about to commence. The huge security operation mounted there against possible agitators had caused more than 1,500 police officers to be transferred from London to Scotland.

Unlike those of the IRA, the multiple attack of 7 July 2005 came without any warning. It occurred during London's rush hour at four separate locations with the specific intention of stretching the ambulance and other emergency services to breaking point and causing the maximum number of casualties. Because of the proximity of the London press, the newspapers gave the attacks full coverage. The first occurred at 8.51 am in a Tube train moving through a tunnel close to Aldgate station before entering Liverpool Street station, where several Underground and over ground lines converged. Five minutes later another explosion took place inside a Tube train moving in the deep tunnel between King's Cross and Russell Square stations. A third came twenty minutes later in yet another Tube train as it was entering Edgeware Road station. The final explosion, thirty minutes after, was in a no. 30 bus packed with commuters forced above ground by the closure of the Underground net-work. In all cases the bombs, which contained 10lb of explosive, were carried in rucksacks by young men who, supremely confident of their Mohammedan God, were willing to sacrifice their own lives when detonating them.

The explosions in the Tube trains marked the first bomb attacks during the 142-year history of the world's largest underground railway system. With at least 49 people killed outright and 700 injured, the casualty levels recalled the air raids during the Second World War. The first blast in the Circle line train approaching Liverpool Street station was described by construction worker Terry O'Shea:

> There was a loud bang and we felt the train shudder. Then smoke started coming into the compartment. It was terrible. People were panicking, but they calmed down after one or two minutes. As they led us down the track past the carnage where the explosion was we could see the roof was torn off, and there were bodies on the track.[8]

Other witnesses described how everybody instinctively fell to the floor before some opened the inner central doors in order to go to the back of the train before stepping down onto the track and making their way past it into Liverpool Street station.

Most of the passengers had to wait for up to forty minutes, with their clothes shredded, before they were able to move towards the station. Here seven passengers were killed and many injured.

The second blast was more horrific still, occurring in a Piccadilly line train as it travelled through a tunnel from King's Cross to Russell Square, 100ft below ground level. The train was packed with morning commuters and inside the first carriage, where the bomb went off, all the seats were taken and people were crammed together in the standing area by a set of double doors. There was just 6in clearance between the sides of the carriage and the tunnel wall and the explosion turned the compartment into a scene of twisted metal and torn bodies. Some people had severed limbs and there were others with split ear-drums and ruptured internal organs from the explosion's aftershock which bounced off the tunnel walls. Uninjured passengers broke side windows to let in more air and the driver appeared, silencing people so that they could hear as he explained that the only way out for the 800 or so passengers was by way of his carriage door. He led them through it and down onto the rails, where people placed their arms on the shoulders of those directly in front and slowly made their way to the station 500yd away from where they ascended the long flights of stairs to the surface. At Russell Square they were met by waiting ambulance crews who checked them for injuries before contacting their relatives.

Back in the train rescue and forensic staff were forced to work in stifling heat and pitch darkness. When Sergeant Steve Betts of British Transport Police passed what he thought was a pile of clothes it proved to be a woman, all of whose limbs had been blown off, who moaned and asked him for help. Conditions were extremely adverse: along with the heat there were the fumes and the vermin, as well as the constant threat of both the tunnel and carriage collapsing 'that seriously hampered the recovery operation and made life near impossible for the emergency workers'.[9] Three days or more afterwards the air in the tunnel remained choked with dust and soot, and in the carriage where the explosion had occurred there were still body remains with rats and other vermin furiously active. Here twenty-one people died and scores were injured.

The force of the third explosion not only shattered a train as it came into Edgware Road station but tore through a wall and into another train. As in the other cases, all the lights went out and people were left in darkness, except for the glow of their mobile phones by which they tried to check their own injuries. One man, who was already badly injured, had been hurled under the carriages:

for half an hour the choking and shocked survivors, waiting to walk 'down the dark tunnel to safety, had to listen to the trapped man's screams until they stopped'.[10]

The eastbound train caught in the explosion ground to a sudden halt, throwing everyone off their seats. The windows cracked across but did not shatter and through them some could make out a lady ripped to pieces lying between the two trains. When the survivors emerged above ground they were led across the road to the London Metropole Hotel, which acted as an emergency casualty clearing station, where they were examined before the seriously injured were sent to St Mary's hospital close by. There the staff followed pre-arranged instructions which had been drawn up as a result of the earlier Paddington rail crash. There were seven deaths and hundreds injured, thirty-eight of them seriously.

The final explosion occurred at Tavistock Place on a no. 30 double-decker bus packed with commuters, which had been rerouted due to the Tube's closure. A pedestrian, Ayobami Betto, was 50ft away from the bus when the bomb exploded on its top deck. He described how 'the bus went to pieces. There were so many bodies on the floor. The back was completely gone, it was blown off completely, and a dead body was hanging out and there were dead bodies on the road. It was a horrible thing.'[11] He talked of other bodies sitting slumped in their bus seats, some with arms and legs missing and of a lady coming towards him soaked in blood.

The 41-year-old bus driver, George Psarabakis, reported his own impressions. He said there was a bang, then carnage, everything seemed to happen behind him and he tried to help the poor people. There were many injured people and he said that at first he thought, 'How am I alive when everyone is dying around me?' He went on to say what so many other Londoners, must have felt when they returned home, 'I was just relieved to be here and to see my wife and children.'[12]

As chance had it, the explosion brought the bus to a halt near the head-quarters of the British Medical Association whose walls were splattered with blood. From there doctors and officials, many of whom had not been involved with practical medicine for years – all dressed in their immaculate conference suits, rushed out to treat the injured in the street. They took the casualties into the grand courtyard of the BMA building where a 'field hospital' was set up, and about twenty of the wounded were laid out on tables and wrapped in table cloths brought from the meeting rooms. In this attack thirteen people died, with dozens wounded.

In a city that had experienced sustained German air assaults during two world wars, followed by prolonged attacks from the IRA, the reactions of most

Londoners to this latest, bloody attack were true to type. Most set about trying to find out how they could return home, for they had no doubt they would somehow return to work the next day.[13] When they discovered it was impossible to use their mobile phones – the security services had jammed the networks to prevent further bombs being set off remotely, and to facilitate calls between the emergency workers – they began persuading roving TV camera crews to play their cameras on personal placards such as 'David Crook. Call your brother.'

As in the past, leading figures also did their utmost to rally morale. Metropolitan Police Commissioner, Sir Ian Blair, made his way around the TV stations emphasizing that a sophisticated emergency plan was being implemented (whatever that meant), although characteristically he reported six explosions rather than the four actual ones. Prime Minister Tony Blair returned from Gleneagles to give encouragement in what was described as a tense and taut address, in the course of which he said, 'Whatever they do it is our determination that they will never succeed in destroying what we hold dear'.

London Mayor Ken Livingstone, interviewed while still in Singapore celebrating the granting of the next Olympic Games to London, declared that the bombers' objective was to turn Londoners against each other.[14] However, calling upon her own experiences of attacks going back many years, the Queen's responses were exemplary: her flag was quickly lowered to half-mast at Buckingham Palace and she declared that 'her thoughts were with the injured, some of whom she had already been able to see and talk to', adding that events such as these simply reinforce our sense of community, our humanity and our trust in the rule of law. The next day she showed her disregard for the bombers by travelling in an open Land Rover as she led a day of commemoration for the dead of the Second World War.

Elsewhere, responses were both pragmatic and defiant. On the afternoon of the bombing, with the Docklands light railway out of action, a Dunkirk-style evacuation was quickly mounted by a flotilla of river cruisers for the employees at Canary Wharf, while at the Stock Exchange brash dealers gave out a typical two-fingered message to the terrorists, asking, 'Is that all you've got?'

For the security services, once the likelihood of repeat attacks was largely discounted the hunt was on for the attackers. At the time 6,000 closed circuit television cameras had been in operation, 2,500 of them in central London positioned both in the streets and at railway stations. Hundreds of feet of film had to be scanned, and 400 extra police were drafted in for an operation unequalled in scale since the height of the IRA campaign 30 years before. This immense task could have stretched from days into weeks had not the police received a remarkable bonus when the parents of the youngest suicide bomber contacted Scotland Yard's emergency helpline at about 10.00 pm on the night of the attack to report that their son, who had been travelling to London with three friends, had not been heard of since. Initially the parents were allocated a family liaison team amid fears that their son was a victim, before suspicions grew that he might himself be one of the terrorists.

The breakthrough came at 8.00 pm on 9 July when, after trawling through hundreds of hours of film, the police found a picture of the missing 18-year-old at King's Cross station along with three other men, all carrying large ex-army style rucksacks. Their identity was subsequently confirmed from documents which they had deliberately left at the scene of the bombings. The four were Lindsey Germaine, a Jamaican-born Briton who had lived during the previous seven weeks in Aylesbury, and three others of Pakistani origin: Mohammed Sidique Khan, aged 30, from Leeds, Shehzad Tanweer, aged 22, and Hasib Hussain, aged 18, from Dewsbury, West Yorkshire.

A classic terrorist cell was likely to number between twelve and twenty men, and the authorities were already aware of another British-born Pakistani whom they believed had masterminded the attacks and who was thought to have fled the country. The bombers' spiritual mentor, who would have prayed with them and assured them that their deaths in action would be the quickest and most certain route to paradise, was never discovered, but his success was seen in the bombers' pride at leaving evidence of themselves at the bomb sites. Furthermore, on the morning of the attacks they had apparently shaved off their body hair in a ceremony of religious purification.[15]

In Aylesbury, Lindsey Germaine had lived with his partner Samantha Lewthwaite and their baby son, following Lindsey's earlier employment in Huddersfield, West Yorkshire as a carpet fitter. Samantha came from a well-established Aylesbury family and her sister worked for the local newspaper, but she had converted to Islam and adopted the traditional flowing black gowns. In the time leading up to the attacks Lindsey was always at home during the day, when they played loud music causing people to knock at their house door to complain, but they never opened it although they would eventually turn the noise down.

Mohammed Sidique Khan at 30 was the oldest of the four and the ringleader. Married with a 14-month-old daughter, he was a primary school mentor and youth worker. The other two bombers regularly attended the youth centre in Lodge Lane, Leeds, where Khan worked and where one witness, speaking to the *Guardian*, said, 'There were meetings, meetings, meetings – there didn't seem to be much youth work going on. People came in from outside the community to these meetings. There were people going in there who had nothing to do with youth work.'[16]

The third bomber was Shehzad Tanweer, aged 22, a university student who planned to go into sports science, who visited Sidique Khan there. He loved cricket and apparently came from a loving family background where his father had a string of successful businesses, including a fish and chip shop. At the end of the previous year Shehzad had attended an Islamic school in Pakistan near Lahore, with the intention of staying there for nine months and learning the Koran by heart. However, after just three months he returned to Britain to work part-time in his father's fish and chip shop. Hasib Hussain, the youngest of the four men had also visited Pakistan and was something of a loner, an under achiever at school who caused problems at home and had also attended the Lodge Lane Youth Centre.

All four bombers were 'clean skins' with no convictions or apparent terrorist involvement, which made them excessively difficult to locate. While a closer investigation of the young men responsible for the worst terrorist attack on London so far confirmed how they were sufficiently disconnected from their British cultural roots to seek a triumphal martyrdom, first impressions were of their relative normality. There was the cricket lover whose father ran a fish and chip shop, a married man closely connected with a youth project associated with a primary school, a Jamaican with a wife and baby with a penchant for loud music and a 'gentle giant' and keen cricketer whose parents voluntarily contacted the police after he had not returned from a trip to London. Together with the problems of locating other British-born terrorists – whether directed from outside the country or not – the British security forces faced the increased difficulty of combating suicide bombers who, unlike previous terrorists, did not fear capture or death. How, for instance, could effective action be taken against suspect packages on the London Underground when men were ready to detonate them in their own laps?

Al-Qaeda gained further advantage from the attack after the bombers' deaths. During their visit to Pakistan, Sadique Khan and Shehzad Tanweer had been afforded the honour of recording videotaped statements for al-Qaeda's communications department. On 1 September 2005, three months after his death, that of Khan was broadcast on the Qatari-based Arabic news station, Al Jazeera. Its message to the station's many listeners went as follows.

> I and thousands like me are forsaking everything for what we believe.
> Our driving motivation doesn't come from tangible commodities
> that this world has to offer. Our religion is Islam – obedience to the
> one true God.... democratically elected governments continuously
> perpetuate atrocities against my people all over the world. And your
> support makes you directly responsible ... and until you stop the

bombing, gassing, imprisonment and torture of my people we will not stop this fight. . . . I myself, I make [calling] to Allah . . . to raise me amongst those whom I love, like the prophets, the messengers, the martyrs and today's heroes like our beloved Shekh Osama Bin Laden . . .[17]

On the first anniversary of the London bombings al-Qaeda released another tape made by Khan's fellow bomber Shehzad Tanweer, entitled 'The Final Message of the Knights of the London Raid', expressing similar views. It concluded with the threat, 'What you have witnessed now is only the beginning of a series of attacks, which, inshallah, will intensify and continue until you pull all your troops out of Afghanistan and Iraq . . .'.[18]

In the event, Londoners responded to the 7/7 attacks (and the later statements by the suicide bombers) with a phlegmatic composure never evident in Spain after the Madrid attacks nor for that matter (admittedly following far more numerous ones) in Israel. Although in 2005 London was probably a more racially diverse city than at any time in its long history – a fact supported by the names of the correspondents to *The Times* during the week following the attack – the letters not only reflected attitudes beyond any instinctive fury at the attacks but also qualities of objectivity and detachment characteristic of a mature democracy. The arguments in those submitted by Londoners – fully aware of their city's great importance and responsibility at such a time – were no less well founded than others.

Unsurprisingly some called for strengthening the powers of the security forces. Mr Alan Jaggs from Lancashire wrote that 'It is time to move to identity cards. They may not solve all problems, but will go some way to help us knowing who is in our country' (letter of 8 July). Dr Charles Tannock, a London MEP, drew attention to the utility of identity cards following the Madrid bombing which led to the rapid tracking down of a terrorist sympathizer (letter of 12 July). Another London correspondent, Michael Joyce, went further, believing identity cards to be of dubious effectiveness and recommending a national database for all British citizens, including their DNA, both 'for combating crime and assisting in the pursuit and conviction of terrorists' (letter of 12 July). The final (and strongest) words on this theme came from a Londoner, Mr Daljit Sehbal, who observed that:

we live in exceptional times, when religious fanatics are prepared to kill innocent people in the misguided belief of doing it for a religious cause. . . . Exceptional dangers require exceptional measures. Let Parliament and the judiciary give support and necessary powers to the police to confront this danger and help the security services to save the lives of our citizens' (letter of 12 July).

Much the largest group was concerned with the purpose and effects of such attacks. Mr Roger Hancock from Raglan, Gwent was wholly unconvinced that 'by killing and maiming innocent people going about their daily business the governments concerned will convert to fundamentalist Islamic states' (letter of 9 July). Sir Peter Smithers, writing from Switzerland, stressed the dangers of such an attack; whereas the 7/7 bombing was relatively modest compared with that on the twin towers, Britain's administration was largely centred in London and therefore 'to destroy Central London would come close to putting Britain out of action for a long time' (letter of 9 July). With regard to the purpose of such attacks, Dr Nick Megoran from Cambridge made the intellectual distinction between what he saw as Tony Blair's disingenuous suggestion that the terrorists were trying to change our way of life, to the accurate one that they were attempting to change our foreign policy (letter of 11 July.)

Mr Bilal Patel from London needed no such distinction, pointing out that the al-Qaeda website explicitly stated that the attacks were in revenge for British actions in Afghanistan and Iraq. Richard Beeston of London followed suit in his belief that 'the suffering and casualties unleashed in a war of doubtful legality have angered and radicalized millions throughout the Muslim world and it may not be surprising that Britain in particular has become a target of this hostility' (letter of 13 July). Correspondent David Lockie was also sure that 'the link between the invasion of Iraq and the deaths in London was direct and manifest' (letter of 15 July).

Such assertions were sharply contradicted by Dr Christopher Grey from the Home Counties, who said that 'attempts to de-couple particular geopolitical events from terrorist attacks are in my view as misguided as attempts to link them' (letter of 15 July). Other writers took a different approach, positively approving of the American and British operations in Iraq, Afghanistan and the Balkans, and acknowledging that the London attacks were a price worth paying. Nick Ioney pointed to the American/British operations removing oppressive regimes from power (email of 13 July) and Arnold Berman warned that 'any weakness now in our will to support these vulnerable countries will grant the fundamentalists the victory they crave' (email of 9 July). Other correspondents commented on the proper role of the media in such circumstances, and there were enthusiastic tributes from Americans to Londoners' imperturbable responses.

Such letters helped to demonstrate that while the suicide bombers' attack on London was the most deadly terrorist attack so far, it had not dented

Londoners' sangfroid or the confidence of the country as a whole in the capital's ability to withstand such assaults. However, with British society possibly moving to lower levels of tolerance, it can no longer be guaranteed that repeated or different attacks might be met with such equanimity, especially as it is only to be expected that al-Qaeda will seek to launch novel and even more deadly ones.

A chilling demonstration of this came in 2006 with a bombing plot that from London's Heathrow was planned to bring unprecedented death and destruction in the skies above Europe. Liquid explosives, formed from a mixture of hydrogen peroxide and other ingredients available on the commercial market, were to be carried onto planes in plastic bottles whose contents were dyed to look like fizzy drinks. On selected planes departing from Heathrow over a two-and-a-half-hour period disposable cameras would trigger initial small explosions that would in turn detonate the larger quantities of explosives contained in the bottles. The resultant holes torn in the planes' fuselages were expected to result in catastrophic failure leading to the death of all their passengers and crew, thereby bringing international air traffic to a standstill. Fortunately, the plot was discovered and on 4 April 2008 eight British Muslims were tried at Woolwich Crown Court in East London. The bombers' range of targets was in fact found to extend beyond London's commercial aviation to Heathrow's new control tower, as well as Canary Wharf, Fawley, Croydon, Kingsbury gas and oil refineries and even to nuclear power stations.

Once more the confidence of the attackers was demonstrated by their digital videos prepared for broadcast after the event. One by Abdullah Ahmed Ali, a leading member of the airlines' group, included the statement, 'You have nothing but to expect that floods of martyr operations, volcanoes of anger and revenge and raping among your capital and yet, taste what you have made us taste for a long time and now you have [to] bear the fruits that you have sown'.[19]

This time the chief terrorists in the liquid-explosives plot were themselves Londoners or men working in London. Ali attended university in London and after graduating went to Pakistan to work for a British charity in a refugee camp there; he came under police surveillance in June 2006 before purchasing an East London flat that became his cell's bomb factory. Ali's compatriot, Assad Al Sarwar, who also recorded a martyrdom tape, was more obvious terrorist material, a 30-year-old drop out from London's Brunel University who lived with his parents in High Wycombe and alternated between Britain and Pakistan. He purchased 40l of hydrogen peroxide, which he boiled down to bomb strength before he and Ali were arrested on 9 August 2006 in Walthamstow's town hall parking lot. A third member of the cell, Mohamed

Gulzar, a native of Birmingham and Portsmouth, was apparently the group's supervisor but fled the country with his friend Rahid Rauf, whose uncle was also an al-Qaeda operative. The five other defendants in the case included Tanvir Hussain, who went to secondary school with Ali at Waltham Forest College. By 2003 Hussain was showing signs of the religious extremism that became fully apparent in his martyrdom video in which he declared, 'People are going to die, but it's worth the price ... you know, I only wish I could do this again ... you know, come back and do this again, and just do it again and again until people come to their senses and realise, don't mess with Muslims'.[20]

The vast spread of London's conurbation with its militant preachers and areas of undoubted deprivation make it fertile ground for such a cell. The activities of this group, however, went beyond the capital to extend to other associates in both Britain and Pakistan, including weekend camps and prayer meetings at a Tablighi Madrassa in Dewsbury, West Yorkshire, while in the USA they attended a variety of Tablighi Jamaat sessions.

Currently London's security forces face a constant challenge to identify young men disillusioned with Western life, who become subject to a militant fundamentalist version of the Muslim religion and are willing to pledge themselves to sacrifice their lives in an attempt to destroy hated Western institutions. Fortunately, even such committed young men on occasions not only reveal their intentions but make mistakes, such as an abortive attempt in 2007 upon the Tiger Tiger nightclub in Leicester Square when their car bombs did not fully ignite.

Realistically, whatever the strength of the security forces and the extent of the surveillance measures in operation, it is impossible to locate all such terrorists in time. As Dame Eliza Manningham-Buller, then Director of MI5, acknowledged with regard to the London shoe bombers, 'we will continue to stop most of [the terrorist attempts], but we will not stop all of them'.[21] This raises a further related problem; in spite of the immense pressures on the security forces to reduce such risks, they have to avoid undertaking measures which cumulatively impinge on the traditional freedoms and privileges of Londoners. This becomes all the more difficult when, for instance, lawyers of the victims of the 7/7 attacks continue to use their skills to prove irresponsibility or, at the least, a lack of effectiveness by the security or emergency services of the time.

Epilogue

Whatever his talents at forecasting future trends, H G Wells's dire predictions for the early strategic bombing of London and other great Western capitals to bring about the destruction of European civilization – in some ways like the passing of King Arthur's Camelot – did not, of course materialize.[1]

What Wells had not fully anticipated was that the German Zeppelins and bombers of the First World War would be unable to bring wholesale destruction to a city the size of London. Nor for that matter would the much-improved but still medium bombers of Hitler's Luftwaffe, even when supplemented by his V weapons. Although at the opening of the Blitz on 14 September 1940 Mollie Parker-Downes's despatches from London left Americans in no doubt about Londoner's lack of sleep ('there are no longer such things as good nights; there are only bad nights, worse night and better nights'),[2] they also emphasized their continuing determination and ability to keep going. Such reports did more than this; they led to a consideration of the British capital that went beyond its industrial and commercial achievements to a more elevated position as Britain's representative for world freedom and democracy.

Whatever its perceived image, during two world wars the classic 'scattered city' of London proved too much for its aerial attackers, and Londoners who lived in their boroughs – the clusters of proud overgrown villages that made up their city – were for the most part able to carry on with their traditional patterns of life. This continued to be the case at the end of the so-called 'swinging sixties' when, after the rationing and austerity of the early post-war years, the capital became the 'must have' target for the IRA's car bombs and, later, their spectacular explosions aimed at the financial heart of the city.

By the early twenty-first century the capital had acquired new enemies, religious fundamentalists – whether inspired by al-Qaeda or not – who viewed London as one of the world's most sinful and heretical communities. Despite the suicide-bomb attacks on 7 July 2005 that caused serious loss of life, Londoners – more diverse than ever – still responded with their traditional decency and calmness which they had shown during the previous century and within two days of the 7/7 attack the capital's public services had returned to normal.

From the nature of recent evidence about other fundamentalist plots there is every likelihood that London will, at some future time, experience new attacks. However, dangers need not be confined to military ones, and the financial convulsions of recent years – predicted by H G Wells even to the hording of gold at times of crisis[3] – have brought fresh and different threats to the capital. These have occurred while London has acquired a higher national profile than at any other time since the Second World War. Its elected mayors – modern successors to the redoubtable Lord Mayor Thomas Fitz Thomas and accomplished media performers, wield more power than many British ministers of state, or even heads of state in some medium-sized countries. As a result, London is not only an obligatory target for such groups as al-Qaeda, but due to its size and the range of its monetary activities, for instance, it is always liable to attract the envy, if not strong opposition, of some home-based politicians who would curb its powers in the same way as monarchs tried to in the past. In this regard on the 10 May 2010 at a time of political uncertainty incumbent Mayor Boris Johnson felt compelled to strike a public note of warning that whatever objectives a new political administration might have with London paying £20 billion in tax on its earnings to the benefit of the rest of the country, its function as wealth creator should never be overlooked.[4]

Throughout its history London has always had to be on its guard and especially so today. Terrorists will surely acquire new weapons, they might conceivably gain access to more powerful explosives and sources of gas (for attacks like those already made on the Tokyo underground), acquire potent bacteriological weapons, like anthrax or ricin, for release into the capital's water supplies or, worst of all, construct 'dirty' nuclear bombs able to be carried in a suitcase or brought up the Thames in small craft capable of inflicting wide-spread damage on central London.[5] Alternatively, they might learn how to insert destructive viruses into computer storage and information systems that could paralyze political and commercial activities. Yet even in a worst-case scenario London still retains the advantages of its immense size, with most of its localities likely to be unaffected.

On the other hand, with its vast population – including economic refugees – representing a vast melting pot of humanity there are always likely to be a number of men and women susceptible to fundamentalist indoctrination; for co-existent with the opulence of leafy Chelsea and Kensington, London has pockets of child poverty deeper than anywhere else in the country.

Notwithstanding this, the application of over zealous security measures against such dangers also poses a threat to the very fabric of London life. This was recognized by H G Wells when he described how, at the time of his fictional bombing attacks, there was no city 'anywhere in which the ordinary law and society procedure had not been replaced by some form of emergency control'.[6] As one London paper expressed it recently, 'such measures not only run a risk for a free society but what some see as a misguided war on terror is the inevitable erosion of individual civil liberties'.[7] Entrepreneurial and hardworking Londoners have surely not outfaced a century of attacks to have their long-held privileges and cherished freedoms reduced in such a way.

The traditional – and best – protection for London (in addition to the necessary security measures) continues to lie in the fierce pride felt by Londoners for their city and to ensure that as far as possible, everyone – whether aspiring or successful, whatever their origins or status – can feel they have a genuine opportunity to take part in its innumerable commercial ventures. As Londoners rather than wealthy tourists, they should always be able to enjoy their city's unique range of leisure activities, including its sport, in the time-honoured way.

In such an environment, whatever new attacks are mounted against the city they are bound to fail, as they did during the last century and have throughout London's long history.

Notes

Prologue

1. Air Commodore A D Garrison, 'The First Battle of Britain', *Australian Defence Force Journal*, no. 91, 37.
2. Bede I, Book II, Chapter III, p. 215 (Loeb Classical Library, 1930).
3. Hugh Clout (ed.), *The Times History of London* (2004), pp. 136–7.
4. Major E Linnarz, *I was London's First Zepp Raider* (December 1938), p. 450.

Chapter 1

1. Message placed in a weighted streamer and found on the sands near Canvey Island.
2. *The Mayfly* broke her back after emerging from her shed and was roundly dismissed by Admiral Sturdee at the subsequent court of inquiry as the work of a lunatic. Andrew P Hyde, *The First Blitz* (2002), pp. 11–12.
3. Airships of over 1 million cu ft of gas were built by the Zeppelin, Schutte-Lanz and Luft-Fahrzeng-Gesellschaft companies.
4. H A Jones, *The War in the Air* (vols II–V, 1928–35), Vol. III, p. 77.
5. Douglas Robinson, *The Zeppelins in Combat* (1971), p. 21.
6. Ibid., p. 50.
7. *The Times*, 21 January 1915.
8. *Kolnische Zeitung*, 21 January 1915.
9. Jones, *The War in the Air*, Vol. III, p. 93.
10. Ibid., Appendix III.
11. Ibid.
12. This terrifying journey was told in remarkable detail by airship captain Trensch von Buttlar-Brandenfels in his book *Zeppelins over England* (1931), pp. 64–7.
13. Michael MacDonagh, *In London during the Great War* (1935), p. 82.
14. Joachim Breithaupt, 'How we Bombed London', *Living Age* (January 1928).
15. Jones, *The War in the Air*, Vol. III, p. 132.
16. Robinson, *The Zeppelins in Combat*, p. 138. The reference is to the German publication *Oldenburger Verlagshaus Lindenallee* (1926), p. 83.
17. Robinson, *The Zeppelins in Combat*, p. 165.

18. Jones, *The War in the Air*, Vol. III, p. 225.
19. Frank Morison, *War on Great Cities* (1937), p. 102.
20. Jones, *The War in the Air*, Vol. III, p. 227.
21. Raymond Laurence Rimell, *Zeppelin, a Battle for Air Supremacy in World War 1* (1984), p. 139.
22. Imperial War Museum, 'Pilots' Reports Relating to Destruction of Zeppelins', letter of Second Lieutenant W J Tempest, Ackworth Grange, 15 September 1920.
23. Robinson, *The Zeppelins in Combat*, pp. 195–6.
24. Ibid., p. 203.
25. Ibid., p. 204.
26. Neil Hanson, *First Blitz, the Secret German Plan to Raze London to the Ground in 1918* (2008), p. 30.
27. Imperial War Museum, 'Pilots' Reports Relating to the Destruction of Zeppelins', report of Lieutenant L P Watkins.
28. Ian Gardiner, *The Flat Pack Bombers, The Royal Navy and the Zeppelin Menace* (2009), p. 123.
29. The airships just got larger. Following Strasser's death proposals were put forward for a monstrous airship with a capacity of 3,813,480cu ft and a length of 780ft, scheduled to be delivered in June 1919, seven months after the end of the war. This would in turn be dwarfed by the intercontinental airliner *Hindenburg* which was to be 761ft long with 5,307,000cu ft of hydrogen. In fact, after the crash of the British airship R101 the Zeppelin company rejected hydrogen for helium gas and designed a much larger ship with 7 million cu ft of helium, the L129 *Hindenburg*, which the American authorities refused to supply. The Nazis were, therefore, forced to continue with hydrogen for the *Hindenburg*, a circumstance that much contributed to the disastrous fire that destroyed it.

Chapter Two

1. Brian Gardner, *Up the Line to Death, The War Poets 1914–18* (1964), p. 73.
2. Raymond H Fredette, *The First Battle of Britain 1917–18* (1966), p. 37.
3. Major Freiherr von Bulow, *Die Luftwacht*, nos 5–8, 1927, 331.
4. Ibid.
5. Hyde, *The First Blitz*, pp. 97–8.
6. Jones, *The War in the Air*, Vol. III, Appendix III, Table B.
7. Barry D Powers, *Strategy without Sliderule* (1976), p. 53.
8. Hyde, *The First Blitz*, p. 87.
9. Jones, *The War in the Air*, Vol. V, pp. 21–2.
10. Hyde, *The First Blitz*, p. 97.

11. Jones, *The War in the Air*, Vol. V, p. 25.
12. Fredette, *The First Battle of Britain*, p. 55.
13. More standardization was desperately needed, for, in December 1916, the army and navy had on order 9,483 aircraft of 76 varieties along with 20,000 engines of 57 kinds. John H Morrow, *The Great War in the Air* (1993), p. 185.
14. Jones, *The War in the Air*, Vol. V, Appendix VI, p. 487.
15. Ibid., p. 489.
16. Ibid., p. 59.
17. Fredette, *The First Battle of Britain*, p. 137.
18. Jones, *The War in the Air*, Vol. V, p. 84.
19. Major General E B Ashmore, *Air Defence* (1929), 'Table of Aeroplane Raids', pp. 171–2.
20. Jones, *The War in the Air*, Vol. V, p. 88.
21. Hanson, *First Blitz*, p. 226.
22. Ibid., pp. 308–17. Devastating fire raids with a new electron incendiary device of almost pure magnesium were planned for the late summer of 1918 but they were never implemented for fear of reprisals against German cities.
23. Ibid., p. 344.
24. Jones, *The War in the Air*, Vol. V, Appendix II.
25. Ibid., Vol. III, Appendix IV. The cost was £803,489 with 120 people killed and 367 injured.
26. C M White, *The Gotha Summer* (1986), p. 209.
27. Fredette, *The First Battle of Britain*, p. 218.
28. Jones, *The War in the Air*, Vol. V, p. 153.

Chapter Three

1. Ashmore, *Air Defence*, p. 106.
2. Hanson, *First Blitz*, p. 11.
3. Walter Raleigh, *The War in the Air* (1922), Vol. 1, p. 410.
4. W S Churchill, *The World Crisis* (1923), p. 341.
5. House of Commons Debates, 1913, Column 59.
6. Martin Gilbert, *Winston S Churchill* (1971), Vol. III (1914–16), p. 240.
7. Jones, *The War in the Air*, Vol. III, p. 79.
8. So called because of the weight of its shell.
9. These guns were highly dangerous to the civilian population, as their shells were solid shot.
10. General Sir Frederick Pile, *Ack Ack, Britain's Defence against Air Attack during the Second World War* (1949), p. 45.

11. Jones, *The War in the Air*, Vol. III, p. 84.
12. Lieutenant Colonel A Rawlinson, *The Defence of London 1915–18* (1923), pp. 24–7.
13. Ashmore, *Air Defence*, pp. 4–5.
14. Rawlinson, *The Defence of London*, pp. 34–41.
15. Brigadier N W Routledge, *Anti-Aircraft Artillery 1914–15* (1994), p. 8.
16. Jones, *The War in the Air*, Vol. III, p. 122.
17. Ibid., p. 162.
18. Christopher Cole and E F Cheesman, *The Air Defence of Britain 1914–1918* (1984), p. 93.
19. Air Chief Marshal Sir Philip Joubert de la Ferté, *The Third Service – The Story Behind the Royal Air Force* (1955), p. 30.
20. Hanson, *First Blitz*, p. 57.
21. Ashmore, *Air Defence*, p. 40.
22. Jones, *The War in the Air*, Vol. V, p. 74.
23. Henry Buckton, *Forewarned is Forearmed, History of the Royal Observer Corps* (1993), p. 35. These were found to be even more effective when used with the new Barr and Stroud height finders.
24. Cole and Cheesman, *The Air Defence of Britain*, p. 313.
25. Jones, *The War in the Air*, Vol. V, pp. 73–6.
26. Ashmore, *Air Defence*, p. 57.
27. Ibid., p. 60.
28. Ibid., p. 83.
29. Ibid., p. 89.
30. Jones, *The War in the Air*, Vol. V, p. 153.
31. In August 1918 with the possibility of German raids resuming it was agreed that the Home Defence Force should be raised to twenty squadrons. Cole and Cheesman, *The Air Defence of Britain*, p. 459.
32. Jones, *The War in the Air*, Vol. V, p. 153.
33. Ibid., p. 87.
34. Hanson, *First Blitz*, p. 160.

Chapter Four

1. Richard Morris, *The Man Who Ran London in the Great War. The Diaries and Letters of Lieutenant General Sir Francis Lloyd, GCVO, 1853–1926* (2010).
2. Hanson, *First Blitz*, p. 225.
3. *The Times*, 3 June 1915.
4. Arthur Marwick, *The Deluge, British Society and the First World War* (1991), pp. 346–7.

5. *Illustrated London News* appeared every Saturday.
6. Michael MacDonagh, *In London during the Great War*, p. 14.
7. *The Times*, 2 June 1915.
8. J E Preston Muddock, *A Brief Record of the London Special Constabulary, 1914–19* (1920), pp. 12–14.
9. Ibid., p. 23.
10. *The Times*, 25 September 1915.
11. *Daily Mirror*, 9 September 1915.
12. *The Times*, 22 April 1915.
13. *The Times*, 26 September 1916. Other leaders on bombing appeared on 13 November 1915, 17 January 1916, 15 February 1916, 14 June 1917, 1 October 1917, 7 December 1917 and 2 November 1918.
14. *The Times*, 8 September 1917.
15. *Daily Mail* issues of 6, 7, 8, 25 and 28 September 1917.
16. *The Times*, 26 and 27 September 1917.
17. Nial Ferguson, *The Pity of War* (1988), p. 221.
18. Marquis Alice Goldfarb, 'Words as Weapons', *Journal of Contemporary History* (1978), cited in Ferguson, *The Pity of War*, p. 220.
19. MacDonagh, *In London during the Great War*, p. 16.
20. *The Times*, 19 February 1918.
21. Letter of W A Phillips to James N Todd dated 9 September 1915, Imperial War Museum Documents, 84/52/1.
22. Letter of Miss Finucane describing the Zeppelin raid of 17 August 1915, Imperial War Museum, Misc 208, Mem 3020.
23. Letter of Mrs M Rattray from St Thomas' Hospital, Imperial War Museum, 99/37/1.
24. Diary of Mrs Purbrook, August 1914–November 1918, Imperial War Museum Documents 97/3/1.
25. John Gregg, *The Shelter of the Tubes, Tube Sheltering in Wartime London* (2001).
26. Diary of R Saunders, Imperial War Museum, 6570 79/15/1.
27. Letter of P Braham to his wife, 3 March 1918, Imperial War Museum, 99/84/1.
28. *The Times*, 26 September 1917.
29. MacDonagh, *In London during the Great War*, p. 151.
30. A T Wilkinson, Imperial War Museum collection 78/51/1.
31. MacDonagh, *In London during the Great War*, p. 64.
32. The Revd M F Foxell, unpublished book on mankind and war, Imperial War Museum documents 05/29/1.

33. Letter of J H Stapley, technical editor Southern Counties Cycling Union, Imperial War Museum documents P/391.
34. Mrs Purbrook, Imperial War Museum documents 06/53/1.
35. J B Evans, RAMC, Imperial War Museum document 3280, Con Shelf.
36. *The Times*, 1 October 1917.
37. *The Times*, 15 October 1915.
38. Miss W L B Toner, Imperial War Museum documents P472.
39. Lance Corporal S G Pittaway, letter of 10 April 1916, Imperial War Museum documents 06/34/02.
40. Lieutenant A G Stevenson, letter of 17 June 1915, Imperial War Museum documents B6/77/1.
41. MacDonagh, *In London during the Great War*, p. 74.
42. A T Wilkinson, Imperial War Museum documents 78/51/1.
43. Letter from 'Stew' to Tim from 47 St James' Road, Battersea, Imperial War Museum documents Misc. 239, item 3384.
44. Letter of 3 September 1916 by A Lockwood, Imperial War Museum Documents 02/27/1.
45. Letter of Mrs M Daynell-Browning, 4 September 1916, Imperial War Museum Documents 92/49/1.
46. Letter of Lieutenant W Leefe Robinson VC of 22 October 1916, Imperial War Museum Documents 90/3/1.
47. C T Newman MM, Imperial War Museum documents 03/5/1.
48. Letter of J B Evans of 22 November 1917, Imperial War Museum documents 3280, Con Shelf.
49. MacDonagh, *In London during the Great War*, p. 91.
50. R Saunders, private papers, letter from Fletching, 17 September 1914, Imperial War Museum Documents 6570, 79/15/1.
51. G R Sims, 'The London Front I', *Daily Chronicle*, 22 January 1918.
52. G R Sims, 'The London Front II', *Daily Chronicle*, 22 January 1918.
53. MacDonagh, *In London during the Great War*, p. 259.

Chapter Five

1. Pile, *Ack Ack*, p. 31.
2. Joubert de la Ferté, *The Third Service*, p. 48.
3. Cabinet Minutes WC233 of 24 August 1917, Appendix II.
4. W K Hancock, *Four Studies of War and Peace in this Century* (1961), p. 48.
5. Jones, *The War in the Air*, Vol. VI, Appendix I; the complete report is contained in pp. 8–14.
6. Report to the British Cabinet, 17 August 1917, by General Jan Smuts into 'Air Organisation and the Direction of Aerial Operations'.

7. David Divine, *The Broken Wing* (1966), p. 120.
8. Smuts' Air Organization Committee was followed by his Aerial Operations Committee, reconstituted as the War Priorities Committee, finally to become the Air Policy Committee. Jones, *The War in the Air*, Vol. VI, 13–19.
9. *The Times*, 27 October 1917.
10. Jones, *The War in the Air*, Vol. V, p. 30.
11. Andrew Boyle, *Trenchard, Man of Vision* (1962), p. 222.
12. Air Vice-Marshal Tony Mason, *Air Power: A Centennial Appraisal* (1994), p. 31.
13. Jones, *The War in the Air*, Vol. VI, p. 111.
14. Sir Charles Webster and Noble Frankland, *History of the Second World War: The Strategic Air Offensive Against Germany, 1939–45* (4 vols, 1961), Vol. 1, p. 40.
15. Maurice Baring, *Flying Corps Headquarters 1914–1918* (1930), p. 275.
16. Boyle, *Trenchard*, p. 315.
17. During a day raid by DH9s on Mainx on 31 July the 12 bombers that set out were attacked by up to 40 German fighters – only 2 returned, Jones, *The War in the Air*, Vol. VI, p. 141.
18. Sir John Slessor and B Liddell Hart, *History of the Second World War* (1970), p. 590.
19. Mason, *Air Power*, p. 41.
20. Derek Wood and Derek Dempster, *The Narrow Margin, The Battle of Britain and the Rise of Air Power 1939–40* (1963), p. 65.
21. Peter King, *Knights of the Air* (1989), p. 207.
22. Webster and Frankland, *History of the Second World War*, Vol. 1, p. 52.
23. E L Woodward and R Butler, *Documents on British Foreign Policy 1919–39* (1949), Vol. 1, Third Series, pp. 672–3.
24. Boyle, *Trenchard*, p. 525.
25. Ibid., p. 566.
26. Ashmore, *Air Defence*, p. 147.
27. Ibid., p. 149.
28. Ibid., pp. 150–5.
29. Group Captain W F MacNeece Foster, 'Air Power and its Application', *JRUSI* (LXXII, May 1928), 247–61.
30. Hansard, House of Commons 5s vol. 270: 632.
31. Divine, *The Broken Wing*, p. 192.
32. Denis Richards, *Royal Air Force 1939–45* (3 vols, 1953), Vol. I, p. 7.
33. Ibid., p. 25.
34. Webster and Frankland, *History of the Second World War*, Vol. 1, p. 76.

Chapter Six

1. Wing Commander Dennis McHarrie, 'Luck', *Poems of the Second World War* (1985), p. 116.
2. John Killen, *The Luftwaffe, A History* (1967), p. 125.
3. Len Deighton and Max Hastings, *Battle of Britain* (1980), p. 5.
4. Gavin Lyall, 'Dowding', in Field Marshal Sir Michael Carver (ed.), *The War Lords: Military Commanders of the Twentieth Century* (1976), pp. 206–7.
5. Harald Penrose, *British Aviation, Ominous Skies 1935–39* (1980), p. 68.
6. Len Deighton, *Fighter, The True Story of the Battle of Britain* (1977), pp. 39–40.
7. Ibid., p. 142.
8. Webster and Frankland, *History of the Second World War*, Vol. 1, p. 147.
9. Deighton and Hastings, *Battle of Britain*, p. 77.
10. Ibid., p. 92.
11. Squadron Leader Peter Brown, *Honour Restored, The Battle of Britain, Dowding and the Fight for Freedom* (2005), p. 28.
12. H C G Matthew and Brian Harrison (eds), *Oxford Dictionary of National Biography* (2004), Vol. 16, p. 776.
13. Brown, *Honour Restored*, p. 25.
14. Boyle, *Trenchard*, p. 722.
15. The detailed accounts of Dowding's removal contained in Brown's *Honour Restored*, pp. 161–223 can be supplemented by those in Vincent Orange's *Dowding of Fighter Command* (2008), pp. 206–22.
16. Mason, *Air Power*, p. 53.
17. Patrick Bishop, *Fighter Boys* (2003), p. 169.
18. Ibid., p. 94.
19. Deighton and Hastings, *Battle of Britain*, p. 115.
20. Ibid., p. 165.
21. Deighton, *Fighter*, p. 183.
22. Basil Collier, *The Battle of Britain* (1962), p. 76.
23. Killen, *Luftwaffe*, p. 135.
24. Collier, *The Battle of Britain*, pp. 94–5.
25. Deighton and Hastings, *Battle of Britain*, p. 151.
26. David Wragg, *Bombers* (1999), p. 38.
27. Collier, *The Battle of Britain*, p. 122.
28. Brown, *Honour Restored*, pp. 88–9.
29. Winston S Churchill, *The Second World War* (6 vols, 1951), Vol. II, *Their Finest Hour*, p. 329.

Chapter Seven

1. Gavin Ewart, 'The Bofurs AA Gun', *Poems of the Second World War*, p. 35.
2. Terence H O'Brien, *History of the Second World War, Civil Defence* (1955), p. 587.
3. Pile, *Ack Ack*, p. 57.
4. Ibid., p. 55.
5. The units involved were the 7th Essex Regiment, 4th City of London (Royal Fusiliers), 6th City of London (City of London Rifles), 7th City of London (St Pancras Rifles), 20th London (Queen's Own) and 21st London (1st Surrey Rifles).
6. Pile, *Ack Ack*, p. 115.
7. Routledge, *Anti Aircraft Artillery*, p. 68, Table xi.
8. Pile, *Ack Ack*, p. 90.
9. Routledge, *Anti Aircraft Artillery*, p. 373.
10. Pile, *Ack Ack*, p. 107.
11. Routledge, *Anti Aircraft Artillery*, p. 387.
12. *The Battle of Britain August–October 1940* (1941), p. 17.
13. Richard Haigh and Denis Richards, *The Battle of Britain* (1989), p. 268.
14. Deighton and Hastings, *Battle of Britain*, p. 169. It was subsequently found that 'of thirty two Big Wings launched by 12 Group only seven met the enemy and only once did a Big Wing arrive first at its intended point of interception', Symposium at Royal Air Force Staff College Bracknell, 25 June 1990.
15. Haigh and Richards, *The Battle of Britain*, p. 272.
16. Adolf Galland, *The First and the Last* (1955), p. 73.
17. Ken Delve, *Fighter Command 1936–1968, An Operational and Historical Record* (2007), p. 33.
18. Pile, *Ack Ack*, p. 173.
19. Webster and Frankland, *History of the Second World War*, Vol. 1, pp. 131, 132.
20. Ibid., p. 4.
21. Deighton and Hastings, *Battle of Britain*, p. 217.
22. Bishop, *Fighter Boys*, p. 405.
23. Ibid., p. 405.
24. Ibid., p. 406.

Chapter Eight

1. Tom Harrisson, *Living Through the Blitz* (1976), p. 59.
2. Montgomery H Hyde and G R Nuttall, *Air Defence and the Civil Population* (1938), p. 3.

3. 'A Supreme Effort for Peace', Labour Party Manifesto of 29 October 1938.
4. O'Brien, *History of the Second World War*, p. 292.
5. The surface brick shelters were generally not as popular as the Underground, Quentin Reynolds, *The Wounded Don't Cry* (1941), p. 175.
6. O'Brien, *History of the Second World War*, p. 72.
7. W Eric Jackson, *London's Fire Brigades* (1966), p. 89.
8. O'Brien, *History of the Second World War*, p. xvi.
9. Peter Stansky, *The First Day of the Blitz, September 7 1940* (2007), p. 12.
10. O'Brien, *History of the Second World War*, p. 388.
11. Alfred Price, *Blitz on Britain, 1939–45* (1977), p. 78.
12. Joanna Mack and Steve Humphries, *London at War, The Making of Modern London, 1939–45* (1985), p. 40.
13. Cyril Dermaine, *The London Blitz, A Fireman's Tale* (1992), pp. 17–26.
14. Stansky, *The First Day of the Blitz*, p. 42.
15. Jim Wolveridge, *Ain't It Grand* (1981), pp. 69–71.
16. Constantine FitzGibbon, *The Blitz* (1957), p. 63.
17. Ibid., pp. 63–4.
18. These were officially defined as major fires that were spreading.
19. Ben Robertson, *I Saw England* (1941), pp. 111–23.
20. O'Brien, *History of the Second World War*, p. 681, Appendix IV.
21. R M Titmuss, *Official Volume on Problems of Social Policy, History of the Second World War* (1950), p. 190.
22. Ibid., Appendix 8, pp. 560–1.
23. The WVS was responsible for the first 'Meals on Wheels' scheme, Katharine Bentley Beauman, *Green Sleeves, The Story of the WVS/WRVS* (1977), p. 63.
24. Titmuss, *Official Volume on Problems of Social Policy* , p. 272 n.
25. Ibid., p. 277.
26. C M Kohan, *Works and Buildings* (1952), p. xvi.
27. Ministry of Health circular 2450, 9 August 1941.
28. O'Brien, *History of the Second World War*, p. 420.
29. M J Gaskin, *Blitz, The Story of the 29th December 1940* (2005), p. 169.
30. Ibid., p. 200.
31. Ibid., p. 259, evidence of B J Rogers, Imperial War Museum document 129.
32. Ibid., p. 280.
33. Ibid., p. 295.
34. By August 1941 all fire watchers were reorganized into Herbert Morrison's so-called Fire Guard, Mike Brown, *Put that Light Out* (1999), p. 103.
35. O'Brien, *History of the Second World War*, pp. 593–8.

36. Edwin Webb and John Duncan, *Blitz Over Britain* (1990), p. 117.
37. C M MacInnes, *Bristol at War* (1962), pp. 87–8.
38. O'Brien, *History of the Second World War*, p. 418.
39. There were seventy-one major raids on London during the early Blitz.
40. Gavin Mortimer, *The Longest Night, The Bombing of London on May 10 1942* (2005).
41. Ibid., p. 308.
42. Ibid., pp. 313–14.

Chapter Nine

1. Michael Leitch, *World War Two Songs* (1966), pp. 136–7.
2. Tom Harrisson, *War Factory* (1943), Prologue, Note on Mass Observation.
3. Titmuss, *Official Volume on Problems of Social Policy*, p. 350.
4. FitzGibbon, *The Blitz*.
5. Ibid., p. 268.
6. Angus Calder, *The People's War* (1969).
7. Harrisson, *Living Through the Blitz*, p. 281.
8. Angus Calder, *The Myth of the Blitz* (1991), p. 2.
9. Clive Ponting, *1940 Myth and Reality* (1990).
10. Robert Mackay, *Half the Battle, Civilian Morale in Britain during the Second World War* (2002), p. 6.
11. Titmuss, *Official Volume on Problems of Social Policy* , p. 111.
12. Jonathan Croath, *Don't You Know there's a War On?* (2005), p. 219.
13. Titmuss, *Official Volume on Problems of Social Policy*, p. 136.
14. Ibid., p. 369.
15. FitzGibbon, *The Blitz*, pp. 29–30.
16. Ibid., p. 31.
17. Mass Observation Report 447, 'Interim Report on ARP in Kilburn, 9/10/40'.
18. Angus Calder, *The People's War*, p. 197.
19. Mass Observation Archive, Sussex University, Box 9 (Folder 9T), Air Raids.
20. Mass Observation Archive, Sussex University, Box 5A, Observer CF.
21. Mass Observation Archive, Sussex University, Box 5A, Observer HP.
22. Mack and Humphries, *London at War*, p. 92.
23. Ibid., p. 93.
24. Harrisson, *Living Through the Blitz*, p. 306.
25. Grace Foakes, *Life with Reuben* (1975), p. 66.
26. Mass Observation Archive, Sussex University, Air Raids 1938–41, Box 6A.

27. Mass Observation Archive, Sussex University, Air Raid 1938–41, 'Report of P V Smith on Effect of Raids, 8/9/40'.
28. Mass Observation Archive, Sussex University, Air Raids 1938–45, Box 5 LE, 15/8/40.
29. Mass Observation Archive, Sussex University Air Raids 1938–45, Box 5, 25/6/40.
30. Mass Observation Archive, Sussex University Air Raids 1938–45, Box 6, 1/10/40.
31. Mass Observation Archive, Sussex University, Air Raids 1938–45, Box 6, 21/10/40.
32. Mass Observation Archive, Sussex University, Air Raids, Monday 4/11/1940, Observer FE.
33. Mass Observation Archive, Sussex University, Air Raids, 6G, 12/6/40.
34. Mass Observation Archive, Sussex University, Air Raids, Friday August 23 1940.
35. Mass Observation Archive, Sussex University, Air Raids, The City, February 3 1941.
36. Mass Observation Archive, Sussex University, Air Raids, Box 9N, 16/4/41.
37. Mass Observation Archive, Sussex University Air Raids, Box 9, 20/9/40.
38. Mass Observation Archive, Sussex University Air Raids, Saturday August 31 1940.
39. Ibid.
40. Mack and Humphries, *London at War*, p. 67.
41. Mass Observation Archive, Sussex University, Air Raids, 24/8/40.
42. Mass Observation Archive, Sussex University, Air Raids, 'Night of Thurs 28–29 August 1940'.
43. Mass Observation Archive, Sussex University, Air Raids, Box 6E, 28/8/40.
44. Harrisson, *Living Through the Blitz*, p. 75.

Chapter Ten

1. Mack and Humphries, *London at War*, p. 135.
2. Albert Seaton, *The Russo German War 1941–45* (1971), p. 62.
3. Henry Probert, *Bomber Harris, His Life and Times* (2001), p. 140.
4. Ibid., p. 223.
5. Hitler's order of 14 April 1942 to the Luftwaffe forces in the West, Rothnie Niall, *The Baedeker Blitz, Hitler's Attack on Britain's Historic Cities* (1992), p. 11.
6. O'Brien, *History of the Second World War*, p. 432.
7. Ibid., p. 437.

8. Norman Longmate, *The Doodlebugs, The Story of the Flying Bombs* (1981), p. 21.
9. Ibid., p. 90.
10. Ibid., p. 23.
11. Ibid., p. 42.
12. 'Interim Report of 17 May 1943' by Duncan Sandys to the War Cabinet.
13. Ibid., p. 50.
14. Benjamin King and Timothy Kutta, *Impact, The History of Germany's V Weapons in World War II* (1998), p. 185.
15. Steve Darlow, *Sledgehammers for Tintacks* (2002), p. 199.
16. Ibid., p. 17.
17. Longmate, *The Doodlebugs*, p. 86.
18. King and Kutta, *Impact*, p. 192.
19. David Irving, *The Rise and Fall of the Luftwaffe, The Life of Field Marshal Erhard Milch* (1973), p. 231.
20. R V Jones, *The Wizard War* (1978), p. 353.
21. O'Brien, *History of the Second World War*, p. 650.
22. King and Kutta, *Impact*, p. 211.
23. O'Brien, *History of the Second World War*, p. 653.
24. Pile, *Ack Ack*, pp. 338–9.
25. Routledge, *Anti Aircraft Artillery*, p. 412.
26. Ibid., p. 315.
27. Ibid., p. 412.
28. Longmate, *The Doodlebugs*, p. 449.
29. Ibid., p. 415.
30. Brian Cull with Bruce Lander, *Diver! Diver! Diver! RAF and American Fighter Pilots Battle the V-1 Assault over South-East England 1944–5* (2008), pp. 8–9.
31. Bob Ogley, *Doodlebugs and Rockets, The Battle of the Flying Bombs* (1992), p. 200.
32. David Johnson, *V1, V2 Hitler's Vengeance on London* (1991), p. 115.
33. Longmate, *The Doodlebugs*, p. 445.
34. Report by Air Chief Marshal Sir Roderic Hill to the Secretary of State for Air, 17 April 1948, supplement to the *London Gazette* of 19 October 1948.
35. Longmate, *The Doodlebugs*, p. 473.
36. Darlow, *Sledgehammers for Tintacks*, p. 200.
37. Longmate, *The Doodlebugs*, pp. 474–5.
38. Roy Irons, *Hitler's Terror Weapons, the Price of Vengeance* (2002), p. 180.
39. Longmate, *The Doodlebugs*, p. 42.
40. General Dwight D Eisenhower, *Crusade in Europe* (1948), p. 260.

Chapter Eleven

1. Felicity Goodall, *Voices from the Home Front* (2004), p. 293.
2. *The Times*, 22 September 1920.
3. Sir William Congreve, *Treatise on the Congreve Rocket System as Compared with Artillery* (1827).
4. King and Kutta, *Impact*, p. 6.
5. Major General Walter Dornberger, *V2* (1954), p. 38.
6. Ibid., p. 39.
7. Gregory P Kennedy, *Germany's V-2 Rocket* (2006), p. 11.
8. Volkhard Bode and Gerhard Kaiser, *Building Hitler's Missiles* (2008), p. 9.
9. Norman Longmate, *Hitler's Rockets, The Story of the V2s* (1985), p. 34.
10. Dornberger, *V2*, p. 20.
11. Ibid., p. 29.
12. Ibid., p. 91.
13. Longmate, *Hitler's Rockets*, p. 52.
14. Kennedy, *Germany's V-2 Rocket*, p. 29.
15. Longmate, *Hitler's Rockets*, p. 97.
16. Ibid., p. 99.
17. Bode and Kaiser, *Building Hitler's Missiles*, p. 67.
18. Longmate, *Hitler's Rockets*, p. 101.
19. King and Kutta, *Impact*, p. 314.
20. Kennedy, *Germany's V-2 Rocket*, p. 42.
21. Longmate, *Hitler's Rockets*, p. 123.
22. Ibid., p. 129.
23. Ibid., p. 146.
24. King and Kutta, *Impact*, p. 223.
25. Bode and Kaiser, *Building Hitler's Missiles*, p. 63.
26. O'Brien, *History of the Second World War*, p. 668. More than twice the number of V2s landed on Antwerp than London, causing significant damage and casualties there.
27. Geoffrey Brooks, *Hitler's Terror Weapons From V1 to Vimana* (2002), p. 17.
28. Pile, *Ack Ack*, pp. 386–8.
29. The story of the anti-V2 activities by British Spitfires is contained in Craig Cabell and Graham A Thomas, *Operation Big Ben, The Anti-V2 Spitfire Missions, 1944–5* (2004).

Chapter Twelve

1. Peter Taylor, *Provos, The IRA and Sinn Fein* (1997), p. 153.
2. Martin Gilbert, *Winston S Churchill 1945–65* (1988), p. 4, speech of 9 May 1945.

3. Ibid., p. 7.
4. John Baylis, *Ambiguity and Deterence, British Nuclear Strategy 1945–1964* (1995), p. 34.
5. Ibid., p. 36.
6. A R Oppenheimer, *IRA The Bombs and the Bullets. A History of Deadly Ingenuity* (2009), p. 1.
7. Richard English, *Armed Struggle, A History of the IRA* (2003).
8. The Green Book quoted in Brendan O'Brien's *The Long War, The IRA and Sinn Fein 1985 to Today* (1993), p. 289. A fuller version including conditions and rules is to be found at the Appendix to Martin Dillon's *25 Years of Terror, The IRA's War Against the British* (1994).
9. The ideas that circulated among the Provisional IRA have been discussed at length in Professor Richard English's book *Armed Struggle*, pp. 120–33.
10. David McKittrick and David McVea, *Making Sense of the Troubles* (2000), p. 27.
11. Ibid., p. 83.
12. Dillon, *25 Years of Terror*, p. 162.
13. McKittrick and McVea, *Making Sense of the Troubles*, p. 88.
14. Ibid., p. 128.
15. Dillon, *25 Years of Terror*, p. 217.
16. Oppenheimer, *IRA The Bombs and the Bullets*, pp. 163–4.
17. McKittrick and McVea, *Making Sense of the Troubles*, p. 290.
18. Ibid., p. 198.
19. English, *Armed Struggle*, p. 285.
20. *Sunday Times*, 2 May 1993.
21. Dillon, *25 Years of Terror*, p. 283.
22. This dual problem is discussed at some length in Malachi O'Doherty's *The Trouble with Guns, Republican Strategy and the Provisional IRA* (1998), pp. 197–200.

Chapter Thirteen
1. Jason Burke, *Al-Qaeda* (2000), p. 244.
2. Leslie Macfarlane, 'The Right of Self-Determination in Ireland and the Justification of IRA Violence', in Paul Wilkinson (ed.), *International Library of Terrorism, British Perspectives* (1993), Vol. 1, p. 112.
3. *The Times*, 8 July 2005, article by Sean O'Neill and Daniel McGrory.
4. *Sunday Times*, 9 October 2005, article by David Leppard.
5. *The Times*, 8 July 2005, article by Michael Evans.
6. Ibid.

7. It has subsequently been found out that West Yorkshire police had the fingerprints of the terrorist ringleader, Mohammed Sidique Khan, on file. He had been arrested for separate offences when he was 11 and 18.

8. *Independent*, 8 July 2005, article by Tom Judd and Ed Caesar.

9. *Independent*, 9 July 2005, article by Jason Bennetto.

10. *The Times*, 8 July 2005, article by Ben Macintyre.

11. Ibid.

12. *Guardian*, 9 July 2005, article written by Owen Bowcott and Mark Honigshaum.

13. *The Times*, 8 July 2005, article by Ben Macintyre.

14. *Guardian*, 8 July 2005.

15. *The Times*, 15 July 2005, article by Sean O'Neill and Stewart Tendler.

16. *Guardian*, 15 July 2005, report by Sandra Laville, Audrey Gillan and Dilpazier Aslam.

17. Bruce Hoffman, 'Radicalization and Subversion: Al Qaeda and the 7 July 2005 Bombings and the 2006 Airline Bombing Plot', *Studies in Conflict and Terrorism* (2009), 1103.

18. Ibid., 1004.

19. Ibid., 1105.

20. *Guardian*, 9 September 2008, article by Peter Walaker and Vikram Dodd.

21. *Intelligence and Security Committee Report into the London Terrorist Attacks of 7 July 2005* (2006), p. 39.

Epilogue

1. H G Wells, *The War in the Air* (1908), p. 349.

2. Fortnightly letter from London by Mollie Parker-Downes published in the *New Yorker* of 14 September 1940.

3. Wells, *The War in the Air*, p. 351.

4. *Daily Telegraph*, 10 May 2010.

5. *Daily Telegraph*, 23 March 2010.

6. Wells, *The War in the Air*, p. 353.

7. *Financial Times*, 4 May 2010.

Select Bibliography

Reports and Accounts

Hill, Sir Roderic, *Report on Air Operations by Air Defence of Great Britain at Fighter Command in Connection with the German Flying Bomb and Rocket Offensive 1944–5*

On Target, The Great Story of Ack-Ack Command, official souvenir, 1955

'Report of Bombing Restriction Committee 1943'

'Zeppelins, Original Account', Library of the Royal Aeronautical Society, presented by Miss R M Frampton, 15 June 2004

Journal and Newspapers Articles

Baxter, I M, 'Description of the Allied Bomber Offensive on Germany and of German Air and Civil Defence Systems', *Military Illustrated* (June 2000), 16–23

Beach, J, 'The British Army, the Royal Navy and the "Big Work" of Sir George Aston 1904–1914', *Journal of Strategic Studies* (February 2006), Vol. 29, No. 1, 145–68

Castle, I, 'Zeppelins over London', *Military Illustrated* (September 2006), 8–15

Chapman, R, 'Unsung Heroes, British Anti-Aircraft Command and Crews 1940–41', *Military Illustrated* (May 1995), 29–32

Emmerson, A, 'The Plessey Tunnel Factory', *After the Battle*, No. 139 (2008), 32–43

Harding, Thomas, 'Full speed ahead for the warship that can defeat London single-handedly', *Daily Telegraph*, 15 August 2007, p. 12

Hobbs, D, 'Air Superiority, A Personal View', *Air International* (January 2007), 26–31

Homes, Ray, 'An obituary of an intrepid airman who rammed a German bomber over London to ensure it did not attack Buckingham Palace', *Times Register*, 29 June 2005, p. 57

Jackson, Michael N, 'The Anti Aircraft Corps', *Stand To!* (September 1997), 22–3

Juniper, D, 'Gothas over London', *RUSI Journal* (August 2004), Vol. 148, 74–80

Kender, M, 'The London Balloon Apron', *Stand To!* (January 2002), 12–16

Kennedy, M, 'Sex, fear and looting; survivors disclose untold stories of the Blitz', *Guardian*, 5 October 2006, p. 9

Mordon, J, 'Crime in the Blitz', *Military Illustrated* (March 2007), 16–23

Smith, Edward G, 'Bombing for Peace or the Greatest Illusion', *The Author* (1933)

Smith, Michael, 'RAF axes Tornado squadron in face of Treasury squeeze', *Daily Telegraph*, 1 February 2002, p. 9

Books

Allen, H R, *The Legacy of Lord Trenchard*, 1972

Ashmore, Major General E B, *Air Defence*, 1929

Baylis, John, *Ambiguity and Deterrence, British Defence Strategy 1945–64*, 1995

Beauman, Katharine Bentley, *Green Sleeves, The Story of the WVS/WRVS*, 1977

Bell, Amy Helen, *London was Ours, Diaries and Memoirs of the London Blitz*, 2008

Berko, Anat, *The Path to Paradise, The Inner World of Suicide Bombers and their Dispatchers*, 2009

Best, Geoffrey, *Churchill and War*, 2005

Bishop, Patrick, *Fighter Boys*, 2003

Blake, Lewis, *Red Alert, South East London 1939–45*, 1982

Boyle, A, *Trenchard, Man of Vision*, 1962

Brooks, Geoffrey, *Hitler's Terror Weapons From V1 to Vimana*, 2002

Brooks, Stephen, *Bomber, Strategic Air Power in Twentieth Century Conflict*, 1983

Brown, Mike, *Put that Light Out, Britain's Civil Defence Services at War 1939–45*, 1999

Brown, Squadron Leader Peter, *Honour Restored, The Battle of Britain, Dowding and the Fight for Freedom*, 2005

Bryant, Kenneth, *Streatham's 41, an Account of the German V1 Offensive Against England*, 1945

Bushby, John R, *Air Defence of Great Britain*, 1973

Cabell, Craig and Thomas, Graham A, *Operation Big Ben, The Anti-V2 Spitfire Missions, 1944–5*, 2004

Calder, Angus, *The People's War*, 1969

——, *The Myth of the Blitz*, 1991

Chamberlin, E R, *Life in Wartime Britain*, 1972

Clark, Ronald W, *The Role of the Bomber*, 1977

Cole, Christopher and Cheesman, E F, *The Air Defence of Britain 1914–1918*, 1984

Collier, Basil, *The Defence of the United Kingdom,* 1957

——, *The Battle of Britain*, 1962

——, *A History of Air Power*, 1974

Collier, Richard, *The City that Wouldn't Die*, 1959

Coogan, Tim Pat, *The IRA*, 2000

Cooper, Geoffrey, *Farnborough and the Fleet Air Arm*, 2008

Cragin, R Kim and Daly, Sarah A, *Women as Terrorists*, 2009

Cross, Robin, *The Bombers, The Illustrated Story of Offensive Strategy*, 1987

Cross, Vince, *Blitz, The Diary of Edie Benson, London 1940–41*, 2001

Cruall, Jonathan, *Don't You Know There's a War On? Voices from the Home Front*, 2005

Cull, Brian with Lander, Bruce, *Diver! Diver! Diver! RAF and American Fighter Pilots Battle the V-1 Assault over South-East England 1944–5*, 2008

Deighton, Len, *Fighter, The True Story of the Battle of Britain*, 1977

Delve, Ken, *Fighter Command 1936–1968, An Operational and Historical Record*, 2007

Dickins, Gerald, *Bombing and Strategy, the Fallacy of Total War*, 1946

Dillon, Martin, *25 Years of Terror, The IRA's War Against the British*, 1994

Divine, David, *The Broken Wing*, 1966

Dobinson, Colin, *Fields of Deception, Britain's Bombing Decoys of World War 2*, 2000

——, *AA Command, Britain's Anti-aircraft Defences of the Second World War*, 2001

Douhet, Guilio, *The Command of the Air*, 1943

Dupuy, Trevor Nevitt, *The Air War in the West Sept 1939–41*, 1964

Easdown, Martin with Genth, Thomas, *A Glint in the Sky, German WW1 Air Attacks on Kentish Towns*, 2004

Emden, Richard van and Humphries, Steve, *All Quiet on the Home Front*, 2003

Emme, E M, *The Impact of Air Power*, 1959

English, Richard, *Armed Struggle, A History of the IRA*, 2003

FitzGibbon, Constantine, *The Blitz*, 1957

Fletcher, Hanslip, *Bombed London, A Collection of Thirty-eight Drawings*, 1947

Franks, Norman, *RAF Fighter Command 1936–68*, 1992

Fredette, R H, *The First Battle of Britain 1917–18*, 1966

Gardiner, Ian, *The Flat Pack Bombers, The Royal Navy and the Zeppelin Menace*, 2009

Gardner, Brian, *Up the Line to Death, The War Poets 1914–18*, 1964

Gaskin, M J, *Blitz, the Story of the 29th December 1940*, 2005

Gentile, Gian P, *How Effective is Strategic Bombing?*, 2001
Gibbs-Smith, Charles H, *The Aeroplane, An Historical Survey*, 1960
Gilbert, Martin, *Winston S Churchill 1945–65*, 1988
Goldstein, Laurence, *The Flying Machine and Modern Literature*, 1986
Goodall, Felicity, *Voices from the Home Front*, 2004
Gordon, Thomas, *Ruin from the Air, the Atomic Mission to Hiroshima*, 1977
Gregg, John, *The Shelter of the Tubes, Tube Sheltering in Wartime London*, 2001
Grey, C G, *A History of the Air Ministry*, 1940
Griehl, Manfred, *German Bombers over England 1940–44*, 1988
Hanson, Neil, *First Blitz, the Secret German Plan to Raze London to the Ground in 1918*, 2008
Harris, Clive, *Walking the London Blitz*, 2003
Harrisson, Tom, *Living Through the Blitz*, 1976
Hastings, Max, *Bomber Command*, 1979
Hawton, Hector, *Night Bombing*, 1944
Henrey, Robert, *The Siege of London*, 1946
Henshall, Philip, *Hitler's Rocket Sites*, 1985
Hicks, Karl, *Bombing 1939–45: the Air Offensive Against Land Targets*, 1990
Hildebrandt, A, *Balloons and Airships*, 1973
Hill, Maureen, *The Blitz, Photographs by the* Daily Mail, 2002
Hooton, E R, *Phoenix Triumphant, The Rise and Rise of the Luftwaffe*, 1994
Hough, Richard and Richards, Denis, *The Battle of Britain*, 1989
Howard, Michael (ed.), *The Theory and Practice of War. Essays presented to Captain BH Liddell Hart*, 1965
Hughes, Major General B P, *Between the Wars 1919–39*, 1992
Hyde, Andrew P, *The First Blitz*, 2002
Jackson, W Eric, *London's Fire Brigades*, 1966
Jacobsen, C G, *The Nulcear Era*, 1982
Johnson, David, *The City Ablaze*, 1980
——, *V for Vengeance, The Secret Battle of London*, 1981
Jones, H A, *The War in the Air*, vols II–V, 1928–35
Jones, Neville, *The Origins of Strategic Bombing*, 1973
Joubert de la Ferté, Air Chief Marshal, Sir Philip, *The Third Service – The Story Behind the Royal Air Force*, 1955
Kennedy, Gregory P, *Germany's V-2 Rocket*, 2006
Kerr, Judith, *Bombs on Aunt Dainty*, 2002
Killen, John, *The Luftwaffe, A History*, 1967
Kincome, Brian, *A Willingness to Die*, 1999
King, Benjamin and Kutta, Timothy, *Impact, The History of Germany's V Weapons in World War II*, 1998

King, H F, *Armament of British Aircraft 1909–1939*, 1971

Knoke, Heinz, *I Flew for the Fuhrer*, trans. John Ewins, 1943

Kurzman, Dan, *Day of the Bomb*, 1986

Langley, Andrew, *The Bombing of London 2005*, 2006

Lewis, Cecil, *Sagittarius Rising*, 1936

——, *Sagittarius Surviving*, 1991

Lindqvist, Sven, *A History of Bombing*, 2001

Longmate, Norman, *How We Lived Then, A History of Everyday Life during the Second World War*, 1971

——, *The Doodlebugs, The Story of the Flying Bombs*, 1981

——, *The Bombers*, 1982

——, *Hitler's Rockets, The Story of the V2s*, 1985

Macdonald, Peter G, *Stopping the Clock, Bomb Disposal in the World of Terrorism*, 1977

Mack, Joanna and Humphries, Steve, *London at War, The Making of Modern London 1939–45*, 1985

Mackay, Robert, *Half the Battle, Civilian Morale in Britain During the Second World War*, 2002

McKercher, B J C and Ion, A Hamish, *Military Heretics, the Unorthodox in Policy and Strategy*, 1994

Marwick, Arthur, *The Deluge, British Society and the First World War*, 1991

Mason, Air Vice Marshal Tony, *Air Power, A Centennial Appraisal*, 1994

Miksche, Ferdinand Otto, *Is Bombing Decisive?*, 1943

Morris, Captain Joseph, *The German Air Raids on Great Britain 1914–18*, 1926

Mortimer, Gavin, *The Longest Night: the Bombing of London on May 10 1941*, 2005

Mosley, Leonard, *Backs to the Wall, London Under Fire 1939–45*, 1971

Munson, Kenneth, *German Aircraft of WW2*, 1978

Narracott, Arthur, *Air Power in War*, 1945

Neumann, G P, *The German Air Force in the Great War*, 1969

Nixon, Barbara, *Raiders Overhead*, 1980

O'Brien, T H, *History of the Second World War, Civil Defence*, 1955

O'Doherty, Malachi, *The Trouble with Guns, Republican Strategy and the Provisional IRA*, 1998

Ogley, Bob, *Doodlebugs and Rockets, The Battle of the Flying Bombs*, 1992

Orange, Vincent, *Dowding of Fighter Command*, 2008

Palmer, Alan, *The Kaiser, War Lord of the Second Reich*, 1978

Pape, Robert Anthony, *Bombing to Win, Airpower and Coercion in War*, 1996

Parsons, Martin, *Air Raids*, 2000

Penrose, Harald, *British Aviation: The Pioneer Years*, 1967

——, *British Aviation: The Great War and Armistice 1915–19*, 1969

——, *British Aviation: Widening Horizons 1930–34*, 1979

——, *British Aviation Ominous Skies 1935–39*, 1980

Philpott, Ian M, *The Royal Air Force, an Encyclopaedia of the Interwar Years, Vol. 1, The Trenchard Years 1918–29*, 2005

Pile, General Sir Frederick, *Ack Ack, Britain's Defence against Air Attack during the Second World War*, 1949

Poolman, K, *Zeppelins over England*, 1960

Popham, H, *Into Wind*, 1969

Price, Alfred, *Blitz on Britain 1939–45*, 1977

Probert, H, *The Battle Rethought, A Symposium of the Battle of Britain*, 1990

——, *High Commanders of the RAF*, 1991

——, *Bomber Harris, His Life and Times*, 2002

Raleigh, Walter, *The War in the Air, Vol. 1*, 1922, the Official History of the part played in the First World War by the Royal Air Force

Rashid, Ahmed, *Taliban*, 2001

Rasmussen, Steen Eiler, *London the Unique City*, 1982

Rawlinson, Lt Col A, *The Defence of London 1915–18*, 1923

Ray, John, *The Night Blitz 1940–1941*, 1996

Reckill, Rachel, *Stepney Letters*, 1991

Reynolds, Bertha and Chris, *The London Gunners Come to Town*, 1995

Reynolds, Quentin, *They Fought for the Sky*, 1938

——, *The Wounded Don't Cry*, 1941

Richards, D, *Portal of Hungerford*, 1977

Riedel, Bruce, *The Search for Al Qaeda*, 2008

Rimell, Raymond L, *Air War over Great Britain*, 1987

Robbins, Gordon, *Fleet Street Blitzkreig Diary*, 1944

Rothnie, Niall, *The Baedeker Blitz, Hitler's Attack on Britain's Historic Cities*, 1992

Routledge, Brigadier N W, *Anti-Aircraft Artillery 1914–15*, 1994

Royse, Dr M W, *Aerial Bombardment and the International Regulation of Warfare*, 1928

Saundby, Air Marshal Sir Robert, *Air Bombardment: The Story of its Development*, 1961

Siemes, J, *The Day the Bomb Fell*, 1984

Sledman, Henry W, *Battle of the Flames: The Story of the Bombing of London*, 1942

Slessor, J C, *Airpower and Armies*, 1936

Spaight, J M, *The Beginnings of Organised Air Power: A Historical Study*, 1927

Stansky, Peter, *The First Day of the Blitz, September 7 1940*, 2007

Titmuss, R M, *Problems of Social Policy, History of the Second World War*, 1950

Trensch von Buttlar Brandenfels, *Zeppelins over England*, 1931

Ward, A, *Resisting the Nazi Invader*, 1997

Wasley, Gerald, *Plymouth, A Shattered City*, 2004

Webb, Edwin and Duncan, John, *Blitz Over Britain*, 1990

Webster, Sir Charles and Frankland, Noble, *History of the Second World War: The Strategic Air Offensive against Germany 1939–45*, vols 1–4, 1961,

Wells, H G, *The War in the Air*, 1908

Werrell, Kenneth R, *Death from the Heavens: A History of Strategic Bombing*, 2009

White, C M, *The Gotha Summer*, 1986

Whitehouse, Arch, *The Zeppelin Fighters*, 1966

Whiting, Charles, *Britain under Fire: the Bombing of Britain's Cities*, 1986

Wilkinson, Paul, *Terrorism: British Perspectives*, 1993

Woolf, Arthur Leonard, *The Battle of South London*, 1946

Wragg, David W, *The Offensive Weapon, the Strategy of Bombing*, 1986

Wright, Joanne, *Terrorist Propaganda*, 1991

Ziegler, P, *London at War 1939–45*, 1995

Index

Ack-Ack 93, 94, 95, 112, 137
Adams, Gerry 170, 174, 175, 178
Air Board 63
Air Force Apprentice School 68
Air Force Cadet College 68
Air Force Staff College 68
Air Ministry 68, 74, 81, 139, 144
Air Raid Precautions Committee 71, 105, 106
air-raid wardens 107, 108
airships 7, 8
Air Staff 83
Aitken, Max, Lord Beaverbrook 52, 79
Aldgate station 185
Allied Expeditionary Air Force 148, 160
al-Qaeda 181, 183, 185, 190, 191, 192, 193, 195, 196
Anderson shelter 107, 144
Anglo-Irish Accord (1985) 176
Anti-Aircraft Command 37, 95
anti-aircraft guns 1, 10, 38, 45, 117
Ashmore, Major General Edward 'Splash' 40, 41, 42, 43, 45, 70, 71
Attlee, Clement 169, 170

Baldwin, Stanley 68, 71, 93, 94, 106
Balfour, Arthur 51, 69
Balkans 93, 192
Beaverbrook, Lord see Aitken, Max
Behneke, Rear Admiral Paul 8, 20, 35

Belfast 119, 172, 175
Belgium 10, 21, 27, 32, 42, 66, 84, 147, 149, 158, 160, 161, 165
Bentivegni, Captain Richard von 29, 32
Bentley Priory 73, 83, 97
Berlin 51, 68, 89, 90, 138, 141, 155, 169
Biggin Hill 68, 89
Billing, Noel Pemberton 63, 65
Birmingham 116, 119, 121, 174
Blair, Sir Ian 184, 188
Blair, Tony 178, 188, 192
Blitz 98, 109–21, 123–33, 137, 144, 145, 146, 160, 195
Blizna 157, 159, 164
Bloody Sunday 172, 173
Bomber Command 73, 81, 82, 88, 102, 141, 142
Brandenburg, Captain Ernst 23, 24, 25, 26, 27, 32, 33, 43, 44
Braun, Wernher von 152–3, 155, 157, 158, 164
Breithaupt, Captain Joachim 12, 13, 14
Brighton 99, 176
Bristol fighters 44, 45
Britain 9, 10, 11, 12, 14, 15, 17, 18, 21, 22, 26, 28, 29, 30, 64, 78, 98, 102, 118, 135, 139, 143, 153, 154, 169, 170
Britain, Battle of 81, 85, 88, 99, 147

British Expeditionary Force 21, 27, 35
Buckingham Palace 37, 115

Cabinet Office 158, 177
Canary Wharf 178, 188, 193
Chamberlain, Neville 74
Channel, English 83, 85, 86, 92, 100, 143
Chatham 30, 39, 65
Cherwell, Lord 141, 143, 144, 145, 155, 160
Chichester-Clark, James 172
Churchill, Winston
    proposals for London's defences 36, 37
    support for RAF 68, 69
    highlights London's inadequate defences 72
    increased fighter demands 79–81, 82, 83, 85, 90, 95, 100, 105, 114, 115, 130, 135, 138
    initiates investigation into Peenemunde 141, 145, 146, 155, 159
    acknowledges end of weapon attacks 164
    pays tribute to London 169
City of London 2, 27, 47, 109, 112, 116, 117, 118, 121, 131, 177, 178, 180
Civil Defence 105, 106, 109, 111, 115
Coastal Command 73
Committee of Imperial Defence 69, 95, 105, 141
Commons, House of 68, 120, 121, 164, 175
Coventry 116, 119
Croydon 39, 87, 89, 130, 193
Czechoslovakia, Czechs 84, 102, 147, 153, 163

Daily Express 48
Daily Mail 28, 48, 52, 78, 117
Daily Mirror 48
Degenkolb, Gerhard 154, 156, 157
Deptford 15, 55
Derry, Apprentice Boys of 172
docks, London 8, 109, 110, 111, 131
doodlebugs 143, 145, 146, 147, 148, 160
Dornberger, Walter 152–8, 161, 162, 163, 164
Dornier Do 17 80, 110
Dover 24, 25, 31, 36, 39, 87, 119
Dowding, Air Marshal Sir Hugh 73, 74, 79, 80–90, 95, 97
Downing Street Declaration (1993) 178
Dublin 176
Dunkirk 25, 36, 80, 82, 90, 124
Duxford 89, 98, 99, 100

'Eagle's Day' 86, 87, 99
East Anglia 38, 39, 82
East End 1, 2, 27, 31, 47, 56, 111, 121, 131
Edgware Road station 185, 186
Eisenhower, General Dwight 149
Essex 38, 44, 111, 148

Falkenhayn, General von 11, 12
Fighter Command 73, 77, 80, 81, 82, 84, 85, 88, 90, 95, 100, 101
First World War 7, 23, 29, 46, 47, 53, 70, 71, 78, 82, 83, 93, 101, 129, 131, 151, 153
Flying Fortress 110, 139, 142
France 11, 21, 35, 40, 48, 66, 67, 69, 77, 78, 80, 81, 84, 93, 105, 138, 149, 153, 157, 160, 161, 165
French, Field Marshal Lord 39, 40, 52

George V, King 48, 53, 55
Germany 7, 21, 26, 35, 45, 52, 64, 66, 67, 72, 73, 78, 107, 131, 136, 137, 138, 139, 141, 149, 151, 155, 157, 159, 165, 169
Giant 31, 32, 33
Goering, Reichsmarschall Hermann 79, 83, 84, 86, 87, 88, 89, 90, 92, 97, 98, 99, 100, 140
Good Friday Agreement (1998) 178
Gotha GIV bomber 22, 23, 25, 27, 28, 29, 30, 31, 32, 33, 34, 40, 43, 44, 46, 59, 63, 66, 101
Grosskampfflugzeug 21–2

Hague Convention 35
Haig, Field Marshal Sir Douglas 28, 32, 33, 39, 65, 66
Halifax bombers 29, 74, 155
Hampden bomber 74, 89
Handley Page 33, 67
Harmsworth, Alfred, Lord Northcliffe 52, 66
Harmsworth, Harold, Lord Rothermere 52, 66
Harris, Sir Arthur 'Bomber' 135, 136
Harwich 27, 29, 39, 148
Hawker Fury 77
Hawker Hurricane 79, 80, 81, 82, 86
Hawkinge aerodrome 86, 87
Heathrow airport 178, 193
Heinkel He 111 80, 110, 119, 143
Heinkel He 112 79
Henderson, General Sir David 25, 35, 36, 64
Hendon 38, 39
High Seas Fleet 13, 14
Hill, Air Marshal Sir Roderic 146, 161, 164

Himmler, Heinrich 156, 158
Hitler, Adolf 72, 83
    launches air attacks on Britain 86, 89
    orders London Blitz 90, 94, 98, 121
    switches Luftwaffe to the East 121
    Baedeker raids 136, 138, 139, 140, 142
    supports V weapons against London 155–65
Hoeppner, General Ernst von 22, 23, 27, 29, 32
Holland 148, 149, 161, 163, 165
Home Defence Squadrons 69, 80
Home Guard 121
Home Intelligence Unit 123, 124
Hornchurch 54, 88, 89
Hounslow 39
Hull 10, 31, 119
Hurricane 77, 80, 81, 85, 86, 88, 89, 100, 101, 102

IRA 170, 172
    bombs London 174–7
    operations halted 178, 179, 180, 181, 183, 185, 187, 188, 195
Ireland 102, 170
Ireland, Republic of 170
Italy 72, 78, 137

Japan 72, 149, 169
Jones, Dr R V 138, 141, 143, 156, 159, 160
Joynson-Hicks, William 43, 65
Junkers Ju 88 80

Kaiser Wilhelm II 9, 11, 26, 27, 35
Kammler, SS Grupenfuhrer Hans 156, 157, 158, 161, 162, 163

Kampfgruppe 100 116, 117, 119
Kendall, Wing Commander Douglas 141, 158
Kerr, Admiral Mark 65
Kesselring, Albert 83, 88, 90, 92, 98, 99, 100
Khan, Mohammed Sidique 189, 190
King's Cross station 121, 185, 186, 189
Kleine, Captain Rudolf 27, 28, 29, 30, 31, 32

Lancaster bomber 74, 110, 155,
Leytonstone 1, 10, 11
Linnarz, Hauptmann Erich 1, 2, 3
Liverpool Street station 185, 186
Lloyd George, David 52, 64, 65, 68
London Ambulance Service 106, 108
London Fire Brigade 32, 106, 117
Lubeck 135, 136, 139
Luftwaffe 74, 77, 79, 80, 83, 84, 85
    attack on airfields and factories 86–90
    daylight assault on London 92, 96–102
    the Blitz 109, 111–12, 116–21, 133, 135, 136, 137
    flying bombs 139, 140, 148, 149

Madrid 184, 185, 191
Mallory, Trafford Leigh 82, 88
Mathy, Heinrich 12, 13, 14, 15, 16, 18, 37
Messerschmidt Bf 109 79, 80, 88
Messerschmidt Bf 110 86
Messerschmidt, Willy 79
Milch, Erhard 139, 140, 142, 143
Mitchell, Reginald 78, 79

Morrison, Herbert 118, 129, 143, 145, 147, 159, 160
    Morrison shelter 144
Mosquito 80, 101, 145
Munich 74, 106
Mustang 137, 145

New Scotland Yard 173, 184, 189
New Zealand, New Zealanders 84, 102, 147
Nordhausen 156, 157, 160, 163
Normandy 143, 145, 158, 159
Northcliffe, Lord *see* Harmsworth, Alfred
Northern Ireland Treaty (1921) 171
North Sea 8, 10, 11, 17, 24
Norway, Norwegians 80, 81, 147

Oberste Heereslitung (OHL) 21, 30, 34

Paddington station 121, 187
Parachute Regiment 172, 173
Park, Keith 82, 83, 85, 87, 88, 89, 90, 97, 100
Parliament 2, 12, 45, 64, 68, 93, 115
Pathfinder 116, 136, 137
Peenemunde 138–42, 152, 153, 155–60, 164, 165
Pile, General Sir Frederick 37, 95, 96, 97, 101, 146, 147, 148, 165
Plymouth 116, 118–19
Poland, Poles 83, 84, 102, 107, 138, 147, 159
Poplar 26, 110, 111
Portsmouth 39, 116, 119, 149
Press Bureau 49, 50, 51, 52
Provisional IRA 170–1, 172, 173, 174

Queen's Concert Hall 120, 121, 132

Republicans, Irish 170, 171, 181
Robinson, William Leefe 40, 57, 58
Rothermere, Lord *see* Harmsworth,
    Harold
Royal Air Force
    founding 65–9
    establishing 70, 72, 73, 74, 80, 81
    defending Britain 85, 86, 88, 94
    bombing of Germany and
        Peenemunde 131, 136, 137,
        141
    counteracting flying bombs 144–7,
        155, 156, 158
Royal Arsenal *see* Woolwich Arsenal
Royal Flying Corps 24, 27, 30, 35, 39,
    47, 63, 66
Royal Naval Air Service 22, 24, 25,
    27, 30, 36, 63, 64, 66
Russia, Russians 121, 135, 163

Sandys, Duncan 141, 147, 161, 164
Scheer, Admiral Reinhard 13, 15, 17
Scott, Admiral Sir Percy 37, 38, 39
Second World War 3, 26, 29, 37, 46,
    47, 78, 102, 149, 185
Sinn Fein 170, 175
Smith, Constance Babington 140,
    141
Smuts, Lieutenant General Jan
    Christian 28, 64, 65, 70
Sopwith Camels 39, 43, 44, 45
Sopwith Pups 27, 39
South Africa, South Africans 102, 147
Soviet Union 102, 170
Speer, Albert von 156, 157, 158, 162
Sperrle, Hugo von 83, 90, 98, 99
Spitfire 77, 79, 80, 81, 83, 85, 86, 88,
    89, 100, 102, 103, 140, 145

Square Mile *see* City of London
Stirling bomber 74, 90
Strasser, Corvette Captain Peter 8, 9,
    11, 12, 14, 15, 16, 17, 18
Stuka dive-bomber 79, 87, 88

Tanweer, Shehzad 189, 190, 191
Thames, River 2, 13, 16, 110, 116,
    117
Thatcher, Margaret 175, 176, 177
The Times 10, 13, 47, 48, 49, 50, 51,
    52, 54, 55, 56, 59, 65, 107, 151,
    191
Thompson, Lord 105, 106
Tirpitz, Admiral 8, 9
Townsend, Squadron Leader Peter
    84, 85, 103
Trenchard, Hugh 64, 65, 66, 67, 68,
    69, 70, 71, 77, 78, 82, 94, 102

Underground, London 31, 54, 107,
    121
Unionists 174, 176, 180, 181
USA 65, 78, 102, 139, 163, 164,
    169
US Eighth Air force 136, 137, 141,
    155
US Ninth Air force 147
Usedom 138, 152, 156

V1 102, 136, 138, 142–3, 146, 147,
    148, 149, 154, 160, 163, 164, 165,
    195
V2 136, 147, 150, 153, 154, 156, 158,
    160, 161, 162, 163, 164, 165, 195
Ventnor 86, 87, 88

Wachtel, Colonel Max 140, 142, 143,
    149
War Cabinet 27, 66, 80

War Office 14, 25, 95
Weir, Sir William 63, 65, 67
Wellington bomber 74, 90
West Ham 1, 10, 109, 119
Western Front 22, 25, 26, 39, 40, 48, 53, 65, 66, 70
Whitelaw, William 173, 174
Woolwich Arsenal 37, 45, 109, 110, 116, 121

X-GERAT 101, 116, 136

Zeppelin
  initial raids 1, 2, 9
  limitations 12, 13, 14
  vulnerability 15, 16, 17, 19
  superseded by bombers 22, 23, 25, 29, 31, 33, 34
  improved defences 36, 37, 38, 40, 43, 45
  psychological reactions 46, 47, 49, 50, 51, 52, 53, 55, 57, 58, 63, 101, 151, 195